Victims in the News

Victims in the News

Crime and the
American News Media

Steven M. Chermak

Westview Press

BOULDER • SAN FRANCISCO • OXFORD

Copyright © 1995 by Westview Press, Inc.

Published in 1995 in the United States of America by Westview Press, Inc., 5500 Central Avenue, Boulder, Colorado 80301-2877, and in the United Kingdom by Westview Press, 12 Hid's Copse Road, Cumnor Hill, Oxford OX2 9JJ

Library of Congress Cataloging-in-Publication Data
Chermak, Steven.
   Victims in the news : crime and the American news media / Steven M. Chermak.
      p.   cm.
   Includes bibliographical references and index.
   ISBN 0-8133-2496-3 (hc). — ISBN 0-8133-2497-1
   1. Crime and the press—United States.   2. Victims of crime—
United States.   I. Title.
PN4888.C8C48   1995
070.4'49344—dc20   94-46207
                                                                                        CIP

Printed and bound in the United States of America

   The paper used in this publication meets the requirements
(∞) of the American National Standard for Permanence of Paper
   for Printed Library Materials Z39.48-1984.

10   9   8   7   6   5   4   3   2   1

Contents

List of Tables   vii
Preface   ix
Acknowledgments   xi

1 The News Media, Public Concern, and Crime Victims   1

Converging Issues, 2
Research Significance, 10
Notes, 12

2 Constructing Crime News   13

The Production of News at the *Tribune* and the Nightly, 14
The News Filtering Process, 18
Conclusion, 40
Notes, 41

3 News Images of Crime, Victims, and Defendants   43

A Day at the Nightly, 44
Prevalence of Crime in the News, 47
Crime as an Element of News, 49
Crime Victims and Defendants in the News, 58
Characteristics of Crime Victims as Elements of News, 62
Characteristics of Defendants as Elements of News, 74
Contrasting Images of Victims and Defendants, 80
Conclusion, 82
Notes, 83

4 How Crime Victims Affect the Media 85

Crime Victims and Media Selection Decisions, 86
Crime Victims and the Production of News, 88
Crime Victims as Sources, 93
How Crime Victims Are Contacted, 96
Conclusion, 107
Notes, 107

**5 The Presentation of Crime and Victims in Print and
in Electronic Media** 109

Print and Electronic Media Formats, 110
The Presentation of Crime Compared to Other News Topics, 113
Types of Crimes Presented, 117
Sources Used for the Presentation of Crime, 122
Presentation of Victims and Defendants, 126
Conclusion, 132
Notes, 132

**6 The Presentation of Crime and Victims in
Different Sized Cities** 133

Overall Presentation of Stories in Different Media, 134
Types of Crime Presented in Each City, 139
News-Item Sources Used for the Presentation of Crime, 144
Sources Used Within Crime Stories, 146
Presentation of Victims and Defendants Across Cities, 151
Conclusion, 165
Notes, 166

7 The News Media in Society 167

The Powers of the Watchdog, 167
Muzzling the Watchdog, 170
The Costs of Crime News Production, 176

Appendix: A Note on Research Methodology 183
References 189
About the Book and Author 199
Index 201

Tables

2.1 News-Item Sources Cited   15
2.2 Evaluation of Police and Court Organizations in News Stories   22
2.3 Crime Incident Sources   29
2.4 Presentation of Criminal Justice Stages   30
2.5 Characteristics of Different Story Types   34

3.1 Types of Crime Stories Presented   47
3.2 Topics of News Stories Presented   48
3.3 Topics of Stories Presented Without Sports and
       Business Sections   49
3.4 Crime Categories   50
3.5 Type of Crime in Crime Stories   51
3.6 Newsworthy Categories of Crime   54
3.7 Victim and Defendant Characteristics   60
3.8 Victim Characteristics   64
3.9 Type of Harm Presented   71
3.10 Defendant Characteristics   76

4.1 Incident, Victim, and Defendant Sources   89
4.2 Victim Source Information   92

5.1 Presentation of Crime in Newspaper and Television Media   114
5.2 Categories of Crimes Presented in Newspaper and
       Television Media   118
5.3 Source Comparison in Newspaper and Television Media   124
5.4 Victim and Defendant Demographic Characteristics in Newspaper
       and Television Media   127
5.5 Type of Harm Reported by Newspaper and Television Media   131

6.1 Number of Index Offenses Known to the Police   135
6.2 Type of News Story in Nine Media Organizations   136
6.3 Level of Crime Story in Nine Media Organizations   137

6.4   Types of Crimes Presented in Nine Media Organizations   140
6.5   Types of Crimes Presented in Combined Media Categories   141
6.6   News-Item Sources in Newspapers   145
6.7   Incident Sources Cited in Crime Stories in Combined Media
         Categories   147
6.8   Victim Sources Cited in Crime Stories in Combined Media
         Categories   148
6.9   Defendant Sources Cited in Crime Stories in Combined Media
         Categories   149
6.10 Local and Nonlocal Victim Characteristics in Crime Stories in
         Combined Media Categories   154
6.11 Local and Nonlocal Defendant Characteristics in Crime Stories
         in Combined Media Categories   157
6.12 Local and Nonlocal Types of Harm in Crime Stories in
         Combined Media Categories   160

Preface

Historically, crime victims have been a neglected asset of the criminal justice system. Although the capability to process cases is dependent on the willingness of victims to report crime to the police and cooperate with prosecutors, criminal justice professionals have exploited this important asset. Over the past three decades, dramatic changes in attitudes about crime victims have occurred, resulting in modifications in how the system uses them in the criminal justice process.

Similarly, there has been a growing interest in the news media's role in the administration of justice. Much has been written on crime in the news media over the past thirty years. Content studies of what is presented to the public about crime, ethnographic studies of the news-production process, and interviews with news personnel provide some background understanding of how the news media affects the criminal justice system.

This book capitalizes on the increased interest in these two areas and reports on how these topics intersect. The primary purpose of this book is to present information on how victims are presented to the public in print and electronic news media. In addition, the news-production process was observed to understand why specific victim images are presented to the public. This book combines three research methodologies—content analysis, ethnography, and interviews—to examine the presentation of crime, victims, and defendants in the news.

Crime is a sensational topic. News organizations try to capitalize on public interest in gore by providing a steady supply of the most revolting crime available. Demand influences how crime news is produced. Individuals in criminal justice organizations—police officers, prosecuting attorneys, and judges—are the primary sources that reporters use for attribution in crime stories. These sources provide a self-serving, distorted image to reporters to manipulate public perceptions of the organization. This book considers how the relationship between news and source organizations limits how crime is presented in the news.

News media use victims to increase the marketability of the news product. The status of crime victims can increase the likelihood that specific images get presented. Crime victims—if they are young or old, are willing to go on camera, or are able to visualize their pain with emotional quotes—increase the newsworthiness of a news story. A narrow portrait of victims is provided in the news media; one that has helped change the status of victims in the criminal justice system.

Steven M. Chermak

Acknowledgments

Many individuals deserve thanks and credit for the completion of this book. Professors David Bayley, David Duffee, Graeme Newman, Bob Hardt (all at the University of Albany) and Scott Christianson provided guidance when I was first struggling with this topic. They also encouraged me to continue to refine my interest in this area. I am indebted to Eric Riksheim, David Lataski, Dennis Rome, and four reviewers for helpful suggestions. Gina Lake was instrumental in preparing the final manuscript for press. I thank her for her computer expertise and tireless work with numerous revisions.

SMC

1

The News Media, Public Concern, and Crime Victims

Walking innocently across the street, a young child is killed tragically by gunfire. As the surviving family members begin to struggle with the realities of murder, they are asked by the news media to make a public obituary to the deceased victim. Journalists hope the family members can articulate their pain, suffering, and confusion in a newsworthy fashion so others can attach some meaning to the family's loss. The newsworthiness of this crime increases significantly if members of the family weep on camera, provide a descriptive photograph, or express their pain dramatically in words.

The presentation of crime in the news media results from a complex decisionmaking process involving a variety of individuals and organizations that have conflicting interpretations of events. Representatives from news and criminal justice organizations are the principal agents who define the images offered, making decisions about which crimes are filtered out of the news-production process, which are given small amounts of space, and which are presented as the most important stories of the day. Other interested individuals, such as crime victims, are thought to have infrequent, direct access to this process. Crime victims—along with defendants, protesters, and participants in unusual activities—are considered "unknowns" by the news media (Gans 1979: 14).

The research discussed in this book documents the role crime victims play in the production of news about crime. Previous research has generally overlooked the specific role victims play in the generation of crime stories. The present research examines the methods used by reporters to convince victims to participate in newsmaking and specifically, when crime victims are used as news sources, explores how frequently they are relied on for story information and the type of information they are asked to provide.

In addition, the present study examines the presentation of crime victims in popular print and electronic media.[1] Few research studies have examined the details of the offenses that are presented, especially details about the crime victims themselves (Mawby and Brown 1984: 82), focusing instead on the aggregate presentation of crime news. Little is known about how victims are presented in the news, whether their presentation varies by type of medium or across the media of different-sized cities, and how the image of victims compares with that of defendants. This book fills these gaps by examining the characteristics of victims presented in the news, the frequency with which victims are portrayed, and where they are presented.

These issues are examined using a multimethodological approach. Traditionally, media studies have examined either the presentation of crime news or the organizational processes used to generate stories (Ericson, Baranek, and Chan 1987, 1989). Each type of study uses a distinct methodology. Presentational studies rely primarily on content analysis (in which the frequency of certain words, phrases, and themes is calculated); process studies use ethnography or interviews.

This book combines all three of these methodologies to examine how the presentation of victims and the process used to generate stories vary across print and electronic media in cities of different sizes (for a discussion of the research methodology, see the Appendix). Content analysis of six print and three electronic news organizations from different cities provides information about what is presented to the public about crime, victims, defendants, and sources. A total of 2,664 crime stories were content-coded for the presentational analysis; of these, 2,158 were in newspapers, and 506 were from television. Ethnographic observation of the news-production process in a print and electronic organization was undertaken, and interviews of news and criminal justice personnel were conducted to assist with the interpretation of the content findings. In order to protect anonymity, both organizations and individuals have been given fictitious names. The observed newspaper and television organizations will be referred to as the *Midwest Tribune* and the Midwest Nightly, respectively.

Converging Issues

Over the past two decades, the public, criminal justice professionals, and government officials have become increasingly concerned about the treatment of crime victims. A number of factors have contributed to this concern, including a growing crime problem, the development of advocacy groups lobbying for change, and legislative response to public and interest group pressure. In part, the concern has been spawned by the sensationalism of certain stories in the news media that have accentuated some of the problems experienced by crime victims.

Correspondingly, the presentation of crime topics in various media has received increased academic scrutiny. For example, a historical meta-analysis of crime and media studies indicated that the total amount of research conducted during the past twenty years was more than double that of the prior seventy years (Marsh 1989: 508). Academics have used content and ethnographic methods to study how crimes are presented in the news, how organizations produce stories, and whether a daily bombardment with crime news influences how the public thinks about crime. The news media are frequently cited as publicizing crime and influencing, even misguiding, the public about it.

The academic literature has, however, ignored an important aspect of crime reporting: how crime victims and the news media overlap. This research was designed to study that topic.

The Public and the Media

People form their opinions about crime in a variety of ways. Approximately 35 million people annually in the United States are victims of crimes (Bureau of Justice Statistics 1994). These victims can comment firsthand on what it means to be traumatized by crime. Others perpetrate crimes, and their opinions are formed in part from their experiences as perpetrators. Still, others work daily as criminal justice practitioners, making arrests, prosecuting or defending suspected offenders, and supervising convicted defendants. When they think about the problem of crime in society, all of these individuals rely on their personal experience in forming their opinions.

Most people, however, do not have such direct daily exposure to crime and form their impressions about crime, criminal justice, and victims indirectly. The vast majority of people in fact, rely on the mass news media for information about crime and its victims (President's Commission on Law Enforcement and Administration of Justice 1967; Meyer 1975; Sherizen 1978; Skogan and Maxfield 1981). A study by Graber (1980: 49-50), for example, found that 95 percent of the respondents surveyed cited the mass media as their primary source of information about crime and criminal justice, and another study indicated that nearly half of the respondents had read or watched a crime story the previous evening (Skogan and Maxfield 1981: 140). This reliance on various media for forming crime images is accentuated by the popularity of criminal justice themes in television shows, literature, movies, and comic books (Newman 1990).

"Many people spend more time in 'mass mediated' interaction than in direct 'live' interaction with other people," according to Ericson, Baranek, and Chan (1991: 13). In 1985, for example, over 60 million newspapers were circulated daily, and 99 percent of U.S. households had radios (Stanley and Niemi 1988). Whereas before 1950 television sets were found in fewer than 10 percent of all U.S. homes, by 1985 they were found in 98 percent of homes and were viewed for an average of more than seven hours a day (Stanley and Niemi 1988). Americans will watch, on average, seven years of television in their lifetimes (Elias 1986).

Common sense tells us that the issues portrayed in the media can affect the public and policymakers. The media's influence on the criminal justice system has been acknowledged in such diverse policy areas as drug arrests (Belenko, Fagan, and Chin 1991), police crackdown behavior (Sherman 1990), homicide prosecutions (Pritchard 1986), citizens' fear of crime (Graber 1980), juvenile justice (McGarrell 1988), passage of computer crime laws (Hollinger and Lanza-Kaduce 1988), and death penalty executions (Stack 1987; but see Bailey and Peterson 1989; Bailey 1990). Others have gone beyond simply acknowledging this influence to advocate working with the media to inform public opinion (American Bar Association 1988; Barak 1988).

Much literature exists on the role of the media in shaping public opinion. Studies have examined such diverse areas as the media's effect on voting behavior, the effect of good news versus bad news, and the media's influence on issues addressed in legislative policy. Researchers have also compared types of media, examined the effects of different reporting styles, and considered how individual characteristics exacerbate those effects. The results from these studies have been inconsistent.

Some research has documented the media's influence on public opinion and criminal justice decisionmaking (Berk, Brookman, and Lesser 1977; Einstadter 1979; Fisher 1989; Gordon and Heath 1981; Haskins and Miller 1984; Pritchard 1986). For example, Forst and Blomquist (1991) argued that the news media invented social concern for missing children, resulting in political pressure to make changes in the system. Jacob and Lineberry (1982: 112) found that "trends in front page reports of crime contributed to and reinforced the growing salience of crime on the urban (and national) political agendas during the 1960s and 1970s." Moreover, other research has illustrated the power of the media in concocting a "crime wave."[2] Fishman (1978), for example, looked at reports of a rash of crimes committed against the elderly in New York City in 1976. Over a seven-week period, this theme was emphasized by all New York City media and even received national media attention. The public response consisted of a general outcry for protection of the elderly. The mayor pledged to make the streets safe for the elderly, additional staff were allocated to special police squads, community meetings were held, and bills were introduced in the legislature (Fishman 1980: 5). The actual number of crimes against the elderly, however, had not changed, and some types of crimes had actually decreased. Other researchers have documented such media-created crime waves in the areas of mugging (Hall et al. 1978) and sexual assault (Voumvakis and Ericson 1984).

Although many researchers have concluded that the news media play an important role, equal numbers question its agenda-setting ability (Chaffee 1975; Dobb and MacDonald 1979; McGuire 1986; Sacco 1982). Cumberbatch and

Beardsworth (1976) argued that researchers have overestimated the ability of the media to influence the public and policy. Protess, Leff, Brooks, and Gordon (1985: 35) found that an investigative reporting series on rape generated no new policies to deal with the abuses uncovered.

Do media messages affect public opinion and policy decisions? After reviewing this literature, Surette (1992: 87) concluded that the nature of the relationship between the news media and policymaking is still unclear. The quest for a direct effect of the media on public opinion is too simplistic. According to Ericson (1991: 221), "The mass media have diverse and conflicting influences: and moreover, . . . these influences are a function not only of mass media organization, content, and mode of presentation, but also of the broader social networks of which they, their sources, and their readers are a part." All individuals have their own "socially constructed reality," which they use when interpreting, reacting to, and being exposed to messages in the media. This reality is shaped by personal experiences, interactions with other individuals, interactions with groups, and exposure to different media (Altheide 1984; Ericson, Baranek, and Chan 1991; Quinney 1970; Surette 1992; Tuchman 1978). The relative importance of these items depends on people's reliance upon them. For example, crime victims attend more closely and react differently to crime stories than does the general public (Dobb and McDonald 1979; Garafalo and Laub 1978; Skogan and Maxfield 1981). It is nearly impossible for journalists, writers, and artists to predict whether members of their audience will read an item, how they will read it, and how they will react to it (Newman 1990).

By studying news content, we can develop an understanding of how the media portray crime and victims. It cannot be assumed, however, that the audience sees the same picture as the researcher (Graber 1980). There seems to be some relationship, although not specified, between what the media produce and their effect on the public and on political decisionmaking. In some circumstances, for some people, there is such a relationship. At a minimum, the media provide frames of reference for perceiving our world (Ericson 1991; Surette 1992), helping to define what issues are significant (Altheide 1984; Lotz 1991). Thus, in order to understand the growing interest in crime victims, it is important to decipher the portrait provided within these frames.

The Evolution of Crime Victims

At one time, crime victims played an active role in the criminal justice system. As the colonies were being settled in the seventeenth century, a system of private prosecution existed in which victims did some of their own detective work and provided direct assistance to prosecutors (Gittler 1984; Hudson 1984; Karmen 1990; McDonald 1976, 1977). Victims also had direct input into how a defendant should be punished. Restitution paid directly to the victim was a popular form of punishment, some offenders were bound into servitude to the victim, or the state was paid by the victim to incarcerate the offender (McDonald 1976, 1977).

As state power increased, victims' input into criminal justice decisionmaking decreased. The police, courts, and correctional components of the criminal justice system were influenced by the Beccarian notion that harm should be measured according to its effect on society rather than on the individual (Hagan 1982; McDonald 1976, 1977; Ziegenhagen 1977). The police were organized to suppress crime and protect society (Wickersham Commission Reports 1931: 17); private prosecution was superseded by the advent of the public prosecutor (Gittler 1984); and penitentiaries were built, making restitution to the victim obsolete and increasing the popularity of punishment by incarceration (Gittler 1984; McDonald 1976). The goals of this system were to deter, rehabilitate, and punish criminals, not to make restitution to or vindicate the victim (McDonald 1977: 296).

Victims were used to provide crime reports to the police and to testify on behalf of the state; recovery of losses was relegated to civil tort remedies (Gittler 1984; Hudson 1984). Over time, the victim's role was nearly eliminated as plea bargaining became increasingly popular (Karmen 1990). Many victims felt they were being victimized twice because of this limited role combined with endless delays, continuances, and financial burdens such as time lost from work (Bard and Sangrey 1986; Elias 1986).

More recently, however, crime victims have started to reemerge as critical participants in the criminal justice system (Elias 1986). Beginning in the 1970s, there has been growing public concern for crime victims, which has sparked federal, state, and local legislative initiatives (Acker 1992; Karmen 1984, 1990; Roland 1989; Skogan, Lurigio, and Davis 1990; Viano 1987). Among the important factors in the reemergence of victims have been heightened public concern for victims, the development of interest groups, and the acknowledgment of the victimization problem by legislators and researchers. Another factor that has contributed to the increased public awareness of crime victims is their portrayal in the media. Evidence of each of these factors present in the crime victims' movement is discussed to illustrate the changing role of the victim in society.

Public Concern. A rapidly rising crime rate and increased urban disorder have stimulated public awareness of crime and violence in society. The actual number of individuals victimized by crime has increased, and, more important, people have come to perceive themselves as potential victims (Carrington and Nicholson 1984: 4). The rising crime rate, coupled with dissatisfaction with controversial Warren Court decisions that protected and extended the rights of defendants, has helped convince the public to accept conservative solutions to crime (Karmen 1990; Viano 1987). Crime victims have been linked with the conservative crime control ideology to counterbalance the expansion of defendants' rights, and victims have been used to provide "legitimacy and justification for restrictive measures" (Viano 1987: 442).

Interest Groups. Interest in crime victims has grown alongside concern for other individual rights. General discontent with perceived government oppression has fueled feminist, racial, and other groups to organize in protest. These broader social movements have incorporated the needs of special groups of crime victims, such as the feminist incorporation of rape victims. The growth of these more general rights movements influenced crime victims to organize nationally into a movement of their own. Organizations such as the National Organization for Victim Assistance, Mothers Against Drunk Driving (MADD), and Parents of Murdered Children were founded to coordinate victim advocacy and support efforts. These movements have assisted in raising public awareness about the needs of crime victims and have promoted the development of programs structured to assist victims (Anderson and Woodard 1985: 221).

Legislative Response. Legislators at all jurisdictional levels have responded to the increased concern about the treatment of crime victims in the criminal justice system. Typically, government officials have probed into the needs and treatment of crime victims at public hearings, then drafted and enacted legislation addressing the problems identified. For example, in December 1982 the President's Task Force on Victims of Crime presented results from hearings regarding crime victims in the criminal justice system. Over sixty specific recommendations were presented with the intent of ameliorating the trauma of crime for victims. Since the publication of this report, most legislative recommendations have been enacted at the federal and state levels (Office for Victims of Crime 1988).

Federal concern for victims has been illustrated by executive branch initiatives and implemented legislation. Evidence of moral support came in Ronald Reagan's 1981 proclamation of the first National Crime Victims' Week (Carrington and Nicholson 1989). Similar state and federal initiatives have been proclaimed annually. In 1982, the Victim and Witness Protection Act was enacted by Congress, advocating the use of victim impact statements, making it a crime to intimidate and harass victims, and establishing fair treatment principles for victims. The Comprehensive Crime Control Act and Victims of Crime Act were enacted in 1984. The latter established a crime victims fund, making money available for crime victim compensation and victim assistance programs (Stark and Goldstein 1985). The Office for Victims was established to administer funds appropriated for these programs as well as to provide aid to victim assistance programs across the country (Young 1989).

State legislators have been equally active in passing reform legislation aimed at assisting victims. For example, all fifty states, the District of Columbia, and the Virgin Islands have established victim compensation programs; forty-seven states have passed legislation allowing input of victims at sentencing; forty-six states have passed legislation that protects victims from intimidation; forty-four states have a victims' bill of rights; forty-three states require that public officials keep victims informed of criminal proceedings; thirty-eight states allow victim input at parole hearings; all fifty states have restitution laws that provide statutory reinforcement of the courts' common-law authority; twenty-six states have enacted legislation that mandates that restitution be ordered unless a judge gives reasons for not issuing an order; and forty-two states have enacted notoriety-for-profit statutes (National Organization for Victim Assistance 1988). Thirteen states have amended their constitution to include a provision regarding victims' rights (Levinson 1992: A18). It has been estimated that in the past decade, over 1,500 pieces of legislation have been passed that promote the interests of crime victims (Gibbons 1988). This increased legislative interest is even more startling when we consider that in 1971, of the nearly 400 recommendations made by the National Advisory Commission on Criminal Justice Standards and Goals for crime reduction and prevention, not one addressed the needs of crime victims (Office for Victims of Crime 1988: 3).

Finally, there has been increased awareness about the needs of special victims with particular vulnerabilities to crime. Legislation has been enacted to meet the needs of these special groups (Anderson and Woodard 1985; Karmen 1990; National Organization for Victim Assistance 1988; Stark and Goldstein 1985). Legislators have assisted child victims by enacting legislation allowing children to testify via closed-circuit television, requiring speedy trials for offenses against children, prohibiting the requirement to corroborate a child's testimony, and liberalizing the rules for children seeking compensation. The needs of female victims of sexual assault and domestic violence have also been emphasized. Sexual assault victims have been protected by enacting rape shield laws, establishing special services for victims, providing additional compensation for medical services, and protecting confidential communications between counselors and victims. Domestic violence reforms have included establishing funds for domestic violence services, facilitating the use of protective orders, and instituting provisions for mandatory arrest. Penalties have been enhanced for crimes committed against the elderly and against children, for drunk driving, and for bias-related crimes.

Research Response. Although victimology was shaped in the 1940s and a number of important studies were produced (Mendlesohn 1963; Von Hentig 1948; Wolfgang 1958), historically, scholars have generally neglected the role of crime victims in the criminal justice system (Gittler 1984). In fact, the President's Commission on Law Enforcement and Administration of Justice (1967: 80) stated that "one of the most neglected subjects in the study of crime is its victim." Research produced since the President's Commission has highlighted the importance of studying victims and provided justification for reforming their treatment. For example, a number of studies have indicated that victims are generally dissatisfied with their treatment within the criminal justice system (Ash 1972; Block 1974; Cannavale and Falcon 1976; Hagan 1982; Hawkins 1973; McDonald 1976, 1977).

Other, simultaneous research indicated the importance of crime victims to the system, acknowledging that victims are the principal gatekeepers of the system (Gottfredson 1989; Gottfredson and Gottfredson 1988; Reiss 1971). The detective as crime sleuth has been found to be a media-generated myth: Arrests are made because of information provided by victims and witnesses (Greenwood and Petersilia 1977; Spelman and Brown 1981). In addition, research indicates that victims' decision to cooperate with the prosecution and the information they are able to provide are key determinants in securing convictions (Cannavale and Falcon 1976; Forst and Hernon 1985).

News Media Contributions. The news media are another important factor contributing to the rediscovery of crime victims (Karmen 1990). Victim advocacy groups have used the news media effectively in bringing the problems victims experience within the criminal justice process to the attention of the public. For example, part of the legislative response to special crime victims can be explained by the media's emphasis on their unique vulnerabilities, which has altered the expectations about, and the treatment of, these victims. For example, during the 1970s rape received a great deal of media attention, which influenced public recognition of the seriousness of sexual assault and contributed to concern for rape victims (Gittler 1984: 118). The growing interest in other special groups of victims, such as child victims, battered spouses, victims of drunk driving, the elderly, and—most recently—bias-related and campus crime victims, has also been thought to have resulted from the media's emphasis on these groups (see Fattah and Sacco 1989: 148-152; Gittler 1984: 118-120; Karmen 1990: 219-275). Attention given to these specific groups has evolved into more general concern for all crime victims (Gittler 1984: 120).

In addition, the news media have contributed to making the general problem of victimization an issue of national concern by publicizing extreme, traumatic cases. Among the most powerful and sensationalized stories are those regarding the victimization of clearly innocent victims and those involving vigilantes. Innocent victim stories are those that present a particular one-sidedness to crime—for example, strong, evil offender preys upon meek, defenseless victim (Lotz 1991). The media's current emphasis on stalkings fits this genre.

A specific example of an innocent victim story that stimulated a direct public response was the Kitty Genovese story. Genovese was stabbed and murdered over a thirty-five-minute period. What was newsworthy about this story was that there were thirty-eight witnesses who could have responded to her cries for help but failed to do so. Public response was strong because the story provided a shocking reality of victimization as well as symbolizing the general unresponsiveness of society toward victims, and the story was able to be captured and presented to a growing television audience (Bard 1985: 45; see also Conklin 1975). Adam Walsh provided the media with another high-profile innocent victim. In 1983, over 55 million Americans viewed the television docudrama of his kidnapping and murder (Karmen 1990: 226). This was perhaps the "triggering event" (McGarrell and Castellano 1991) of a missing children's movement, which has become among the strongest and most influential groups in passing new laws to protect a special class of victims (Karmen 1990).

The media also sensationalize stories involving vigilantes. The emphasis is on victims, unprotected by a system that is supposed to be their guardian, who strike out in heroic fashion. Vigilantes might overreact when protecting themselves, seek retribution for an unjust sentence, or intercede as a Good Samaritan (Karmen 1990). Although acts of vigilantism are rare, stories such as the attempted robbery of Bernard Goetz or Ellie Nesler lashing out at her son's alleged molester receive extensive media coverage. Successful vigilante responses are generally applauded by the news media and the public.

Although the media have been cited for making positive contributions to the reemergence of crime victims, they have also been criticized. The source of the conflict comes from the attempted balancing by the media of the public's right to know with an individual's right to privacy. The media have been criticized for their sensational, "death-knock"[3] coverage of grieving victims; showing bodies, body bags, and bloody scenes; camping out on victims' front lawns; and coming onto a crime scene, cameras rolling, asking how the victim feels (Seymour 1986). Grabosky and Wilson (1989: 115) argued that journalists are willing to be "super assertive, and sometimes manipulative" in order to obtain information from victims, resulting in further traumatization of the victims. The frequency with which these types of problems occur, however, is still unclear because the results by Grabosky and Wilson were based on interviews with fifty-three Australian television and newspaper journalists. In addition to the limited generalizability of the findings, conducting a small number of interviews is not as effective as combining what journalists say with watching what they actually do (Ericson, Baranek, and Chan 1987, 1989).

Research Significance

This book examines the overlap between crime victims and the news media. The presentation of crime victims in the news and their role in the news-production process cannot be understood without considering other aspects of the news-production process and the other content presented within crime stories. This study puts the presentation of victims within a larger context, contributing to our understanding of crime in the news media in six ways.

First, what is presented about crime is determined in large measure by representatives of the different organizations involved in the news-production process. Chapter 2 examines this process, discussing the different factors that constrain the images presented. The information about crime presented in the news media is limited as the result of selection decisions that are influenced by organizational constraints. Representatives of news organizations struggle with criminal justice sources to determine the images that are presented about crime. News organizations are businesses expected to manufacture a product every day. Organizational decisions are made that ensure that the most newsworthy crime story is presented to the public in the most efficient manner. This process influences what is presented about crime. How this process works and the information generated from it are considered. The reasons news media rely heavily on criminal justice sources and the motivations of these organizations to provide information, as well as certain types of information, are also discussed.

Second, all of the elements of a crime story (type of crime, victim, and defendant) are considered throughout this book because each element, separately or in combination, can determine how important a news story is to an organization. Crime victims are only one element of a crime story. The growing media research has highlighted other story information that needs to be examined because the frequent presentation of certain elements of crime can constrain the information provided about victims. Chapter 3 examines the presentation of crime, victims, and defendants in the news and discusses why certain images are presented.

Third, this research examines how the victims' role changes across the type of story and how victims' involvement in the news-production process influences the final product. The presentation of crime and crime victims occurs as a result of a process. The use of victim and family members is contrasted with the information provided by criminal justice and other sources. This book provides a systematic evaluation of the victims' role in the generation of crime stories—such as when organizations contact victims, how they contact them, and for what reason—providing essential clues as to why certain characteristics of victims are presented to the public and others are excluded. Chapter 4 details the role crime victims play in the news-production process.

Fourth, this research makes comparisons across types of media, considering whether the different format needs of an organization affect the images of crime, sources, and crime victims presented in the news. The images of crime, victims, and defendants in print and electronic media are discussed in Chapter 5. Newspaper and television are among the most popular media from which the public obtains its images of crime. Print and electronic organizations, however, have different format needs that must be fulfilled in order to make their product appealing to the largest possible segment of the public. Stories about certain crimes and specific victims are selected and produced to fill the needs of each type of organization.

Fifth, this research examines whether differential access to crime influences the type of crime, the type of victim, and the sources used for the presentation of crime, comparing results across different cities. Crime is a relative problem, distributed unevenly across U.S. cities. People who live in large urban centers have to cope daily with the threat of becoming a victim. In smaller cities, residents may leave their doors unlocked because crime seems nonexistent. The news media that have the responsibility of presenting the local crime portrait have access to varying amounts of serious crime, depending on the city considered. Thus, the final news product depends on the types of local crimes available to the organization. Chapter 6 examines how differential access to crime affects the news product presented.

Finally, the role of the news media in society is examined in Chapter 7. The powers the news media have to inform the public about crime and victims are discussed. These powers, however, are constrained by the structure of the news–production process and source control over the presentation of crime. This book concludes by discussing how these constraints might influence the public's thinking about crime and victims.

Notes

1. The public receives messages from a wide variety of communication sources, including mass media (e.g., television, newspaper, radio), target audience media (e.g., cable television programs), and intrapersonal and interpersonal communication (Bittner, J.R. 1989. *Mass Communication: An Introduction* 5th ed. New Jersey: Prentice Hall). This study considers only the messages offered by television and newspaper organizations that sell primarily to a local audience. Of course, the findings represent only a small portion of the various messages available to the public about crime and victims. These media were chosen, however, because of the availability of their message to mass, diverse audiences.

2. The process whereby journalists link a number of crimes together around a more general theme is typically referred to as a "moral panic" (Cohen, S. 1972. *Folk Devils and Moral Panics.* London: MacGibbon and Kee; Gusfield, J. 1981. *The Culture of Public Problems.* Chicago: University of Chicago Press).

3. Those situations in which relatives of deceased victims are interviewed shortly after finding out about the victim's death (Grabosky, P. and Wilson, P. 1989. *Journalism and Justice: How Crime Is Reported.* Leichhardt: Pluto Press).

2

Constructing Crime News

This chapter examines how crime news is constructed by the various participants directly involved in the news-production process. Crime is a high-priority news topic. Because of its popularity, there is a large news hole that must be filled. The content analysis performed revealed that on average, newspapers covered nine crime stories a day; television stations covered four. News media rely heavily on individuals who can provide the necessary story elements without question. In order to make the production of crime news more manageable, the media routinize their task by putting themselves in a position to get easy access to the sources that can fulfill story needs (Ericson, Baranek, and Chan 1987, 1989; Gans 1979; Tuchman 1973). Establishing cordial relationships with criminal justice sources ensures that the news organization can meet its daily crime story quota, but it also limits the information provided in stories because the information known by these agencies is biased and reflects their own perspective.

The news media have a large number of stories to choose from because crime is consistent and abundant (Tunstall 1971). The vast majority of crimes that become news must first be officially acknowledged by a criminal justice source. The images presented in the news are narrow at first because a large number of crimes are never reported to the police. Then, the production of news involves condensing the crimes made available into a limited amount of news space. The selection, production, and presentation of crime stories are based on a number of discretionary decisions made by both news and criminal justice source organizations. Source organizations develop policies regarding their relationship to the media, decide on the level of access that can be gained by the media organization, and attempt to garner public support by promoting particular programs within the media. Media organizations have an equally large range of possible discretionary decisions to make when selecting stories interacting with a source, and presenting crime stories (Ericson, Baranek, and Chan 1987, 1989). The final news product presented, in an attempt to satisfy public curiosity, is influenced by the cost-benefit calculations made by both the media and the source organization, which have a symbiotic relationship.

The majority of past research that has examined the presentation of crime in the news has focused on news content, failing to link what is presented to the news-production process (Ericson, Baranek, and Chan 1987). Content analysis gives only a partial explanation of the presentation of crime news because it fails to consider how the process eliminates various crimes from presentation (Ericson, Baranek, and Chan 1989; Gans 1979). In order to strengthen the inferences drawn from content analysis, it is necessary to couple the presentation of crime news with how news is produced within an organization. The balance of this chapter discusses the steps involved in the production of news about crime.

The Production of News at the *Tribune* and the Nightly

News organizations are structured so that they can meet the high demand for crime stories efficiently, relying on a variety of news-item sources (those cited as authoring the story) to meet the organizations' needs. Some stories are produced internally by individual reporters, either working a specific beat or generally assigned, who attempt to establish links with a variety of local criminal justice sources who can assist them with their daily mandate. In addition, wire services such as the Associated Press (AP) and United Press International (UPI) are available to both newspaper and television news organizations. Finally, national and international crime stories may be extracted from other national newspapers such as the *New York Times*.

Table 2.1 presents data on the news-item sources used by the nine news organizations in the content analysis.[1] This analysis revealed that the majority of stories were produced by reporters who work within a news organization covering local news (62.7 percent). Wire reports were also frequently used to fill daily crime news space (21.3 percent). Approximately 8 percent of crime stories were elicited from other newspapers.

Midwest Tribune

Such use of item sources was found when observing activities at the *Midwest Tribune*. National and international crime stories included in the *Tribune* were often collected from wire services and articles appearing in other newspapers. Local crime stories were produced internally by three primary sources. First, the majority were produced by reporters on either the police beat or the court beat. The police beat was located on the first floor of police headquarters, tucked out of the way at the end of a corridor. The decentralized structure and limited amount of direct supervision of the news organization gave reporters a

TABLE 2.1 News-Item Sources Cited

Item Source	Total	Percent
Reporter	1,669	62.7
Wire reports[a]	567	21.3
Another newspaper	210	7.9
Editor[b]	59	2.2
Affiliated reporter	31	1.2
Expert	15	0.6
Citizen	13	0.5
Unknown[c]	100	3.8

N = 2,664

[a] Includes AP, UPI, Reuters, Cox, Newhouse, McClatchy, Gannett, and those stories for which wire reports were designated but no specific one was specified.

[b] Includes only those instances in which the editor was clearly identified.

[c] Stories that did not have a source attribution.

Source: All tables used the nine media sources detailed in the Appendix.

large amount of discretion in producing crimes they deemed newsworthy. This beat was staffed from 11:00 a.m. to 6:00 p.m. by two reporters, and another reporter worked the beat until 1:00 a.m., which was the time final stories had to be submitted to be included in the last edition. Police beat reporters produced between three and five crime stories each day. Some of the resources found in the police beat office were two computers linked directly to the main office, a telephone with a direct connection to the newsroom, three other telephones with outside lines, and a television set. The activities of various police and fire departments, emergency medical units, and other news organizations were monitored throughout the day with the assistance of police scanners. In addition, the physical location of the police beat allowed reporters to gain access to police documents such as police blotter reports, arrest documents, and official memoranda, which contributed to their efficient production of crime stories.

It was amazing how reporters could use the different resources simultaneously. For example, Manny Diaz, a reporter employed by the *Tribune* for about three months, was writing a story on a gang-related homicide at the computer while talking to his editor on the direct line to the newsroom about some information he was lacking. When he got off the telephone he asked, "Where did that accident occur?" I gazed at him dumbfoundedly and responded, "What accident?" He walked over to a scanner and turned up the volume for the second police district. No other information came over the scanner, so he decided to call the district. He discovered that an accident had occurred, but it was not newsworthy because it lacked "death, blood, and bodies."

The location of the police beat gave reporters the opportunity to interact with key police sources. Indeed, police reporters rarely had to leave police headquarters to produce their stories because the information they needed was accessible within the building or they could contact all necessary sources by telephone. Police beat reporters started each day on the telephone with sources. Reporters made daily calls to city police districts, specific detective divisions (for example, the homicide division), suburban departments, emergency medical personnel, hospitals, coroners, fire departments, the coast guard, and airport security. These calls were made throughout the day to ensure that late-breaking stories were not missed. All of the sources provided what *they* thought was news. Police reporters also had unrestricted access to arrest sheets, police booking reports, and their primary police source, who was affectionately referred to by reporters as the "mouthpiece." The police mouthpiece was a police spokesperson, had an office located next to the police chief's, and said he spent at "least 40 percent of [his] time dealing with the media."

Police organizations provide the physical space for news organizations and access to official police documents in order to increase their ability to control the images presented about themselves in the news. The police are frequently under scrutiny and are held accountable to the public for their actions. The police, therefore, go to great lengths to shield particular crimes or ineffective police responses from public preview because their presentation might adversely affect the public image of the police.

A number of local crime stories were also produced by court beat reporters. The *Tribune* had two separate beats responsible for court news. One was located at the federal courthouse, the other at the county courthouse. The federal court beat was staffed by one reporter who was expected to cover any newsworthy appeals heard by these courts. The majority of daily court stories came from the county beat, which was located on the first floor of the courthouse. It was regularly staffed by two reporters during courthouse hours. They produced between three and five stories a day. The resources available in this office included two computers, a direct line to the newsroom, and two outside telephone lines.

Court beat reporters typically began their day by checking the court calendar to see whether they spotted any newsworthy cases. Court reporters had convenient access to indictments, motions that were filed, returned search warrants, and appellate decisions. Generally, reporters were not questioned when they walked behind desks to peruse these materials, and they did not have to pay for photocopying when they used county copy machines. Moreover, court reporters had free reign of the hallways and offices behind the courtrooms, which gave them the opportunity to mingle with clerks, prosecutors, and defense attorneys outside the judges' chambers. They also had access to court proceedings and received special privileges if a courtroom was filled with spectators. For example, when a popular area doctor was on trial for illegal prescription drug sales and all seats in the courtroom were filled, the judge announced at the beginning of the session that "any media could sit in the jury box" and held up the proceedings until all of the reporters were settled.

The second major producers of local crime stories at the *Tribune* were general assignment reporters. If either the police or the court beat was short staffed, a sensational news story occurred that required coverage from a variety of angles, or a reporter had a particular interest in a story or series of stories, a general assignment reporter could contribute to daily crime coverage. For example, one day during the court beat observational period, both court reporters took vacation days, and the beat office was locked. A general assignment reporter was sent to the courthouse to cover a case involving the sentencing of the prominent doctor when he was found guilty on 268 illegal drug counts.

Finally, reporters working in suburban news bureaus contribute local crime news. An increasing number of newspaper organizations have established these bureaus to increase the appeal of their newspapers to consumers living in areas surrounding the outer boundaries of a city (Kaniss 1991). A reporter who covers bureau news is responsible for all news occurring within a particular suburban area: political, business, community, and any newsworthy crime stories. The *Tribune* had three suburban news bureaus.

Midwest Nightly

All of the reporters who worked for the Midwest Nightly were on general assignment, and any of them could cover a crime story. Two reporters were available to cover stories that occurred between 9:00 a.m. and 3:00 p.m., and one of these was generally sent to the courthouse to collect sound bites for court stories. Two or three other reporters arrived at 3:00 p.m. to assist in the production of stories for the evening broadcast.

The production of news started each morning when a managing editor and an assignment editor arrived to generate a list of potential stories for the evening newscast. A variety of different sources contributed the stories on this list. First, the managing editor relied heavily on criminal justice sources. The managing editor, the assignment editor, or an intern would call a list of police departments (both city and suburban), fire departments, emergency medical personnel, and other potential disaster organizations (for example, airport security, coast guard) to see whether any crime or tragedy could be added to the list. In addition, police and fire scanners operated throughout the day in a space immediately adjacent to that in which the managing editor and assignment editor made their calls. Although television reporters were given access to criminal justice documents such as police arrest blotter reports and court indictments, these documents were rarely used because fewer broadcast stories than newspaper crime stories had to be produced.

Another of the primary sources the television station used to learn about crime stories was other local and national news media. Print, television, and radio media were monitored throughout the day. Each morning the managing editor perused numerous print media, including the *New York Times* and local city and suburban dailies. The radio was tuned into local news stations, and four television stations were on the entire day, monitoring the affiliated local stations, as well as a cable news station such as the Cable News Network (CNN). Typically, an intern was assigned to keep track of the stories presented during the 12:00 p.m. and 6:00 p.m. broadcasts to ensure that the Nightly had all of the stories from the other news programs. The majority of crime stories presented within these media were added to the final list of potential stories.

The managing editor also kept a file of press releases received for each day of the month. This file was perused each morning, and releases were either added to the list or thrown out. A few crime stories were considered from releases sent by various community action groups, such as Mothers Against Drunk Driving or Citizens Against Crime. Generally, however, these stories were covered only briefly on a slow news day.

Selection decisions about the list of potential stories were made at an afternoon editorial meeting. At this meeting the news director, the managing and assignment editors, the producer and assistant producer, anchors, and reporters discussed the list of potential stories, and decisions were made as to whether and how a story was to be covered. A reporter would be assigned to cover a story only if it was newsworthy enough to be a "package." Packages are those stories in which the anchor briefly introduces the story, then a reporter provides the details using various sources. Packages are the longest stories produced by television news stations, lasting on average between one and two minutes. The other types of television news stories are voice-overs (VOs), voice-over sound on tape (VSOTs), and reads. VOs are those stories in which an anchor reads the story while video is shown, whereas VSOTs are stories in which the anchor reads the story and some sound bites taken from sources are included. Reads are those stories read in their entirety by the anchor without any video. VOs, VSOTs, and reads are much shorter than packages, which were put together by a variety of personnel working for the Nightly—including reporters, anchors, assignment editors, producers, and interns—depending on who was available.

The News Filtering Process

Although crime is an important news topic and all crimes have the potential to become news, a number of crimes are never presented. Organizational decisions are made to determine which crimes are excluded from presentation consideration. News personnel and criminal justice sources struggle among themselves to control what is presented, making a series of discretionary decisions during the steps of the news-production process that eliminate potential crime stories. There are four primary steps in the crime news-production process. The first step is controlled primarily by source organizations, which determine the level of access reporters have to the crimes known by a source. In the second step, news personnel select a range of potential stories from the large number made available by the source organization. As with any other kind of potential news material, the central criterion for choosing crime stories is newsworthiness. Third, news and source organizations struggle to determine what information is to be included in a selected story during the production stage of the news process. Fourth, the constructed crime story competes with other potential stories for news space as news personnel determine how a selected story is finally presented to the public.

The Crime News-selection Process

Source organizations are capable of influencing what is and what is not presented about crime. Source organizations determine the level of access a news organization achieves when selecting crimes for presentation. A source organization has an organizationally determined set of criteria that influence its decisions about the release of story information. The source decides what information should be revealed and in what form, what details should be highlighted or discarded, and when the story should be released (Ericson, Baranek, and Chan 1989: 6). Ericson, Baranek, and Chan's (1989: 11) analysis of source organizations in Canada illustrates that the police have become more open to the media so they can control their environment, protect their organizations' vulnerability, and legitimize their work. Policies regarding certain crimes or victims may be established, for example, that limit or expand the ability to make information known to the media, depending upon the needs of the organization. When the Buffalo police department did not like the media coverage of an investigation into the drug activities of some of its officers, an organizational directive completely eliminated media access to police reports, and source contacts refused to respond to media inquiries, thereby influencing what could be presented about the crimes (*Buffalo News*, February 14, 1990).

Criminal justice sources benefit from establishing and maintaining relationships with reporters because these relationships allow the sources to determine the amount and type of crime information provided to news media (Ericson, Baranek, and Chan 1989). Police and courtroom personnel pass along crimes that reflect their own perspective in which seriousness, dangerousness, and crime fighting are emphasized, thus helping these sources to accomplish a variety of objectives. One objective criminal justice sources attempt to further when releasing story information is punishment. An example taken from my observations at the *Tribune* illustrates how one source used the news media to accomplish this objective. As I was eating lunch one day with a *Tribune* reporter, a district attorney thanked her for attending a shock parole hearing for a woman who murdered her abuser and was sentenced to from five to twenty-five years. The district attorney asked numerous media to attend. The woman's sentence was not commuted. The prosecutor suggested that the presence of the media deterred the elected judge from reducing the defendant's sentence because he did not want to be publicly identified as being soft on crime.

Sources use the news media to further the objective of deterrence. Police departments publicize the use of weekend sobriety checkpoints and holiday speed traps to deter individuals from driving drunk or speeding (Ericson 1991). News follow-ups on the productiveness of these police tools are presented in the hope of deterring future law violators. Police departments allow reporters to ride with officers for the same reason. Steve Barber, a reporter from a large television station, was able to ride with police on a drug crackdown detail. Barber thought this story had some deterrent value: "If people see a massive police effort, we got cameras rolling and we do a story on, say, a major drug bust, it might make some kid think twice when they see the police with their helmets and their goggles, and they go busting in their doors. It might scare them, and maybe it will scare them to a point where they say 'I am not going to get involved in this because I don't want it to happen to me.'"

Sources request news coverage to invigorate a stalled investigation. For example, a county judge held a press conference, which was attended by both *Tribune* and Nightly reporters, about a man who was misrepresenting himself as an attorney. The court was trying to uncover other victims who might have been swindled by this impostor. The judge, when asked by one of the reporters why she was releasing a picture of the suspect even though he had yet to be charged with a crime, responded, "We wanted to get the story out so that other people who were victimized can come forward." Similarly, police departments release pictures of suspects or ask reporters to do crime stopper segments to assist in investigations.

Source organizations also use the media as a public relations tool, informing the public about important activities and awards received. Police organizations rely on the news media to promote a positive image of themselves. When individual police officers receive awards, news media cover the ceremonies. This is significant because the news media rarely cover other award ceremonies despite receiving a large number of news releases announcing such awards. On average, thirty press releases about awards, dedications, and ceremonies are received in the course of a month. Most of these will not even make the list of potentially newsworthy stories discussed during the afternoon editorial meeting, and few are covered. Gary Kundrat, the managing editor of the Nightly and the person responsible for generating the list of stories, explained that although they are important for the people directly involved, these stories are of little significance to the general public.

The news media's willingness to rely on these criminal justice sources results from concerns about their own organizational needs. Organizational resources to cover crime news, such as the number of personnel and the amount of news space allowed per topic, are limited. Easy access to source organizations allows reporters to meet the time, deadline, and format requirements of their medium. News organizations are structured so they meet their needs in the most efficient manner: They set up beats within police and court buildings, establish relationships with police and court sources, and have access to police and court information in order to be able to reproduce what is officially known about crime. Moreover, police and fire scanners are conveniently located and continuously monitored to safeguard against overlooking a potentially newsworthy crime.

Relying on the crimes that are known to the police allows the media to satisfy the heavy news demand for stories on crime with minimal organizational costs and time-consuming complications. It would be more difficult to meet story demands, and what could be provided would be more limited if news media did not have easy access to criminal justice source information.

Reporters are unwilling to publicly criticize criminal justice sources for ineffective responses to crime because they fear losing access to police sources and documents. Rarely do stories examine the causes of crime, the motive for a particular crime, or the effectiveness of the criminal justice system (Graber 1980). Results from the present content analysis revealed that causes of crime were mentioned in approximately 2 percent of the sampled crime stories, motives for crime incidents were presented in about 20 percent of specific incident stories, police effectiveness was evaluated in less than 4 percent of the total number of stories, and courts were evaluated in less than 3 percent of the stories. Table 2.2 presents the cases in which the police or courts were evaluated (either positively or negatively) by the media. This table indicates that even when the police or courts were evaluated in crime stories, the media evaluate their performance on one specific instance. The problem is assumed to be isolated and caused by a "rotten apple" rather than being ongoing and systemic.

An example from the ethnographic analysis illustrates how reporters weigh the costs of pushing a particular issue when evaluating the performance of a source. For example, Manny Diaz from the *Tribune* was faced with weighing a number of costs. Diaz, who puts a story together much as a seasoned police detective puts together a case, received a call from a homeowner who had complained to the police about cars parked illegally on his front lawn when an auction occurred nearby. Even after the homeowner posted warning signs, an unmarked police car parked on his lawn. When the man threatened to tow the car, the officer identified himself and went off to the auction. The man had the car towed anyways. He was then arrested for motor vehicle theft and destruction of property. Diaz met with the police mouthpiece about the story.

TABLE 2.2 Evaluation of Police and Court Organizations in News Stories

Type of Evaluation	Police (in percentages)	Court (in percentages)
Overall positive evaluation	12.3	1.6
Overall negative evaluation	10.3	21.3
Overall mixed evaluation	5.1	0.0
Evaluation in specific instance*	69.1	77.1
Other	3.2	0.0
	N=97	N=61

* This category includes those instances in which police or courts are criticized for performance in a specific situation. For example, a victim might have been angered by an investigation, or a prosecutor might have been criticized for selectively prosecuting a particular individual.

The mouthpiece asked an officer who was involved in the confrontation to attend the meeting, something that rarely happened. After listening to the police side of the story, Diaz thought the officer was lying. Nevertheless, the story was never printed for a few reasons. First, the benefits of doing so were unknown. Diaz did not think the homeowner was telling the whole truth either. Second, the costs could have been great. Diaz was still developing his relationship with the primary police source. He was afraid his access to police information might have been limited or totally cut off. Omitting the story did not leave a news gap on that particular day. Therefore, Diaz decided that not covering the story was in his best interest.

News Media Selection of Newsworthy Stories

News organizations are not isolated from outside influences. They and their employees operate within an environment that affects presentation decisions. It is important to accept that these organizations are private businesses producing news to make a profit for their owners (Altheide 1976; Epstein 1974; Gans 1979). If the product is unappealing, just as in any other business, news organizations have to adapt by reorganizing, realigning, or terminating operations. As Bob Suren, a news director from a television station in a medium-sized city, stated: "Newspapers have to sell newspapers, sell ad space. They are not public utilities. They are businesses. We are a business, and I believe that you do what you have to do, legally, ethically, to get folks to watch your show. . . . We are owned by people that want to make money: they really don't care if I lead with a murder or not; they just want to know if anybody was watching."

A news organization's capability of securing advertising commitments is generally related to the strength of the economy as well as to that organization's ability to demonstrate that it is attracting viewers. The amount of space available for the presentation of news is smaller when the economy is bad because businesses do not have excess money to pay for advertising. Two of the police reporters from the *Tribune* discussed their concerns about the possibility of layoffs because of the receding economy. Manny Diaz was particularly vulnerable because he was one of the reporters hired when the *Tribune* had recently expanded. I later asked Greg Monroe, who had been a police reporter for less than a year, whether the changes in the economy might affect the presentation of crime. He responded in the affirmative: "The news hole is shrinking up. Sure, it is going to affect the total amount of crime news and what gets presented." If the economy remains bad and a news organization is in financial trouble, individuals lose their jobs, which affects morale and the amount of time other reporters have to produce stories.

Print and broadcast organizations compete with other media for advertising dollars by presenting a product they hope will attract the largest percentage of the market share. Television news stations compete directly and intensely for ratings, determined quarterly by services such as the A. C. Nielsen Company and Arbitron. Newspaper sales departments, on the other hand, quote total number of papers circulated when bargaining with advertisers (Pasqua et al. 1990). The total amount of money advertisers are charged is based on the number of readers or viewers. According to Phyllis Kaniss (1991: 103), "The difference in a rating point can mean hundreds of thousands of dollars to a station." News organizations go to great lengths to determine the types of news that will attract the greatest proportion of the audience. Indeed, the *Tribune* was in the midst of a major study that attempted "to measure readership of every element of the newspaper" (*Tribune* document no. 1: 1).

As cities have become increasingly decentralized and the primary clients of news and advertised products have moved to suburban areas, news organizations have had to make adjustments to attract this widespread audience (Kaniss 1991). Historically, news media have adapted in order to continue to capture the highest proportion of the audience when it changed either demographically or geographically. Kaniss (1991: 59) noted that "the local news firm must match its messages to its particular local market, and, even more important, it must draw that market of dispersed and diverse readers together into a common local identity." Crime is an important topic news organizations use to capture transformations in their audience because it bolsters readership and circulation. According to Friendly and Goldfarb (1967: 36), "In a competitive situation where there are bound to be occasional or continual battles for readers and revenue, the usual weaponry is the reporting of crime."

Crime delivered through any medium capitalizes on the public's fascination with gore and pathos (Gans 1979). As Greg Monroe of the *Tribune* commented, for some reason the "public has an insatiable appetite for crime." Crime stories provide real-life drama and entertainment that can stir a host of emotions for different audience members. Crime news can make consumers laugh (the burglar who terrorized a suburban neighborhood by breaking into homes in the evening to steal underwear from the sleeping owners), cry (the minister who spent his entire life advocating for the poor and was doing so when bludgeoned to death), reflect (two teenagers who were killed by another when both drivers had been drinking), and rejoice (follow-up story about the donations a family received for their son whose father had two broken legs and was unemployed and whose mother had recently had a stroke; the son was in the hospital because he was thrown from his bike by two thugs who stole the flowers he bought for his mother on Mother's Day). Whether readers laugh, cry, reflect, rejoice, or read with disinterest depends upon their own socially constructed reality. People are interested in crime, attend to it, form opinions about what they read, and continue to be curious about certain crimes as they pass through the criminal justice system.

The news interests of the audience filter back and are acknowledged by the news organization and its reporters, influencing what is presented about crime. Personnel develop an understanding of the news used to attract consumers. In order to get their stories into the news, as well to get them placed prominently, reporters need to conform to audience pressures (Kaniss 1991). Reporters are paid by news organizations. They must produce stories that sell, rely on sources that are easily established and accessible, and abide by whatever organizational policy might be in place that govern their behavior. Although criminal justice organizations play an important role in influencing story selection decisions, the crimes reporters produce as news must meet an independent set of criteria regarding the newsworthiness of events. Reporters develop an understanding of these criteria over time as they become acculturated to their work. Their interactions with other reporters, sources, and superiors influence their understanding of these criteria. Individual reporters adopt these tacit criteria in order to be rewarded and to have their stories displayed prominently. Past research has identified a range of characteristics of newsworthiness that influence reporters' selection decisions (Cohen and Young 1981; Ericson, Baranek, and Chan 1987; Hartley 1982).

Seriousness. The first measure of newsworthiness is the seriousness of the offense. Crimes of violence are overrepresented in the news (Ericson, Baranek, and Chan 1991; Graber 1980; Humphries 1981; Lee-Sammons 1989; Marsh 1988; Roshier 1981; Sheley and Ashkins 1981; Skogan and Maxfield 1981), whereas property and white-collar offenses are underrepresented (Evans and Lundman 1983; Morash and Hale 1987). The crimes least likely to occur (murder, rape) are those most frequently presented (Graber 1980; Skogan and Maxfield 1981). For example, Graber (1980) reported that murders constituted only 0.2 percent of offenses known to the police in Chicago in 1976 but accounted for 26 percent of crime stories in the *Chicago Tribune*. Sheley and Ashkins (1981), in a study of media crime coverage in New Orleans, found that serious crimes predominated in both print and electronic media.

Incident Participants. The individuals involved in an incident can influence decisions about newsworthiness. The characteristics of the victim or the defendant can increase the likelihood that less serious crimes will be presented in the news. Certain demographic characteristics, such as age and occupation, make a crime more appealing as news. For example, the involvement of victims or defendants who are very young or very old or who occupy a position with a high amount of responsibility to the public—such as a police officer, clergy member, or teacher—increases the likelihood that a crime will be prominently displayed in the news.

Incident Producers. The individuals who produce crime stories can determine the newsworthiness of an event. Research indicates that reporters share similar characteristics demographically and in professional background. For example, Weaver, Drew, and Wilhoit (1986: 683) found that reporters who work for newspaper and television organizations have similar political party affiliations, perceptions of journalist roles and ethics, educational levels, and professional reading patterns. Yet, although these factors place limits on individual decisionmaking, reporters still have some autonomy in doing their jobs because of the nature of news production.

Crime news production, especially by newspapers, provides reporters with the freedom to select and produce stories in the manner they choose. Police and court reporters started and ended their day at a beat office, far removed from their superiors. Because of their independence, individual beat reporters possessed a considerable amount of discretion in how and when they produced news stories. Police reporters from the *Tribune*, after examining a two-inch stack of blotter reports, decided which to pull, which to peruse, and which to follow up on. Individual court reporters decided which indictments, appellate decisions, and other court documents examined they selected, which court sessions they attended, and how long they attended them. Each individual reporter decided how a story was covered, the angle and source(s) used, and the story's lead as well as its length. These decisions were constrained, however, because reporters remained in continual contact with editors, discussing size restrictions and angle possibilities.

Individual reporters sometimes have a personal interest in a type of crime, which increases its likelihood of getting in the news. One of the *Tribune* reporters had a continuing interest in gang activities, so he was more likely to cover gang-related homicides. Covering gang activities and the problems associated with gangs afforded this reporter the opportunity to establish strong relationships with members of the gang task force. His interest made officers actively seek him out when they knew of any major gang developments across the city, allowing him to cover events as they occurred rather than reacting after the fact.

Personal characteristics, such as education, socialization, number of years working on the job, and family situation, can influence what is presented within a story because they influence how a reporter reacts with a source. Reporters choose the types of sources with whom they establish an ongoing relationship as well as those they decide to alienate. I spent a few evenings on the police beat with Mike Palivoda, who worked such a beat only twice a week. The rest of his hours were spent as an evening general assignment reporter. Palivoda, who had been on the job for over twenty years, had a very laid-back approach to contacting sources. Generally, other police reporters would call police and disaster sources frequently throughout the day to capture late-breaking news. Palivoda, however, selected only a sample of the available numbers once or twice during his entire shift. I asked him about his approach. Palivoda explained that he did not need to make all the other calls. He had been on the job so long that he had sources looking for him. "I mean, I got sources that will tell me anything. It takes years of being on the job to build up a trust."

The regular police beat reporters were young and were still in the process of developing source contacts. Diaz grew up on the streets of New York and took advantage of his "street sense" when getting access to an informant. He was much less likely to trust a source, more likely to question authority, and more likely to follow up with other source contacts on the information provided than was Monroe, who was more accepting of the police side of the story and more likely to present the police in a favorable light.

Individual sources use a similar cost-benefit framework when deciding whether to release a story. Sources release information for some stories because they simply do not care what is presented about these stories. Other information is released because it is beneficial and helps accomplish an organizational objective: for example, the district attorney who asked the print and electronic media to attend the shock parole hearing that resulted in a woman being sent back to prison. Other information is withheld because of its sensitive or compromising nature. A court reporter from the *Tribune* became extremely upset when the same district attorney "forgot" to tell her about a hearing that was being held that day regarding a prosecutorial misconduct allegation against him.

Sometimes individuals within the same organization interpret an organization's story release policy quite differently. An ongoing problem between the police beat reporters and one particular source, Lacy Dyer, illustrates this. Dyer, who was in charge of the sex crimes division, refused to provide reporters with any information about rapes or child sexual abuse cases. The reporters thought these crimes should be covered on occasion because they were a significant problem that needed to be addressed. One police beat reporter had noted earlier that rape was a significant problem, was one of the most underreported crimes, and was something the public should know about. Because of Dyer's interpretation of organizational policy, however, police reporters could rarely collect enough information to write about these crimes. One morning, when the police mouthpiece stopped at the reporter's office to drop off a memorandum, the reporters brought up the problem with rape cases and suggested that a meeting with the chief should be forthcoming. "She [Dyer] needs to be aware of what we do for you," Monroe pointed out to the mouthpiece. When trying to explain why Dyer did not provide any information, the mouthpiece said he thought she felt she was acting according to the police organization's policy. He, however, had no problem with giving them the information. "I don't mind providing a victim's name, or even a rape victim's name to you guys. It is up to you to decide what you do with the name. All I ask is that you are balanced and provide both sides of the issue."

Some information is withheld by individual sources regardless of the organization's policy. Police beat reporters choose between five and seven blotter reports that might be newsworthy each day. In order to be able to decide whether a story should be done on any of these reports, the reporters usually ask the police mouthpiece to provide the full report. Usually, the mouthpiece will reject one or two of these requests. The reporters generally do not question this withholding of information because it is done consistently and the mouthpiece provides them with other reports that satisfy their daily story requirements.

Reporters are at the mercy of decisions made by criminal justice sources and individuals directly involved in a crime about the type of information that can be provided about crime. Some police officers, district attorneys, or judges may adamantly refuse to present any information about a certain crime incident or a type of crime. Others might be accommodating, depending on such individual motivational factors as political ambition or revenge. Individual criminal justice sources may use their discretion to exclude access to the critical information necessary to write a particular story because they think such information reflects negatively upon their own performance or on how the public perceives the organization or because they believe certain crimes should not be part of the media's role in informing the public about crime. A reporter can still write a story when access to critical information is limited, but it is much more difficult, and the story is unlikely to become an important news story. Similarly, crime victims possess a considerable amount of influence in determining what gets presented about crime. Crime victims and other outsiders provide a different perspective on a story than do criminal justice sources. A decision to avoid speaking to the media guarantees that the story will primarily reflect a criminal justice perspective. A reporter's decision to contact a crime victim and a decision by that victim to cooperate influence the type of story produced.

Uniqueness. The fourth characteristic that has been found to increase the newsworthiness of events is their uniqueness. Crimes that are so extraordinary that they supply an element of shock, humor, or surprise are more likely to be presented. For example, burglaries rarely fit a reporter's concept of newsworthiness because they are not serious and occur too frequently to be newsworthy on a consistent basis. However, when the burglar commits the crime in order to obtain the underwear of a sleeping, unsuspecting victim, the story is important because of its uniqueness. Similarly, victims who defy the odds and show a particular tenacity of survival, such as a security guard shot ten times who survives, increase the likelihood of the presentation of these crimes.

Salience.   Another factor that affects which crimes reporters think are newsworthy is the salience of the event, determined by its location and the frequency of its presentation. News media concerned with attracting a local audience have to rely primarily on crimes that occur within certain audience boundaries. Crimes that affect local individuals or businesses are of primary importance to the news organization because consumers can identify with the street or location at which the event occurred, avoid those areas that might be considered dangerous, and become concerned about the immediate problems that need to be addressed in their community. For example, the public wants to know what local law enforcement agencies are doing to address the problem of crime and violence in the community. News media provide police organizations with the opportunity to justify their response or at least provide a forum to request additional assistance.

The salience of an event as a newsworthy factor can also be seen in the selection of certain crimes that fit a particular pattern. If large numbers of a specific type of crime occur, reporters search for similar events along the same theme. These events are strung together as a theme because of the public's heightened awareness of them. Carjackings and murders of taxi-cab drivers are examples.

The Production of News

Reporters select from those crimes made available to them according to the criteria of newsworthiness just discussed.   They are then responsible for contacting sources by telephone or in person to determine whether they will participate or can provide information that helps clarify the newsworthiness of an event. Reporters produce the story according to the quality of information provided by the various sources. The ability to cite sources gives a story credibility and conveys the impression that the media are simply acting as a funnel for information. The news media benefit from their reliance on these sources because criminal justice sources, such as police officers or judges, are publicly accepted as authoritative voices on crime issues.   The cultural acceptance of these sources helps to legitimize the news organization and confirms its credibility and objectivity (Ericson, Baranek, and Chan 1989; Tuchman 1973). News media are able to continue to function as conveyors of what is officially known about crime because they appear to be fair and balanced.

The ethnographic observations of the *Tribune* and the Nightly illustrated that police and court personnel are news organizations' primary sources for information contained in crime stories.   This reliance gives these sources additional control over the images conveyed about themselves. That is, even if a department fails to shield a particular incident from the news media and a negative image is selected for presentation, the department can still control the damage by responding directly within a news story. Results from the content analysis are similar to my observations at the *Tribune* and Nightly about the heavy reliance on criminal justice sources (see Table 2.3).[2] The media's dependence on criminal justice sources is illustrated by the fact that over half of the information about crime incidents was provided by police or court sources.[3]

Police departments have significant control of the crime images presented because they are the primary agency relied upon for information when a crime is first reported. Approximately 30 percent of the information about crime incidents was provided by various police sources. Table 2.4 presents results from the content analysis regarding the percentage of crime stories obtained at each stage of the criminal justice process.[4] Crime stories are more newsworthy at the beginning stages of the criminal justice system than they are later, resembling an inverted criminal justice funnel. Official discovery of a crime incident was the most frequent stage cited in crime stories. Since very little information about the crime is known immediately after it is discovered, police departments can manipulate the images offered to their advantage (Chibnall

TABLE 2.3 Crime Incident Sources

Type of source (in rank order)	Percent
Police	29.4
Court	25.3
Defendant	8.9
Not specific[a]	6.9
Victim acquaintance	3.7
Documents[b]	3.7
Victim	3.6
Witness/juror	3.6
Politician	3.0
Citizen	2.6
Media	2.1
Other[c]	1.9
School/church	1.4
Defendant acquaintance	1.3
Hospital[d]	0.9
Expert	0.9
Corrections	0.8

[a] Source cited as "sources say," "officials say," "authorities say."
[b] Police or court documents.
[c] Highway spokespersons, community groups, weather service.
[d] Doctors cited, emergency medical service, and coroner.

1977; Ericson, Baranek, and Chan 1989; Fishman 1980; Grabosky and Wilson 1989; Hall et al. 1978; Sherizen 1978).

The heavy reliance of reporters on police sources has been demonstrated by past research (Sherizen 1978). Ericson, Baranek, and Chan (1991:192) found that police sources accounted for nearly 20 percent of the sources used by news media. A wide range of officers are accessible who can comment on a particular case: patrol officers, detectives investigating a case, a superior from a particular precinct, or the public relations spokesperson. Other sources are cited within stories, but they are used less frequently because of the inherent difficulties of contacting individuals and convincing them to comment, especially when a crime is first discovered. Police organizations increase their opportunity to control the image presented about themselves by assigning officers to represent the department as police spokespersons. The spokespersons interact with news reporters on a daily basis, making decisions about the crimes that should be provided to reporters. The frequent interactions with reporters allow spokespersons to develop an understanding about the type of information that is

TABLE 2.4 Presentation of Criminal Justice Stages (specific incident stories)

Stage of Process	Percent
Discovery of crime	18.7
Investigation	4.2
Arrest	15.4
Charged	13.3
Pretrial	3.0
Plea	2.7
Trial	9.1
Jury deliberation	0.4
Verdict	3.9
Sentence	7.3
Extradition	0.7
Appeal	2.3
Supreme Court decision	0.8
Probation	0.1
Commitment to prison	0.4
Parole behavior	1.8
Pardon request	0.3
Release from prison	1.1
Execution	0.5
Follow-ups[a]	12.7
Other[b]	1.3

N=1,982

[a] Either victim, defendant, or crime follow-ups; for example, a story on the impact a crime has had on a victim's family.

[b] Includes other court settlements.

considered newsworthy and how to present it in a way that protects the preferred image of the department. For example, they may develop an understanding of how information can be provided in a way that helps to satisfy the format needs of each type of media organization. Television and newspaper media have different format requirements that constrain what is presented about crime. One of the primary requirements that must be satisfied in order for a crime to become television news is a video. The police department's spokespersons have the ability to respond to questions from television reporters in brief sound bites that are easy to edit and include in a story.

How the Production of News Evolves

Although the information provided by sources determines what can be presented about a particular crime, the production of crime stories is also affected by other factors such as the time available to produce a story and the space to present it, the news organization's need to satisfy format requirements, and editorial scrutiny of the completed product.[5] News space is limited in both print and electronic media. Crime stories will be excluded when other stories are thought to be of greater interest to the public. Similarly, if a story does not meet the format requirements of a medium, such as a television crime story that lacks quality video, then the length of news space will either be limited or the story will be eliminated from consideration. Indeed, at times, time and deadline pressures do limit what is presented about crime in the news, even though criminal justice sources cooperate. The amount of time a reporter has in which to produce a story determines how many sources will be contacted; since time is short, stories generally have little chance of becoming important. If news reporters did not have established relationships with sources, time and deadline pressures would play an even larger role in what is presented about crime.

Editors exercise a large amount of influence on the reporter's entire decisionmaking process. Reporters are in constant contact with editors throughout the day, updating them on the status of a story and on the willingness of different sources to cooperate. Editors will suggest which stories to pursue, which sources to contact, and which story angle to emphasize. Moreover, editors have the final decision regarding the position of the story within the presented product.

Reporters select potential news stories from the pool of crimes made available. If a reporter decides that a selected story is not newsworthy, the story is eliminated. Some stories are thought to be newsworthy but are excluded because the reporter does not have the time or the resources to produce the story, sources are unwilling to comment, or an editor decides the story is unnewsworthy. However, crimes that make it through each of these obstacles are presented to the public and become the most important crime events of the day.

A homicide that occurs on a slow news day is more likely to receive prominent coverage than it would if it occurred when other news competes. Some news topics—such as a war, a political election, or a natural disaster—ensure that any crime stories covered will be relegated to the back sections of a newspaper. News media try to provide what the public is most interested in on a particular day. A news director interviewed from a television station commented: "What I want to do is to attract as many viewers as possible. If, on any given day, it is crime that is going to do it, then you go after it. If it is another story, then you cover it. Today is tax day, and I have a great tax story, I know that. If some mugging was to come up on some side street, chances are I will ignore that crime, because people's minds are elsewhere and I want to keep their minds focused on what they want to see to get them to watch my newscast."

The crime stories that are presented receive various amounts of news space. Some crimes are especially newsworthy and become important news stories. Others, however, are written simply to satisfy space needs. The estimated level of newsworthiness determines the resources that will be expended to produce the story. Stories that are thought to be particularly newsworthy will be given more space and resources and will be followed over a period of days as they progress through the criminal justice system.

News organizations focus on the extraordinary, the unusual, and the deviant because such stories are more entertaining and more likely to be of interest. The more a crime deviates from what is normal and expected, the more the mainstream media can make it simulate an entertaining Hollywood or tabloid presentation, and the more space and time they will allot to it. The relationship between news personnel and criminal justice sources changes as a story increases in newsworthiness.

Each crime can potentially fill four different levels of news space. The four levels, from low to high, are tertiary, secondary, primary, and super primary. Table 2.5 provides a summary that compares the characteristics of stories in these different levels.

Tertiary Crime Stories. Tertiary-level stories are space fillers that appear in the news every day. Such stories are easy to produce by quickly contacting a few sources by telephone. These are brief, usually less than five story inches in length or twenty seconds when timed, and can easily be disposed of if a more newsworthy crime comes along. Reporters do not usually receive a byline. Compared with the other levels of news stories, tertiary crime stories are not interesting by news standards and would not be expected to influence what the public thinks about crime and its victims. Providing crime with a large amount of tertiary news space, however, helps to illustrate the importance of crime as a news topic because other topics, such as politics and schools, rarely receive tertiary space.

Tertiary crime stories are included daily because they satisfy organizational needs to fill the sections of a newspaper designated for "local briefs" or unexpected news holes left when all of the stories are in. Reporters write these stories because they are required by the organization and they may develop into higher-level news stories.

Reporters from the police and court beats are expected to contribute two or three tertiary-level crime stories each day. Typically, tertiary stories from the police beat are taken directly from a police report, supplemented with one or two source contacts to serve as the authority. For example, when making morning police calls, a police beat reporter received information about a shooting that had occurred. The reporter first asked the mouthpiece to provide the full report, then contacted the investigating homicide detective as a source to which to attribute crime-incident information, and, finally, contacted the coroner to attribute information about the victim. Similarly, tertiary court stories are put together by reporters who briefly sit in on a court session or merely call a bailiff or an attorney.

Secondary Crime Stories. Secondary-level crime stories have the potential to become important news. The reporter goes to greater lengths to generate these stories by exhausting the number of sources that might be able to provide information about the crime. Unfortunately, a reporter is unable to gather the information necessary to increase the importance of these stories, so they end up being nothing more than tertiary stories with one or two additional elements or quotes. Secondary stories take up a fair amount of news space (between six and twelve inches) and consume a larger amount of resources than do tertiary stories. Reporters will receive a byline for these stories, but they are generally considered back-page news.

Secondary stories appear almost every day because they help fulfill organizational story needs. They are generally more burdensome than tertiary stories. The reporter contacts a number of sources, but only limited information can be gathered, either because sources cannot be contacted or because they refuse to provide information (for fear of jeopardizing an investigation or losing their jobs). These stories are also burdensome to the organization because they are not necessarily disposable and do not make very interesting news.

For example, while I was observing activities at the *Tribune*, Manny Diaz went to the east side of the city to cover a gang-related drug shooting that killed one victim and left another in critical condition. Diaz thought the story had the potential to become a higher-level news story because another shooting had occurred in the same area the night before and he hoped to link them together.

He was disappointed. The shooting occurred at about two in the morning outside of a bar. The crime scene was cold: The only things that physically remained were blood stains on the cement and bullet holes in a nearby restaurant. Diaz had to dig. First, he went inside the bar, but neither the patrons nor the waitress saw anything. Fortunately, the night manager was still

TABLE 2.5 Characteristics of Different Story Types

Characteristic	Tertiary	Secondary	Primary	Super Primary
Frequency	Every day	Every day	Infrequently	Rarely
Length/coverage	3-7 story inches	7-14 story inches	14+ inches; covered across a number of days and criminal justice stages	14+ inches; covered across a number of days/weeks and criminal justice stages; numerous stories may appear on same date; anniversary dates provide opportunity to do another story
Level of difficulty	Simple; done by one reporter	More burdensome; done by one reporter	More burdensome; still done by one reporter	Burdensome; numerous reporters work on various aspects
Number of sources contacted	1 or 2	Exhaustive, but sources can't or don't provide much information	Exhaustive	Exhaustive and includes sources not typically contacted such as experts
Type of sources contacted	Only criminal justice lower level (e.g., patrol officer, "police said")	Criminal justice; exhaust other sources but hit dead ends; time constraints	Criminal justice; source able to provide newsworthy information; contact individuals directly and indirectly involved	Criminal justice; also individuals involved; other experts; community members; higher-level sources (e.g. "police chief says")

(continues)

TABLE 2.5 *(continued)*

Characteristic	Tertiary	Secondary	Primary	Super Primary
Byline	No	Yes	Yes	Yes; some reporters noted as contributors
Disposable	Yes	Yes	No	No
Justification	Organizational; nature of the criminal justice system	Organizational; nature of the criminal justice system	Organizational; nature of the criminal justice system; can be informative or entertaining	Organizational; nature of the criminal justice system; can be informative or entertaining

in the bar and agreed to go to the crime scene and explain what he had heard. The manager had some good information but did not want to be identified, so the reporter had to continue to dig. Diaz then proceeded to talk to a number of people on the street, in nearby restaurants, and at gas stations, but no one interviewed was able to provide any relevant information. Back at the crime scene, Diaz saw a woman looking out of a window that overlooked the scene, and he called up to her. She said she did not see much, but she gave him a lead because she knew both of the victims and knew where one of their girlfriends lived. He went to the girlfriend's apartment complex, skirted security, and was lucky enough to bump into one of the girlfriend's friends who was with the two victims immediately before the shooting occurred. She was able to give some details about the crime but did not want to be identified.

The reporter was stuck. He did not have time to go to the hospital to interview the victim's family because it was late in the day. In order to write the story, he contacted a police officer from the homicide division to attribute quotes about the crime, called the hospital for quotes on the surviving victim, and contacted the coroner for quotes about the deceased victim. Most of the information included in the story was collected in about fifteen minutes, although the reporter had worked on the story the entire day. Editors of the *Tribune* placed this story at the bottom of page 4 of the local city section (section 2). It was about seven inches long and had a four-inch headline—close to being a tertiary-level story.

Primary Crime Stories. Primary stories are those that take up primary space. Editors are glad to give the space, and reporters enjoy working on these stories. If the story discussed in the previous section had panned out and the reporter had been able to link the two separate shootings, it *could* have been a primary-level story. These stories are placed in the best sections of the paper, either the front page or the front page of the metro section, and editors give reporters more leeway in the amount of space used. With tertiary and secondary stories, on the other hand, reporters are told the amount of space they have before they start writing. A reporter generally labors on a primary story for the entire work day, and a comprehensive list of sources that might have information about the crime is exhausted. There are a number of newsworthy elements to these stories, a reporter is sometimes able to tie the story into some larger community concern, and the story is often supplemented with good pictures or film. These stories occur infrequently. When they do happen, they are covered across a number of criminal justice stages.

The popularity of crime as a news topic can be partially explained by the nature of the criminal justice system. If a crime is discovered and reported, its discovery only represents the initiation of the criminal justice process. Each crime goes through a number of stages in order to be fully processed by the system. This may take weeks, months, or years. Because of this spinning out, crime stories are ongoing, and the same story (especially a higher-level story) might be recycled at each stage of the process. A crime story might be written when a homicide victim is discovered. A few days later, another story might update the investigation. If a suspect is arrested, an arrest story might be done, then another on the suspect's arraignment. If the suspect pleads, another story is presented. If the defendant is tried, stories on opening remarks, important witnesses, closing remarks, and the verdict might be done over a number of days or weeks. The media could also be present at sentencing, incarceration, parole hearings, and release.

Since the criminal justice process is arduous, media organizations have a steady supply of newsworthy crime stories throughout its duration. Clearly, certain stages (discovery, arrest, arraignment, and sentencing) are more newsworthy than others because they are definitive. Arraignment begins the court process, and sentencing ends it. Most stories report on either the police (38 percent) or court (44 percent) stage.

Although court cases are rarely resolved by trial (Smith 1986), Table 2.4 indicates that news media coverage of the trial stage occurs frequently (in 9.1 percent of crime incident stories) because trials usually span a number of days or weeks. When a crime is a primary news story, a trial gives the media organization the opportunity to continually bring the public into the courtroom, updating it on the trial's progress. Also, a trial gives the news organization a wealth of information with minimal effort. Reporters can attend the trial at their convenience and write a story based on whichever witnesses testify after they arrive.

An example from the ethnographic observation shows how easily important primary stories can remain in the news through a number of criminal justice stages. While I was observing the Nightly, a former member of a motorcycle gang was being tried for the murder of his stepdaughter. He had raped her on an earlier occasion; when she threatened to go to the police, he murdered her. This story was in the news from the discovery up until the trial. The Midwest Nightly had a reporter at the courthouse to cover the trial. Separate stories were done on opening arguments, key prosecution witnesses, expert testimony, defense rebuttal witnesses, and concluding remarks. These stories were in the news every weekday for over three weeks. On some days, the Nightly did not have enough staff to send a reporter to cover a particular aspect of the trial. A crime story was still prepared for airing by having a reporter or the assignment editor call the prosecution, defense, and bailiff about what had occurred on that particular day, and film from previous days was used to finish the story. Similarly, if court reporters from the *Midwest Tribune* missed the testimony of a certain witness, a decision by a judge, or a verdict, they could still write a story for the newspaper by contacting either of the attorneys involved or the court bailiff because of their general familiarity with most newsworthy cases in the court system. Because of the high public interest in these cases, primary stories are covered on numerous occasions, and the nature of the criminal justice process allows this to occur.

The best example of a primary-level story occurred while I was observing the *Tribune* with Manny Diaz. The crime involved a woman, six months pregnant, who was hit in the stomach with a brick by a family friend who was arguing with another family member about the length of a woman's skirt. The baby was born prematurely, lived for two or three hours, then died; its death was ruled a homicide. This story had a number of newsworthy elements. First, the crime was serious, and seriousness is a key factor in determining whether any crime becomes news. A second newsworthy element was the status of the victim. Old people and young people are seen as special victims who deserve special protection. A third newsworthy element was that the incident happened just before Mother's Day, and the reporter emphasized the fact that the victim was a mother whose child was taken from her so close to her special day. Another element was the stupidity of the incident. Diaz attempted to lead with the fact that the baby was murdered as a result of an argument about the length of a skirt. Finally, this story was tied to the larger community concern about abortion by discussing the legal status of a fetus. The final decision on the lead ended up being the abortion tie rather than the skirt length because of an editor's preference.

The story took an entire day to assemble. Diaz found out about the story from the police mouthpiece, who provided him with the report. He then called a sergeant in the district in which the incident occurred, the captain in charge of the district, and the homicide detectives who were investigating the case. After he called the coroner for information about the deceased victim, he contacted the hospital about the status of the mother. He asked an attorney whether the friend could be charged with murder and asked the district attorney whether she would be charged. He also contacted a national abortion organization. Finally, Diaz was able to talk with the mother and to obtain permission to send a photographer to her house to take a picture. This story ended up on the front page of the city section (where the mother's picture appeared) and was the lead story on the news of all of the area television stations.

Super Primary Stories. Super primary stories are sensational crime stories with national and international newsworthiness. When a mayor, such as Marion Barry, is arrested for smoking crack, or a sports celebrity, such as Mike Tyson, is convicted of rape, these are super primary stories. They constitute what Samuel Walker (1989) called the celebrated cases of the criminal justice system. Not only is a lead story written that describes the incident, but three or four follow-ups to that story occur on the same day the crime is discovered. For example, in one edition there might be a community-impact story, a victim-impact follow-up, an analysis of the causes of the crime, procedural issues that might come up at the trial, and an editorial. A number of personnel from the organization will be diverted to cover different aspects of these stories. Reporters exhaust the sources who can provide information about the incident, and each reporter who assists is noted as contributing to the story. Later, other sources are contacted to generate the follow-up stories.

The sources used in these stories are individuals the public perceives as having the most power in the organizations concerned. Part of the reason these stories have the potential to influence how the public and politicians think about crime involves the credibility of the sources cited. Police chiefs, the mayor, or other politicians are asked to provide story information when a super primary story affects their department or city. Comments provided by the police chief will be viewed as more significant than those made by patrol officers.

Super primary stories are long stories that fill vast amounts of news space, are usually covered for a number of days after the occurrence of the incident, and continue to be at least a primary story at each successive stage if the case moves through the system. In addition, reporters might produce follow-up stories on anniversary dates related to the crime, such as how the pain continues for a mother one year after her daughter was murdered. Organizational resources are set aside to continually develop different aspects of the story. After a large amount of coverage, one reporter will usually be assigned to cover any additional follow-ups over a period of time as a super primary case moves into the court system. Although rare, these crime stories are the most intriguing, entertaining, and potentially intrusive stories produced by news media.

Super primary stories are the news stories that are talked about, watched, and the most likely to affect the impressions people have about crime. Furthermore, the importance of other stories similar to the presented super primary story is raised because the story piques the public's interest. For example, the Rodney King case was a super primary story because the viciousness of his beating was captured on video. Because of the public's interest in the King incident, a number of other police brutality cases were promoted to a newsworthy level.

A super primary story occurred while I was observing the Nightly. At the beginning of my research, the Milwaukee police discovered serial murderer Jeffrey Dahmer. Dahmer's story was super primary for a number of reasons. There were a large number of victims (seventeen), he used unusual methods to dispose of his victims (boiling their skulls to preserve them and destroying their dismembered parts by sticking them into a vat of acid), the crime scene was macabre (bones, body parts, and smells), and the manner in which Dahmer was initially captured was unusual (one of his victims escaped and flagged down police). Dahmer's story was aired across the country that evening and appeared on the front page of newspapers the morning after; moreover, it remained in the news for weeks after his discovery. The news intensity generated by this super primary case was extraordinary, as illustrated by the two dailies in Milwaukee, the *Journal* and the *Sentinel*, presenting a total of 205 stories in the nine days following Dahmer's arrest (July 24, 1991-August 2, 1991).[6]

News stories about Jeffrey Dahmer were more important in Milwaukee because of the location of the crime. The case remained in the news longer and more stories were produced because reporters had the local angle. This angle, however, also contributed to the importance of Dahmer's murders in the city in which the *Tribune* and the Nightly were located. Dahmer grew up near there, giving *Tribune* and Nightly reporters a different type of local angle. Reporters contacted his family, friends, teachers, past employers, and neighbors, making it an even bigger story than it was in other cities and giving reporters the opportunity to try to link Dahmer's activities with something that had occurred in his past.

Later, when it was discovered that the police had bumbled an opportunity to put an early end to Dahmer's killing spree, the story continued to grow in importance. Dahmer confessed to killing his first victim as a youth who lived near the area of the *Tribune* and the Nightly, which made it an even larger story because the family of that victim still lived there. It was such a big story that about ten satellite trucks and seventy-five news organizations covered the dig for the bones of this victim. For about two weeks, this small town in Midwest U.S.A. was known as the place where Jeffrey Dahmer began his career as a serial murderer. A large number of stories were produced from this town over a number of days. During the nine days after Dahmer's arrest, the *Tribune* carried a total of thirty-two news stories, nearly half of which appeared on the paper's first page or on the first page of the city section.[7] These stories covered the actual dig and the number of bones it produced, psychological evaluations of Dahmer's behavior when he was young, the economic benefits to the community of having a large influx of reporters eating at its restaurants and staying at its hotels, and the two little girls who made about a $25 profit selling lemonade to reporters and interested bystanders observing the dig. News coverage of the Dahmer story allowed me to witness a sensational story and to see a victim's family involved in such a story.

Conclusion

Reporters select those crimes made available to them by the police according to the criterion of newsworthiness. In making their selections, the media have their own independent set of criteria for determining the newsworthiness of a story, and these affect an editor's story selection, production, and assignment decisions, as well as a reporter's decisions about what angle to use, the selection of sources, and how much follow-up to do when reporting a story. Subsequently, the criteria affect the lengthy editing process a story must go through. The media may choose not to present a story if it does not fall within one of their organizationally driven criteria. After the final selection, news media selectively use the source organizations' version of the "truth" to produce a story.

The more selection criteria a story satisfies, the more likely it is that the story will be presented and be given more space. The majority of stories are routine tertiary and secondary stories produced to fulfill organizational needs. Other crime stories, however, are exciting and intriguing—they represent what the public craves. The reason the production of crime stories varies according to the importance of the story is that the latest news on a super primary story, such as the continuing bone count in Jeffrey Dahmer's backyard, will capture audience attention more effectively than a single murder that involves an ordinary, everyday drug dealer. News organizations are willing to commit a larger number of financial and personnel resources to super primary stories because of their ability to attract more consumers.

Notes

1. In contrast to newspapers, which list authorship directly under the headline of most stories, it was much more difficult to determine the news-item sources used by television stations because often the source is not mentioned. Thus, the prevalence of reporters as item sources is overestimated because it appears that television reporters are the source; however, the information may have been taken from a wire report or a newspaper.

2. Only information that was directly attributed to a source was coded. For each crime story, up to nine sources were coded: three who commented about the actual incident (results provided in Table 2.3), three who provided information about the victim, and three who provided information about the defendant (results provided in Chapter 4). If more than three sources provided information on the incident, the victim, or the defendant, the first, third, and fifth sources for each type of information were coded.

3. The large number observed in the content analysis underestimates the media's dependence on criminal justice sources. Table 2.3 also indicates that nearly 7 percent of the sources cited in this analysis were "not specific." These instances occur when reporters attribute the information to "sources," "authorities," or "officials." This same sort of attribution occurred frequently with reporters at the *Tribune*. Reporters use these catchall source attributions in stories because the credibility of the source is not as important to the story, or the source is a criminal justice that refuses to be identified.

4. This analysis examines only those specific incident stories in which there was a clear violation of the law. Program, policy, and statistical stories and editorials were excluded.

5. Similar ideas to those presented in this section have been presented in a chapter I wrote for an anthology on the social construction of crime (Barak, G. 1994. *Media, Process, and the Social Construction of Crime* New York: Garland Publishing, Inc.).

6. This figure was determined by analysis of a database known as Datatimes, which allows the researcher to select various topics according to specific dates (Datatimes. 1992. *Datatimes*. Oklahoma City: Datatimes). The total number of stories that fit the researcher's criteria is determined. For the present analysis, the number of stories that mentioned Dahmer was requested.

7. Ibid.

3

News Images of Crime,
Victims, and Defendants

This chapter focuses on what the media present about crime and why specific stories are not filtered out of the news-production process. A continuing primary-level trial, the apprehension of a suspect, or the anniversary of a particularly heinous crime can limit the space and resources available for new crimes because the existing stories have already piqued the interest of consumers. Some crimes, because of their appeal, are front-page news; other crimes are never even considered. Some are considered but never produced, and some crimes are produced into stories but never presented. Even though the latter two groups of stories are never presented, a consideration of their potential inclusion helps to show why so much crime of specific types gets into the news, which types of crime are automatically excluded, and how the production of news can contribute to what is presented. In order to understand the presentation of crime, it is important first to examine which crimes are considered but excluded. This is one of the primary advantages of using observational data to supplement content findings. I begin by discussing an entire news day at the Nightly in order to underscore the types of crimes that have news potential, the reasons some were presented and others excluded, and how the presentation of crime can be narrowed by the news-production process.

After considering the crimes initially available, reporters go through their daily routine and make source contacts, deciding what should be presented about crime. The final presented product might be affected by the other crime and news topics available, time and space constraints, or the willingness of a source to cooperate. This chapter examines what is presented and why. Three of the most important characteristics of a crime incident are considered.

A Day at the Nightly

For a half-hour newscast, excluding commercials, twenty-two to twenty-three minutes are available in which to present the day's events. Weather and sports consume a large portion of the available news minutes (eight to ten). In the time that remains, stations try to attract audience members by broadcasting local, national, and international stories. Crime news is part of the enticement.

First, most crimes are automatically filtered out because they are not newsworthy. Generally, a range of crimes is considered *potentially* newsworthy. On this particular news day, the managing editor presented thirty-nine story ideas during the afternoon editorial meeting that had been accumulated from making telephone calls, watching other stations' newscasts, listening to the radio, and reconsidering stories carried over from the previous day and not yet covered. Of those thirty-nine stories, nineteen crime-related ones were listed by the managing editor because he thought they had potential news interest.

Only one of the nineteen stories was national in scope; it was a follow-up to the Dahmer story, which had been in the headlines steadily for over two weeks. The rest of the crimes included on the list originated locally. Five were court cases: the murder of a young girl by her stepfather, a capital murder case, a rape trial, the arraignment of a legislative aide arrested as a john in a police crackdown on prostitution, and a lawsuit filed against the mayor by the police chief for infringing on his ability to manage "his" department. Another five crime stories were on the list as status checks (crimes that are presented when discovered, then follow-up contacts are made to see whether any new information is available). Status checks were made on four separate homicides and a jewel heist involving a $17,000 jewel. Stories on five crime prevention activities going on around the city were on the list. These activities included a group protesting allegations of child abuse at a child-care center, an awareness march about black-on-black crime, a police department's annual arrest day, an annual event called "A Night out Against Crime," and a reward offered by a telephone company for information about the theft of cables. Another suggestion on the list was for a reporter to ride with the police and get a story on a real arrest, similar to a story that had been done by a reporter at another station. (Often, broadcast media produce and present stories to keep up with the competition.) Finally, two new crimes discovered by contacting police were on the list. One involved four children arrested by the Coast Guard for making a false Mayday call while on a boat, and another involved a man who was arrested for driving drunk and killing an Amish family of six in a horse and buggy.

In the afternoon editorial meeting, decisions are made about which of the potential story ideas should be produced. On this particular day, eleven of the nineteen crime stories were produced by various members of the organization to be considered for presentation. Stories on all five court cases were produced. A thirty-second voice-over about Dahmer's latest day in court was put together from footage supplied by CNN. The story involving the stepfather who murdered his daughter was put together as a package lasting a minute and a half. Another primary story, approximately one minute long, was done on the murderer who was sentenced to death. This capital case was considered a primary story because of the emotional reactions to the verdict by the victim's family. A mere twenty-second voice-over on the rape trial was produced because the suspect had recidivated while on parole, but the case was just beginning and no testimony was given. A twenty-second read was produced about the police chief's lawsuit. It was only a read because no video was available. The arraignment of the legislative aide was also covered.

There were two reasons for the production of all of the court cases. First, the audience was already familiar with them: Each case was ongoing, and the station had, at one time or another, presented all of them. Second, television court cases absorb few personnel resources. Since cameras are permitted in courtrooms, stories are easily put together by one reporter and one cameraperson in a single location. Judges, attorneys, police officers, and witnesses are accessible at the courthouse. Reporters can send the cameraperson to different courtrooms to collect video while themselves collecting information by talking to the different available sources or watching witness testimony.

Two of the five status checks were produced as voice-overs. One story covered the funeral of a high-school cheerleader who had been murdered; the other was on the reaction of a police department to one of its officers being involved in a deadly force incident. Stories were not produced on the jewel heist or two separate suburban homicides because no new information was available.

Stories were also produced on two of the five crime prevention events. Video was collected by a cameraperson about the police arrest day as well as the Night Out event, which was supported by the mayor's office. These events were chosen because they allowed the Nightly to strengthen its ties with the police department and the mayor's office, two key information sources. A story was not done on the reward offered by the telephone company because the managing editor did not consider it to be news, nor was it a story provided by an important source. In addition, stories were not done on the child-abuse protest or the awareness march because the station did not have a cameraperson or a reporter available to cover them at the time they occurred. The story on the reporter ride-along was put on the back burner because there would not be enough time to do it.

Finally, a story on one of the two new crimes was produced. The drunk-driving incident was produced as a package, even though this crime occurred in a town almost two hours away and its coverage meant that a reporter and a cameraperson were gone for the whole day. It was an important primary story, however, because the crime was serious, the managing editor knew no other station would travel to get community reaction, and the news director believed it was the best story they had. The story on the four young children was not produced because it was not serious enough to expend resources on during a day with such a large amount of crime news, even though the age of the defendants had some news appeal.

Since no other breaking stories occurred after the editorial meeting, the total number of crime stories produced that *could* have been presented was eleven: Dahmer, the murder by the stepfather, the capital murder, the rape trial, the legislative aide, the lawsuit by the police chief, the cheerleader's funeral, the deadly force incident, the arrest day, the Night Out Against Crime, and the drunk driver. Of these eleven, only six were presented to the public in the evening newscast. The Dahmer follow-up was the second story in the broadcast after a national political story, even though it was starting to become old. The reason for the continuing follow-ups to this super primary story was that the public's attention had been piqued, the public related to it easily, and every other medium continued to cover it. The primary story on the Amish family followed the Dahmer-story in the broadcast. This story turned out to be a good news story because of the video clip the reporter had of the Amish farmer's crushed vehicle. The story would probably have appeared first in the broadcast, but the reporter could not get any community reaction because of the unwillingness of individuals living in the Amish community to comment (the Amish believe that having their picture taken steals their soul). The trial of the stepfather who murdered his stepdaughter was next in the broadcast; however, it was not as good as anticipated, because the mother of the victim never took the witness stand to testify. This primary story was in the daily news for the length of the trial because of competition (every news organization was covering it), because of the crime (seriousness and status of the victim), and because the Nightly had easy access to testimony (cameras in the court were "pooled").[1] The police use of deadly force incident was also presented. The family members of the person killed were in the news the entire weekend, alleging that the police misused force in this instance. The police, in a prepared statement, used the media to respond to these allegations. Next, the death-penalty sentence was aired, continuing a story presented at various stages since the murder had occurred. Finally, a story on the Night Out Against Crime protest was presented. This was not cut from the broadcast because the entire city was involved and the event was supported by the mayor's office.

The other stories—the beginning of the rape trial, the funeral of the cheerleader, the arraignment of the john, the lawsuit against the mayor, and the arrest day—were excluded. Time is limited, so decisions have to be made to exclude some stories that are not very interesting. Two of these stories were not interesting because reporters could not collect any video. The story about the police chief had no video (neither the police nor the mayor wanted to make a comment); the reporter who covered the funeral could not get the police or the family to comment on the case, and there was no new information about the status of the investigation. The three other stories were in the evening news lineup to be presented but were excluded because there was not enough time in the broadcast.

Prevalence of Crime in the News

Crime stories are frequently presented and prominently displayed. The majority appear in the first two sections of a newspaper or at the beginning of a broadcast as routine and feature crime stories. Crimes committed by sports celebrities, such as Mike Tyson, Pete Rose, and Tonya Harding, appear in the sports section. Illegal activities by actors and entertainers such as Pee Wee Herman and Michael Jackson are discussed in the entertainment section. Crimes committed by white-collar criminals, such as Michael Milkin, Ivan Boesky, and a variety of S & L financiers, are relegated to the business section. Unlike other major news topics, crime spans most sections of a newspaper.

Table 3.1 provides data on the type of crime stories presented in this study. The majority of crime stories are specific incident stories, focusing on the crime and characteristics of the defendant and the victim. Nearly 75 percent of the crime stories discussed a specific incident. Legislative activities and policy stories were also presented frequently—about 20 percent of the time. Editorials, citizen opinions, and statistical reports make up a small percentage of the total number of crime stories.

The amount of daily crime news that is presented is large in comparison with other topics. Table 3.2 presents the number and percentage of sampled news stories after combining results from the television and newspaper analysis.[2] Approximately 11 percent of these news stories were crime related, making that category the fourth largest after sports, general interest, and business stories. Other topics such as foreign and political affairs,[3] schools, fires, and the environment were less likely to appear as news.

TABLE 3.1 Types of Crime Stories Presented

Type of Story	Total	Percent
Specific crime incident	1982	74.4
Policy story	555	20.8
Editorials	69	2.6
Crime pattern story[a]	41	1.5
Citizen opinion	10	0.4
Statistical report	7	0.3

N=2,664

[a] Reporter notices a particular pattern and reports on a number of crimes, for example, a story on a number of burglaries that have occurred in a particular neighborhood.

TABLE 3.2 Topics of News Stories Presented

	Total	Percent
Sports	5,627	20.8
General interest[a]	3,691	13.6
Business technology	3,616	13.4
Crime	2,879	10.6
General stories[b]	2,749	10.2
Domestic affairs	1,990	7.3
Foreign affairs	1,966	7.2
Science[c]	1,175	4.3
Schools	889	3.3
International affairs	724	2.7
Deaths[d]	613	2.3
Celebrations[e]	418	1.5
Environment	310	1.1
Automobile accidents	163	0.6
Fires	138	0.5
Presidency[f]	133	0.5

N = 27,081

[a] Includes stories about arts, entertainment, people, gardening, and similar topics.

[b] Stories about specific incidents such as chemical leaks, gas leaks, power outages, and missing persons.

[c] Includes medical and health issues.

[d] Includes accidents, suicides, plane crashes, and deaths from natural disasters.

[e] Includes ceremonies and parades.

[f] Not political stories but stories about activities of the president, such as playing golf.

Sports and business stories are popular with readers. Both have designated sections because of their popularity, and a large amount of news space must be filled. A wealth of international, national, state, and local sports stories are used to fill the sports section. Often, in order to fill the space, newspapers will simply provide a laundry list of stories about particular events. At the height of summer, for example, there are between ten and thirteen professional baseball games each evening, and newspapers report the highlights of each game. These were defined here as stories, although doing so skews the results because other topics, such as crime, are not afforded similar space.[5] Table 3.3 presents content results when the sports and business sections are excluded from the calculations. The prevalence of crime stories, in comparison with other stories without designated sections, is evident. Approximately 16 percent of the total number of stories were crime related. These findings are similar to those of other research, which indicates that crime news is among the most frequently cited categories in the news (Kaniss 1991: 123; Sherizen 1978: 208).

TABLE 3.3 Topics of Stories Presented Without Sports and Business Sections

	Total	Percent
General interest[a]	3,691	20.7
Crime	2,879	16.1
General stories[b]	2,749	15.4
Domestic affairs	1,990	11.2
Foreign affairs	1,966	11.0
Science[c]	1,175	6.6
Schools	889	5.0
International affairs	724	4.1
Deaths[d]	613	3.4
Celebrations[e]	418	2.3
Environment	310	1.7
Automobile accidents	163	0.9
Fires	138	0.8
Presidency[f]	133	0.7

N = 17,838

[a] Includes stories about arts, entertainment, people, gardening, and similar topics.

[b] Stories about specific incidents such as chemical leaks, gas leaks, power outages, and missing persons.

[c] Includes medical and health issues.

[d] Includes accidents, suicides, plane crashes, and deaths from natural disasters.

[e] Includes ceremonies and parades.

[f] Not political stories but stories about activities of the president, such as playing golf.

Crime as an Element of News

A wide range of crimes can be considered news, yet for a number of reasons, some crimes are presented to the public whereas others are filtered out of the process. Content analysis specifically identifies the crimes, victims, and defendants that survive this process. Content analysis in my study revealed that 3,862 crimes were mentioned in the stories that covered a specific crime incident. These crimes were coded according to 72 different crime categories (see Table 3.4).

The large number of crimes listed in Table 3.4 was collapsed into similar category classifications for analytical purposes. Narrowing the categories occurred in a two-step process. First, each of the 72 categories was collapsed into one of 26 categories. These categories, the number and percentage of crimes within each category, and the results of combining the categories are presented in Table 3.5. Most index crime categories (murder, assault, rape, robbery, burglary, and larceny) are presented separately in this table. Arson and motor vehicle theft were combined into an "other index offenses" category. Shootings were reported separately, even though they could conceivably be

TABLE 3.4 Crime Categories

Murder	Elder abuse (domestic)
Nonnegligent manslaughter	Domestic violence
Stranger rape	Bias related (race)
Marital rape	Political
Date rape	Misdemeanor
Assassination	Bias related (sexual orientation)
Robbery	Driving while intoxicated
Assault	Disorderly conduct
Burglary	Environmental law violation
Larceny	Harassment
Motor vehicle theft	Trespass
Kidnapping	Contempt
Terrorism	Perjury
Extortion	Obstruction of justice
Conspiracy	Rioting
Arson	Traffic offense
Forgery	Shooting
Fraud	Corrupting a minor
Embezzlement	Prison/police brutality
Bribery	Criminal negligence
Corporate crime	Tampering
Fencing	Medical malpractice
Hostage situation	Cockfighting
Weapons violation	Attempted murder
Escape from custody	Corruption
Vandalism	Gross sexual imposition
Soliciting murder	Cruelty to animals
Prostitution	Pornography/obscenity
Drug sale	Competitive bidding violation
Drug like (possession of	Building code violation
drug paraphernalia)	Resisting arrest
Gambling	Reckless endangerment
Tax evasion	Espionage/treason
Suicide	Smuggling (money, arms)
Child abuse	Murder accomplice
Stranger child abduction	Curfew violation
Elder patient abuse	

considered an index crime, but no specific charges were mentioned in the stories. Drugs were separated from other victimless crimes to illustrate their importance as news.

Some of the categories generated contain a range of similar crimes that were combined because of their infrequent presentation separately. For example, the "crimes against government" category includes acts of terrorism, espionage, and treason. The "crimes against criminal justice" category consists of crimes that affect the operation of the criminal justice system, such as tampering with evidence and intimidating witnesses or victims. Crimes that occur in families,

TABLE 3.5 Type of Crime in Crime Stories

Type of Crime[a]	Crime1[b] (N=1,982)		Crime2[c] (N=1,158)		Crime3[d] (N=722)		All crime[e] (N=3,862)	
	Number	Percent	Number	Percent	Number	Percent	Number	Percent
Murder	543	27.4	256	22.1	125	17.3	924	23.9
Drugs	218	11.0	97	8.4	61	8.4	376	9.7
Forgery/fraud	102	5.1	80	6.9	42	5.8	224	5.8
Assault	99	5.0	68	5.9	37	5.1	204	5.3
Not specific	90	4.5	27	2.3	20	2.8	137	3.5
Sexual assault	89	4.5	54	4.7	41	5.7	184	4.8
Robbery	66	3.3	64	5.5	34	4.7	164	4.2
Crimes against government[f]	61	3.2	18	1.6	8	1.1	89	2.3
Crimes against criminal justice[g]	59	3.0	81	7.0	63	8.7	203	5.3
Other misdemeanor[h]	59	3.0	70	6.0	63	8.7	192	5.0
Embezzlement/bribery	57	2.9	33	2.8	19	2.6	109	2.8
Shootings[i]	56	2.8	13	1.1	12	1.7	81	2.1
Burglary	54	2.7	33	2.8	28	3.9	115	3.0
Other victimless crimes[j]	45	2.3	19	1.6	11	1.5	75	3.0
Harassment/trespass	43	2.2	39	3.4	32	4.4	114	3.0
Kidnapping	43	2.1	26	2.2	14	1.9	82	2.1
Manslaughter	40	2.0	23	2.0	8	1.1	71	1.8
Larceny	40	2.0	15	1.3	18	2.5	73	1.9
Extortion/conspiracy	39	2.0	35	3.0	17	2.4	91	2.4
Other index offenses	39	2.0	21	1.8	15	2.1	75	1.9
Crimes against children[k]	33	1.7	28	2.4	21	2.9	82	2.1

(continues)

TABLE 3.5 *(continued)*

Type of Crime[a]	Crime1[b] (N=1,982)		Crime2[c] (N=1,158)		Crime3[d] (N=722)		All crime[e] (N=3,862)	
	Number	Percent	Number	Percent	Number	Percent	Number	Percent
Driving while intoxicated	32	1.6	21	1.8	14	1.9	67	1.7
Organized crime	22	1.1	17	1.5	9	1.2	48	1.2
Interfamily crime[l]	21	1.1	11	0.9	5	0.7	37	1.0
Police brutality	21	1.1	1	0.1	0	0.0	22	0.6
Bias-related	10	0.5	8	0.7	5	0.7	23	0.6

[a] Presented by rank order of crime1.

[b] First crime mentioned.

[c] Second crime mentioned.

[d] Third crime mentioned.

[e] Combines crime1, crime2, and crime3.

[f] Urban disorder/rioting, terrorism, espionage, treason, and other political crimes.

[g] Perjury, resisting arrest, obstruction of justice, tampering with evidence, and intimidating witnesses/victims.

[h] Vandalism, traffic offenses, cruelty to animals, illegally printing victim's name, and other misdemeanors.

[i] Shooting occurred, but story was not specific as to what the charge would be.

[j] Prostitution, gambling.

[k] Corrupting a minor and gross sexual imposition.

[l] Domestic violence, child abuse and neglect, elder abuse.

crimes against children, and other misdemeanors were collapsed into separate categories. The rest of the crimes were left as single-crime categories.

The second step in the narrowing process involved collapsing the twenty-five categories into eight. To more clearly specify which categories of crime are newsworthy, the crimes in Table 3.5 were collapsed further in Table 3.6. Murder was kept as a separate category because of its frequent presentation. The other violent crime category combines robberies, shootings, and assaults. Drugs, prostitution, and gambling were included in the victimless crime category. Special group crimes are those that affect a special class of victims that are viewed by the public and politicians as being particularly vulnerable to crime and in need of special protection (Karmen 1990). The crimes included in this category were rapes, family crimes, and bias-related crimes. Separate categories were used for the less serious misdemeanors, property offenses, and crimes against criminal justice.

Table 3.6 indicates that murder and other violent crimes are the most newsworthy, accounting for over 40 percent of the crime stories presented. The prevalence of violence in the news is consistent with previous studies that have examined the presentation of crime news (Ericson, Baranek, and Chan 1991; Graber 1980; Humphries 1981; Lee-Sammons 1989; Marsh 1988; Mawby and Brown 1984; Roshier 1981; Sheley and Ashkins 1981; Skogan and Maxfield 1981). Victimless crimes, crimes involving special groups of victims, and white-collar offenses are the next most popular crime stories, in that order. Misdemeanors and property offenses are the least likely to be cited in the news.

A better understanding of which crimes become news can be gained by looking at the content of crime stories according to the different tiers of newsworthiness because higher-level stories are less susceptible to time and resource constraints.[6] Therefore, they are more likely to represent the types of stories used for news appeal. This analysis revealed that murder stories consume a larger percentage of primary news space than of tertiary or secondary space: The percentage of stories that concern murders increases from the tertiary (19.0 percent) to the primary level (29.3 percent). Other violent crimes, such as assaults and robberies, are frequently covered as tertiary crime stories (18.0 percent). They are unlikely to become primary stories (12.5 percent) unless there are other interesting factors. Drug crimes are generally tertiary or secondary stories.

Murder is news. The results of the analysis indicate that nearly one-fourth of the crimes mentioned within crime stories were murders. Crime1 provides the best indicator of which crimes are newsworthy because it most clearly represents which crime was the focus of the story.[7] Murders were the focus in 27.4 percent of the sampled crime stories. The number of murders cited within crime stories *decreased* in frequency from crime1 to crime3. Other crimes, such as the misdemeanor crime categories (other misdemeanors and harassment/trespass), *increased* in frequency from crime1 to crime3 because of

TABLE 3.6 Newsworthy Categories of Crime

Type of Crime	Crime1[a] (N=1,982)		Crime2[b] (N=1,158)		Crime3[c] (N=722)		All crime[d] (N=3,862)	
	Number	Percent	Number	Percent	Number	Percent	Number	Percent
Murder	543	27.4	256	22.1	125	17.3	924	23.9
Other violent crimes[e]	324	16.3	195	16.8	105	14.5	624	16.2
Victimless crimes[f]	263	13.3	116	10.0	72	10.0	451	11.7
Special group crimes[g]	185	9.3	122	10.5	86	11.9	393	10.2
White-collar crimes[h]	181	9.1	130	11.2	70	9.7	381	9.9
Crimes against criminal justice[i]	161	8.1	134	11.6	88	12.2	383	9.9
Misdemeanors	102	5.1	109	9.4	95	13.2	306	7.9
Property offenses	133	6.7	69	6.0	61	8.4	263	6.8
Does not specify	90	4.5	27	2.3	20	2.8	137	3.5

[a] First crime mentioned.
[b] Second crime mentioned.
[c] Third crime mentioned.
[d] Combines crime1, crime2, and crime3.
[e] Robbery, shootings, assaults.
[f] Drugs, prostitution, gambling.
[g] Sexual assault, child, elderly, bias-related victimizations.
[h] Embezzlement, bribery, forgery, fraud, corporate crime, securities violations.
[i] Perjury, resisting arrest, obstruction of justice, tampering with evidence, intimidating witness/victims.

the media's tendency to mention these crimes in passing, as well as of the need for a defendant to have been charged with a number of less serious crimes if the stories are to become news. Although for various reasons not every murder is covered by the media, research has consistently indicated that murders have been a staple in the news over the course of time. For example, murder was found to account for 23 percent of crime stories in 1951 (Humphries 1981: 195), 68 percent in 1968 (Humphries 1981: 195), 40 percent in 1974 (Lee-Sammons 1989: 116), and 26 percent in 1980 (Graber 1980: 39).

Seriousness is an important variable in determining newsworthiness, as is indicated by the continued predominance of murder in the news. Although the media's presentation of murder does not reflect the frequency of that crime in crime statistics, it does indicate what the media think will attract viewers. Murders are more serious than other crimes, both statutorily and in the public's perception. Since news space is limited, news organizations focus on crimes that most seriously affect an individual and are thought by the media to be of greatest interest to the public. As Wilson (1991: 4–5) wrote in his book *Good Murders and Bad Murders,* "The informational market for murder thrives, and the media respond to that market as would any entrepreneur." He expands on this point, remarking that murder is a marketable item that conveys "the intensity of drama, the centerpiece of a true crime story, the remote tragedy of a terrorist attack, and the sardonic humor of a grade B video." News organizations think the public is intrigued by death.

Since murders have such inherent newsworthiness, they stand out when reporters select and produce crime stories. At the beginning of the observational period I spent at the *Midwest Tribune*, Manny Diaz said, as he leafed through the morning police blotter reports, "If it ain't a homicide, then I'm not interested." When police beat or television reporters make daily calls to police divisions, hospitals, and the coroner's office, they look for death: "Do you have any bodies for me?" Court reporters pay the closest attention to any murder that appears on the court calendar. News media constantly follow murder stories across the system to see if anything unknown has been discovered. The managing editor of the Nightly was constantly checking on ongoing cases to see whether the police had any leads or suspects, anyone had been arrested or arraigned, or a case was going to trial.

The heavy presentation of murders assists source organizations as well. The police are presented as pursuing unsolved murders or making an arrest and solving a case, thus fulfilling crime-fighting functions. The more dangerous the streets are perceived to be by the public, the easier it is for source organizations to justify additional spending and budgetary and personnel increases (Wilson and Fuqua 1975). Some police officers also realize that they need the cooperation of victims in order to clear crimes. Therefore, sources are less likely to provide information about living victims for fear doing so could jeopardize an investigation or put the victim in danger, thereby limiting the reporter's ability to produce a story. If the victim is dead, however, this is not a problem. For example, a *Tribune* reporter was asked not to print a story about a police investigation that discovered $7,000 in cash at an elderly woman's home. The police did not know where the woman was; the neighbors had called and said they had not seen her for a few days, which was unusual. The police asked the news organization not to present a story until the status of the woman could be confirmed because they were afraid others might try to break into her home in the hopes of finding leftover cash. If the woman was still alive, a news story might put her in danger.

The newsworthiness of less serious crimes, such as those involving drugs, changes over time depending on the amount of interest in them. It is significant that in my analysis approximately 11 percent of the crime1 stories and nearly 10 percent of the combined category were drug stories (see Table 3.5). These figures are dramatically different from Graber's findings a decade ago. Her research indicated that drugs were mentioned in 0.7 percent of her single category (same as crime1) and 1.8 percent of her combined category (Graber 1980: 22). Drug sale or possession crimes are not as serious as personal violence crimes such as aggravated assault or robbery. They have come to be more serious, however, because of current political and public opinion, which makes them more newsworthy.

Two possible explanations exist for why news media currently use drug stories to capture an audience. First, part of the interest can be explained through a consideration of the sample period and the occurrence of two super primary drug stories that had mass audience appeal. During the first six months of 1990, the period from which the newspaper sample was drawn, both Manuel Noriega and Marion Barry were arrested for drug crimes. Noriega's arrest, arraignment, and pretrial motions were all in the news. Barry was arrested and arraigned, went into rehabilitation, lashed out at the Federal Bureau of Investigation (FBI) for trying to kill him, and decided not to run for reelection; the early parts of his trial were included in the sample, thereby possibly skewing the results. Sixty-five of the 218 drug stories in the sample were stories about either Noriega or Barry. When their crimes are removed from the analysis, the percentage of crime1 drug stories decreases to 7.3. The interest generated by these two stories can be shown by comparing the 1990 crime stories to those from 1991 (which had no outlying cases). Approximately 7 percent of the crime stories from the 1991 sample were drug stories, the same percentage as 1990 when the Barry and Noriega outliers are removed. Even when the super primary drug cases are excluded, however, the number of presented drug stories is significantly larger than that found by Graber (1980).

Second, public interest in drug crimes was high during the period studied because of the "war against drugs." Drugs have become a prominent political, academic, and media issue. Resources have been poured into addressing the latest drug epidemic that is overloading the criminal justice system. Drug arrests have increased dramatically, court calendars are flooded, and prisons continue to be overpopulated. Drugs are much more newsworthy today than they were when Graber conducted her research, so much so that news media coverage of drugs can be considered a prolonged "moral panic."   The newsworthiness of drug crimes has increased significantly because of increased public concern. Table 3.6 indicates that victimless crimes are the third highest category of crime cited because of the increased coverage of drug crimes.

The next most newsworthy categories, special group and white-collar crimes, are worthy of comment. Like drugs, these crimes appear to have increased in newsworthiness. Table 3.6 indicates that over 10 percent of the crimes in the sampled crime stories involved special groups of victims. Moreover, this percentage *underestimates* the newsworthiness of these crimes because it excludes those cases that overlap the other presented categories. For example, if a sixty-five-year-old woman was robbed or an eight-year-old was assaulted, these cases would have been included in the violent crime category. The victims' ages as well as their status as being in a special group, however, were key elements in the promotion of these crimes to a newsworthy level. Past research has indicated that domestic crimes and crimes against women were generally not presented in the media (Roshier 1981: 27). Because of the news media's response to political and public interest, crimes against special groups are currently more likely to be presented in the news than was previously the case.

Table 3.6 indicates that white-collar cases account for nearly 10 percent of the crimes mentioned in the sampled crime stories. Past content research has indicated that white-collar crimes were seldom reported in the news (Evans and Lundman 1983; Graber 1980). Evans and Lundman's research (1983: 533), which compared newspaper coverage of a 1961 corporate price-fixing case with that of a 1976 case, found articles about white collar crime to be less frequently and less prominently displayed than cases involving individual defendants. Graber (1980: 22) found that business crimes accounted for less than 2 percent of the total number of crime stories in her sample. Again, this trend can be explained by the evolving nature of newsworthiness and the adaptation of news organizations to their audience. Political and public consciousness has been heightened by factors such as the Savings and Loan fiasco, high-profile cases such as those of Michael Milkin and Ivan Boesky, and the critical depiction of greed in popular entertainment media (such as the movie *Wall Street*). This heightened consciousness has raised the level of newsworthiness of white-collar crime, thereby stimulating the increase of its coverage.

Crime Victims and Defendants in the News

Seriousness of the crime provides only a partial explanation of why certain crimes are covered as news. An "ordinary homicide," in which an 18–24-year-old black male murders an 18–24-year-old black male might be transformed into a crime story—depending on other news availability—but it will generally be only a lower-level story. This type of homicide occurs too frequently to be important news. Not all homicides are important news, and some do not even become news stories. According to an informant from one of the affiliated stations in the city that was observed, "If we covered every homicide, we would be doing nothing but covering homicides. A lot of these are motivated by passion, at the moment. A lot of them are drug-related. You can try to dwell on the wider implications of why the drug problem is creating such a situation, but you can't cover every homicide—it is just not of interest. You need more unusualness, randomness, indicative of a wider problem." A number of other factors, such as the victim and defendant involved, interact with the seriousness of the crime to determine whether a murder becomes news, the level of newsworthiness it achieves, and the other types of crimes that are presented. The level of newsworthiness increases with each extra element that can be included in the story.

Crime victims and defendants can provide the necessary element that makes less serious crimes newsworthy, as well as increase the newsworthiness of serious crimes, because these factors broaden audience appeal. Demographic characteristics of both victims and defendants can influence which crimes become news because they can make certain crimes more attractive. The demographic characteristics of crime victims and defendants[8] in this study are presented in Table 3.7. Media content results are also provided for victims of fire, automobile accidents, and suicide; and the available official statistics on victims in general, murder victims, and defendants are presented. These data are provided for comparison with the media's presented image of crime victims and defendants.

The content results indicate that most demographic characteristics of both victims and defendants are generally not presented. Race of victim could only be identified for approximately 15 percent of all victims, and the race of the defendant was identified only 25 percent of the time. Marital status for both victims and defendants is less likely than race to be mentioned in a crime story, whereas age and occupation are somewhat more likely to be given. Age is the characteristic most likely to be identified because it is easily gleaned from a police report or court jacket. Marital status and occupation are not usually provided because a reporter would have to rely on additional source contacts outside of the information easily obtained from criminal justice sources and reports; moreover, these characteristics are not of general interest to readers.

Because of these additional burdens affecting reporters' daily routines, the images presented of victims and defendants are vague.

When demographic characteristics are given, crime victims are generally presented in the news as male, white, fairly young (17–25 years old), and married. These findings are similar to past research on the characteristics of victims (Graber 1980; Humphries 1981; Marsh 1988; Mawby and Brown 1984). Females are overrepresented in the news in comparison with their representation in crime statistics. Although official data are unavailable, it also appears that young victims (0–12 years old) are overrepresented. Some stories fail to identify an individual harmed by the crime but mention the name of a business or a corporation. These instances accounted for 6.2 percent of the victims mentioned. Their names are provided because readers can identify with certain types of businesses. For example, bank robberies are often in the news because they are serious crimes. The bank is identified because the majority of the public has been in a bank at some time, probably keeps savings there, and may visit one at least every two or three weeks. Noting the name and address of a bank increases the salience of the story.

Male defendants are overwhelmingly presented in the news, as we would expect from Uniform Crime statistics and past research (Graber 1980; Humphries 1981). Race and occupation of the defendant are rarely identified in the media. White defendants are more likely to be presented in the news, a result that is consistent with official statistics when the "unknown" category is removed. Crimes committed by professionals, politicians, and criminal justice personnel are more newsworthy than crimes committed by students, laborers, or defendants with service jobs. The most frequently cited occupation of crime victims in the news is that of a worker in the criminal justice system. Police officer, judge, and lawyer are important, newsworthy occupations. In addition, victimizations of politicians, students, and helping professionals are more newsworthy than are those of people with service or labor jobs.

Reporters, news organizations, and the public all expect individuals in newsworthy occupations to be held to a higher moral standard. When those individuals violate the law, their crimes have more of an impact and are of more interest to the public than those of ordinary citizens. Likewise, their victimizations are of high interest. Males, professionals, and politicians are more likely to be presented as defendants than as victims, whereas females, students, and helping professionals are more likely to be presented as victims than as defendants. Married victims and defendants are more likely to be presented in the news than are single or divorced individuals.

TABLE 3.7 Victim and Defendant Characteristics

	Content		Official		Content	Official
	All Victims (in percentages)	Fire/Accident Victims (in percentages)	Victim Statistics[a] (in percentages)	Murder Statistics[b] (in percentages)	All Defendants (in percentages)	Uniform Crime Report (UCR)[b] (in percentages)
Sex						
Male	45.3	38.6	37.0	78.0	79.9	81.7
Female	33.4	29.3	21.8	21.9	10.6	18.3
Other[c]	6.2	5.1	X	X	1.1	X
Unknown	15.0	27.0	X	X	8.4	X
Race						
White	7.7	7.8	28.2	48.5	13.4	67.3
Black	5.8	2.5	36.0	48.6	7.9	30.8
Other[d]	2.2	2.5	27.3	1.7	3.1	1.8
Unknown	84.4	87.3	X	1.2	75.5	X
Age						
0 - 12 years	9.2	7.4	X	4.8	0.2	1.7
13 - 16 years	4.8	2.5	62.9	X	3.6	6.3
17 - 25 years	10.3	9.3	73.8/57.8[e]	29.0	16.6	37.9
26 - 35 years	9.4	7.8	34.9	30.8	13.3	32.6
36 - 50 years	7.3	9.3	20.8	21.7	14.7	17.3
51 - 64 years	2.7	7.8	7.9	7.2	5.4	3.5
65 years and older	2.5	4.4	3.9	4.8	1.2	0.7
Not identified	53.3	51.5	X	X	44.9	NA

(continues)

TABLE 3.7 *(continued)*

Occupation						
Professional	4.8	3.4	X	X	8.9	X
Politician	2.1	1.5	X	X	8.9	X
Criminal justice personnel	7.0	6.9	X	X	7.0	X
Helping professions	4.1	0.5	X	X	3.9	X
Student	5.4	5.4	X	X	3.2	X
Labor	1.2	1.0	X	X	2.3	X
Service	2.3	1.0	X	X	0.6	X
Criminal	1.7	0.0	X	X	0.9	X
Entertainer	0.7	3.9	X	X	2.0	X
Unemployed	0.3	0.0	X	X	0.7	X
Other	0.3	0.0	X	X	0.9	X
Not identified	70.2	76.5	X	X	60.6	X
Marital Status						
Married	12.1	7.4	X	X	7.1	X
Divorced	0.8	1.0	X	X	1.1	X
Other	1.1	3.0	X	X	0.8	X
Unknown	86.0	89.7	X	X	91.1	X

X = Not available
NA = Does not apply

[a] This column presents rates per 1,000. The figures were derived from *Criminal Victimization 1990*, Bureau of Justice Statistics, U.S. Department of Justice.
[b] Figures were derived from *Crime in the United States, 1989*, Federal Bureau of Investigation, U.S. Department of Justice.
[c] Includes businesses, corporations, and the government.
[d] Includes Hispanics, Middle Easterners, and Asians.
[e] The statistical source presented rates for 16–20 and 20–24-year-olds.

Characteristics of Crime Victims as Elements of News

Crime victims are influential in determining why certain crimes are selected, how stories are produced, which stories are presented, and which crimes get filtered out of the process. Whether a crime is selected and whether it is promoted to a secondary, a primary, or even a super primary level can be influenced by the status of the victim. Crime victims are in the news because they provide a human-interest element to each story. Their reactions are used by news media to explain what it is like to be involved in crime so that consumers can experience crime vicariously. Crime victims supply an emotional element to a story, and certain characteristics of victims are thought to capture emotions more effectively than others. Specific demographic characteristics defined as inherently emotional automatically grab people's attention. In addition, the impact of a crime on the victim or the victim's family is presented to illustrate what it is like to be affected by crime. These factors are discussed in this section using supporting data from the content analysis. Past research has noted a broad range of factors that might increase the newsworthiness of any crime. Instances in which crime victims conform with these factors are also discussed here.

Demographic Characteristics. Table 3.8 provides data on victim demographic characteristics presented in the news: whether victims are named in crime stories; whether their address is provided; and their sex, race, marital status, age, and occupation. Percentages for specific crime incident stories are presented according to the first victim mentioned in each crime story (Vic1). Column two combines data on all victims mentioned in crime stories (All Victims); column three presents the All Victims variable for newspaper stories only; and columns four through six present tertiary, secondary, and primary results, respectively, from the newspaper analysis.

The results indicate that most demographic characteristics were generally *not* mentioned within crime stories. Therefore, these characteristics were not important elements in the newsworthiness of stories but were used only as identifiers in order to make a story less vague when easily available. Age,[9] race, occupation, and marital status of the victim were rarely provided. A crime victim's name was provided in only about 60 percent of the specific incident stories that involved a victim, and a specific home address was rarely given.

This low frequency of reporting of names and addresses can be explained by two factors. First, I indicated earlier that the majority of crime stories report the discovery of crime. Sources are more likely to withhold specific identifiers at this stage for fear of jeopardizing an investigation by alienating the victim. In addition, a reporter may not have the time to collect this information or the space to provide it. If a number of individuals were victimized by the same defendant—for example, a defendant charged with twelve robberies—the media will generally name only one or two of the victims because of space constraints.

Second, most media organizations have unwritten, and some have written, policies regarding the presentation of rape and child victims' names. The names of such victims will be provided only when they have been murdered. These policies have resulted from the pressure exerted on politicians and media personnel by advocacy groups discouraging the identification of victims (Wolf, Thomason, and LaRocque 1991).

The competitive pressure to attract consumers will, however, sometimes result in media organizations deviating from these policies and overriding concerns voiced by outside groups. Such pressure arises in the coverage of super primary stories because of their heightened awareness and the need for organizations to outclass the competition. For example, the names of the women involved in the William Kennedy Smith and Mike Tyson rape cases were named by both print and electronic organizations in both cases. The reason certain media strayed from policy in these two specific cases was to attempt to surpass the competition or, if they had not done the naming first, to catch up with their competitors.

The results presented in Table 3.8 indicate that the percentage of characteristics reported increases when we compare crime victims' presentation in primary stories with that in tertiary and secondary stories. In certain circumstances, the demographic characteristics of the victim can contribute to whether a crime is covered and to the level of newsworthiness it achieves. One of the informants discussed how certain victims are more important than others so that certain crimes take precedence over others.

> We look for, if there was a shooting or murder, what kind of neighborhood did it happen in, and how did it happen. . . . From our long experience with our covering of shootings and muggings, we do mentally rate the quality of crimes that occur, based on who is involved, how innocent is the "victim." If you determine a crime involves two bad guys doing a drug deal and they are both what we would call scumbags, then you say, both were basically asking for it, both knew the risk involved, and so the quality of that story as far as the tone of that story, the amount of time that is given to it on the air, and the follow-up to it, probably would be less than, say, an innocent bystander shot, or a child shot on a stoop by a stray bullet: these send a story off on a whole other tangent.

Table 3.8 indicates that some demographic characteristics of victims are more likely to be displayed in primary stories than in tertiary stories. Age is an important demographic characteristic that can increase the newsworthiness of a crime. News media pay special attention to the victimization of children and the elderly and are willing to expend additional time and resources to produce

TABLE 3.8 Victim Characteristics

	Vic1[a] (in percentages)	All Victims[b] (in percentages)	All Newspaper Victims (in percentages)	Newspaper Tertiary (in percentages)	Newspaper Secondary (in percentages)	Newspaper Primary (in percentages)
Named						
Yes	66.3	59.2	63.4	58.4	63.3	67.5
No	33.7	40.8	36.6	41.6	36.7	32.5
Address						
None	61.7	65.0	63.6	67.3	61.5	62.8
Specific	4.2	4.1	4.5	7.0	4.9	2.1
General	9.3	8.2	9.7	7.5	11.5	9.1
City	23.3	21.0	20.7	17.0	20.7	23.8
Other[c]	1.4	1.6	1.5	1.2	1.2	2.3
Location						
City	5.0	4.6	3.2	4.4	3.1	2.6
Suburb	4.0	3.8	4.0	3.4	4.2	4.1
Rural	0.4	0.5	0.6	0.2	1.0	0.2
Not identified	90.6	91.1	92.2	91.9	91.6	93.1
Sex						
Male	52.0	45.3	46.1	43.4	44.6	50.2
Female	31.2	33.4	33.0	31.4	34.1	32.3
Other[d]	7.1	6.2	7.2	7.7	8.5	4.7
Unknown	9.7	15.0	13.7	17.5	12.8	12.8

(continues)

TABLE 3.8 *(continued)*

	Vic1[a] (in percentages)	All Victims[b] (in percentages)	All Newspaper Victims (in percentages)	Newspaper Tertiary (in percentages)	Newspaper Secondary (in percentages)	Newspaper Primary (in percentages)
Race						
White	9.6	7.7	4.6	1.5	4.2	7.9
Black	7.6	5.8	3.9	1.2	4.0	5.9
Other*	2.4	2.2	2.2	1.5	2.1	3.0
Unknown	80.4	84.4	89.2	95.8	89.7	83.2
Marital Status						
Married	15.6	12.1	13.8	7.9	15.0	17.0
Divorced	0.8	0.8	0.9	0.5	0.9	1.2
Other	0.3	1.1	0.7	0.7	0.3	1.2
Unknown	83.3	86.0	84.7	90.9	83.8	80.7
Age						
0 - 12 years	9.5	9.2	9.2	6.9	10.3	9.5
13 - 16 years	5.3	4.8	5.3	5.2	4.3	6.7
17 - 25 years	12.2	10.3	10.8	9.1	11.8	10.8
26 - 35 years	12.8	9.4	10.8	10.3	9.4	12.6
36 - 50 years	8.8	7.3	7.9	7.4	7.3	9.1
51 - 64 years	3.7	2.7	3.1	3.7	3.3	2.4
65 years and older	2.8	2.5	2.9	3.9	3.3	1.4
Not identified	44.9	53.3	50.0	53.4	50.4	47.5

(continues)

TABLE 3.8 *(continued)*

Occupation	Vic1[a] (in percentages)	All Victims[b] (in percentages)	All Newspaper Victims (in percentages)	Newspaper Tertiary (in percentages)	Newspaper Secondary (in percentages)	Newspaper Primary (in percentages)
Professional	6.2	4.8	4.5	6.7	3.7	3.9
Politician	3.1	2.1	1.8	2.0	1.6	1.8
Criminal justice personnel	7.5	7.0	7.3	9.1	5.7	7.9
Helping professions	3.5	4.1	5.0	3.9	5.1	2.2
Student	6.1	5.4	5.3	3.2	5.2	7.3
Labor	1.3	1.2	1.3	0.2	1.9	1.2
Service	2.5	2.3	2.7	3.9	2.4	2.2
Criminal	2.0	1.7	1.9	1.7	1.9	2.0
Entertainer	1.2	0.7	0.9	1.2	1.2	0.2
Unemployed	0.3	0.3	0.3	0.0	0.4	0.4
Other	0.4	0.3	0.1	0.5	0.0	0.0
Not identified	65.7	70.2	68.8	67.5	70.7	67.3

[a] First victim.

[b] Combines up to three victims mentioned in a story.

[c] Combines state and county results.

[d] Includes businesses, corporations, and the government.

[e] Includes Hispanics, Middle Easterners, and Asians.

stories about these groups. The media use the added emotion old age or youth brings to the story, increasing the chances that a victimization of either of these groups will be covered. Children, when victimized, are portrayed as being left unprotected by the system, resulting in their loss of innocence. The elderly are people who have long paid their dues and should be allowed to live in peace. Both groups are given special protection in our society and special attention in the media.

The age factor also contributes to a large range of crimes being presented to the public. This connection was tested by considering how age interacted with specific types of crimes. Property offenses are rarely newsworthy; however, when they were committed against an elderly or a child victim, these crimes received at least tertiary coverage. When property offenses were examined by the age of victim and type of story, the results indicated that age was identified *only* when the crime was committed against a child or against someone over fifty. Age is not generally identified when the media present a white-collar offense except when the victim is over sixty-five, conjuring up the image of an unsuspecting elderly victim falling prey to a con artist.

Occupation of the victim is another important factor that can raise the newsworthiness of less serious crimes. The occupation is usually identified only when it is newsworthy, being mentioned less than 30 percent of the time for the victims in the analysis. Victimization of students, criminal justice professionals, and helping professionals is more newsworthy than that of people in other occupations. That is, when people who are responsible for protecting the public (such as the police) are left unprotected and are victimized, their occupation can be an indicator of newsworthiness. A crime is also more likely to be covered by news organizations when guardians of the public (doctors, teachers, and similar groups) are victimized. As in the case of age, the education level of a victim influences whether a crime is presented for public preview.

When occupation is identified, criminal justice professionals as victims are the most likely to be found in the news across all categories of crime. Crimes that are less violent (property offenses, misdemeanors, and similar offenses) are rarely newsworthy. The victimization of a criminal justice professional can, however, raise these crimes to a newsworthy level. For example, since motor vehicle theft is such a common crime, it is not generally considered even potentially newsworthy. However, when the county prosecutor had her car stolen from her driveway while she was sleeping, a *Tribune* reporter produced a tertiary story on the incident, stressing that one of the county's top law enforcement officials had been victimized. Police officers murdered or seriously injured in the line of duty are primary news. When primary murders were examined, it was found that occupation of the victim was infrequently identified (less than 30 percent of the incident stories); when occupation was identified, criminal justice or helping professionals were presented over half of the time.

Victimizations that occur in suburban areas are news because of the threat crimes present in these regions. Crime victims who live in suburban areas are more newsworthy because crimes happen there less frequently and involve more "important" members of society, and suburbanites are often the target market for the products advertised in the media. Table 3.8 indicates that the percentage of victims cited as being from the inner city decreased from the tertiary to the primary level, whereas the percentage of victims from suburban areas increased. Some individual reporters thought serious crimes that occurred in suburban areas were more important because they perceived these victims as being able to react more emotionally than those living in the downtown area, further, a larger portion of the media's audience can relate to the harm to these victims. Fran Karns, one of the court reporters from the *Tribune*, discussed why she was more likely to contact suburban homicide survivors: "Victims are so fatalistic in the inner city: it is almost like they expected it to happen." Other reporters were simply afraid to try to interview victims after dark in certain neighborhoods and included their comments on a story only if they could contact the victims by telephone. When victims are not contacted or cannot supply a reporter with newsworthy comments, the newsworthiness of a story is lower.

The importance of suburban victimizations was dramatically revealed in a story about a ten-year-old girl, Mary Beth Adams, who was abducted and later found murdered. I discussed news coverage of the case with the deceased girl's mother and the suburban news reporter from the *Tribune* who was assigned to cover the story. This was a super primary story that was covered in the news every day for months as the search for the girl was conducted on the local, state, and national levels. I asked the reporter why this case garnered such attention.

That's a good question because I covered another story which involved a black girl, named [Helen Devon], who was a little bit older. The police found her body dismembered, and they convicted her boyfriend of the murder, which was similar to the Adams case but didn't get as much notoriety. A major part of the notoriety of the Adams case was that it occurred in [Jones Point]. [Jones Point] is a pretty rich [suburban] community out on the lake and the people really turned out. You have a lot of retired people who basically sit on their ass and have a lot of money. You got retired bank presidents, retired printers, retired reporters, it is not like the inner city where Helen came from. In the city, you didn't have the same resources, people didn't have the wherewithal like they did with Adams. When the Adams story broke, you had people printing up flyers, you had people calling up friends out of state. It really mobilized a lot differently; to me that was a big part of the story—how the community of [Jones Point] responded to handling this little girl's disappearance. When [Devon] disappeared, you had people handing out flyers, but it wasn't the same thing. In [Jones Point] they geared up like it was a friggin' election, they were putting stuff out. They had thousands of volunteers, they had people calling up, they had the access to the media. . . . Again, I think a lot of it, unfortunately, dealt with the money the people in [Jones Point] had, as compared to other communities that couldn't gather as much. The time was right, they had a lot of people who had a lot of access to money, and they had a lot of access to media.

This suburban homicide generated citywide interest. Each news organization attempted to capitalize on the overwhelming interest in the case, trying to outclass the competition and be the first to add a new twist to the story. Everyone in the city wanted to know what had happened to the Adams girl. The mother of the girl could not believe the attention the case received. She described how no matter where she went, people asked her if she was the mother of Mary Beth Adams. She commented that strangers from all over the city offered to help find her daughter.

Although violent crimes that occur in suburban neighborhoods are more newsworthy than crimes in the city, they are more difficult for the reporter to produce because of limited access to police organizations in the suburbs. Media organizations' relationships with the police in suburban neighborhoods are generally less well established because news coverage of crimes in suburban and rural areas is less frequent. Suburban police do not know how much they can trust the media. In addition, police in suburban areas try to deny that they have a significant crime problem. Numerous reporters who worked for large city media cited problems getting information from suburban police. For example, an informant from a network television station discussed suburban police refusals: "Crime occurs in the suburbs. The types of problems that are in the city are there as well. In fact, the gang problem is moving out to the suburbs. Suburban police would like to make you think they are running them out of the city, but they're not. The suburbs don't want to admit that they are there."

Suburban murders become secondary stories because of the unwillingness by the police to provide the media with unrestricted access. An example from my observance of the Nightly supports this point. A reporter was covering a murder in a suburban township. Clearly, this had the potential to become a primary story because it involved a student who was a cheerleader, and her father, a high-school teacher, was a primary suspect. Although apprehensive, the police chief agreed to be interviewed by the reporter. After we drove for forty-five minutes to the suburb in which the murder had occurred, the interview had to be conducted outside of the department because the police would not allow the reporter inside the building. The interview took less than three minutes. The police chief refused to answer any questions regarding the status of the investigation or about any leads they were working on, and what he did say was "old news." Almost everything he said was edited out for presentation to the public. A potential primary story ended up being presented as a secondary story because of uncooperative source behavior.

Impacts of Crime. Another way victims can provide the type of emotion needed to sell news is through the media's presenting the impact crime has on the victim. There are a number of types of such impact, including financial, property, physical, psychological, and indirect (such as medical bills, transportation to the courthouse, and absence from work). These different types of impact are presented unequally as media content because of the types of crimes generally found in the news; yet an examination of these impacts furthers our understanding of the media's prescription of newsworthiness and fills a gap in existing presentational research. Table 3.9 presents the financial, property, physical, and psychological effects of crimes that are presented in the news. Financial and property impacts are mentioned in less than 5 percent of the crime stories. The reason for the infrequent reporting of financial and property harm is that these types of crime are not considered newsworthy. Crimes without death, blood, or battering are generally not found in the news. Once in a while, however, financial or property effects can be the determining presentational factor if they satisfy the need to entertain. Large amounts of property loss, such as the destruction of a victim's home (arson) or the victim's loss of over a million dollars, increase the newsworthiness of a crime. Very small amounts, such as a woman robbed and beaten for the ten dollars she had in her purse, can also increase the newsworthiness of a crime story because of its senselessness.

The media provide their consumers with infrequent opportunities to gain an understanding of the psychological impact of victimization. The results from the content analysis indicate that psychological effects were mentioned in approximately 1 percent of the sampled stories. This complements other research indicating that "the mass media do not grant much attention to the aftermath of murder" (Wilson 1991: 12). The public cannot understand what it is like to be victimized from the stories considered in this study. The media provide no information about what it is like to be in fear of crime and to be constantly vulnerable to it, and they rarely explain reactions to victimization, even though these are common. Two reasons exist for this neglect. First, reporters do not understand the nature of victimization or the psychological harm that can result from it. Because of this lack of understanding, it is difficult for media to include these elements in a story. Second, it is hard for the public to relate to the psychological harm (Taylor, Wood, and Lichtman 1983).

Physical harm is significantly more newsworthy than any other type of harm because it is the easiest for the public to relate to and the type of crime predominantly presented in the news is murder. The public understands what it means to die and to bleed because, to some degree, these conditionas are part of everyone's reality. Table 3.9 indicates that death is the type of harm most likely to be presented in the news, and the proportion of cases that include death

TABLE 3.9 Type of Harm Presented

Type of Harm	Vic1[a] (in percentages)	All Victims[b] (in percentages)	All Newspaper Victims (in percentages)	Newspaper Tertiary (in percentages)	Newspaper Secondary (in percentages)	Newspaper Primary (in percentages)
Financial amount ($)						
0 - 100	12.2	11.5	11.1	10.0	16.1	3.2
101 - 1,000	11.0	13.9	12.8	13.3	16.1	6.5
1,001 - 35,000	20.7	20.5	20.5	13.3	16.1	35.5
35,001 - 100,000	11.0	10.7	11.1	10.0	12.5	9.7
100,001 - 999,999	7.3	4.9	5.1	13.3	1.8	3.2
Above $1 million	14.6	9.8	10.3	3.3	16.1	6.5
Not specific	23.6	28.7	29.1	36.7	21.4	35.5
(Number of victims)[c]	82	122	117	30	56	31
Property amount ($)						
0 - 1,000	3.5	3.2	3.8	2.6	5.2	2.6
1,001 - 10,000	9.6	7.7	9.0	15.4	3.4	10.5
10,001 - 50,000	3.5	2.6	2.3	0.0	5.2	0.0
50,001 - 99,999	3.5	2.6	3.0	7.7	1.7	0.0
100,000 - 999,999	5.1	4.5	5.3	2.6	6.9	18.4
Home destroyed	3.5	5.8	5.3	0.0	3.4	0.0
Above $1 million	1.8	1.9	2.3	0.0	1.7	5.3
Does not specify	68.4	71.8	69.2	71.8	72.4	57.9
(Number of victims)[c]	114	156	135	39	58	38
Physical harm						
Death	69.5	70.0	70.0	62.4	68.2	77.9
Broken bones	2.0	1.5	1.6	2.0	2.1	1.0

(continues)

TABLE 3.9 (continued)

Type of Harm	Vic1[a] (in percentages)	All Victims[b] (in percentages)	All Newspaper Victims (in percentages)	Newspaper Tertiary (in percentages)	Newspaper Secondary (in percentages)	Newspaper Primary (in percentages)
Cuts	3.3	3.2	3.3	4.6	3.7	1.7
Bumps	0.7	0.5	0.2	0.3	0.2	0.2
Severe trauma	7.1	8.7	8.6	9.5	8.8	7.6
None/minor	1.7	2.0	1.9	2.9	2.3	0.5
Beaten	6.7	4.9	4.3	3.9	5.1	3.7
Sexually abused	5.8	6.2	7.5	8.5	7.8	6.4
Other	0.4	0.3	0.2	0.7	0.2	0.0
Does not specify	2.9	2.7	2.3	5.2	1.6	1.0
(Number of victims)[c]	917	1,488	1,228	306	512	407
Psychological harm						
Fear	27.3	33.3	34.6	66.7	41.7	18.2
Shock	9.1	11.1	7.7	0.0	8.3	9.1
Denial	4.5	8.3	11.5	0.0	0.0	27.3
Anger	18.2	11.1	3.8	0.0	8.3	0.0
Mood shifts	13.6	8.3	11.5	0.0	8.3	18.2
Shaken up	18.2	19.4	19.2	0.0	16.7	27.3
Other	4.5	2.8	3.8	33.3	0.0	0.0
Does not specify	4.5	5.6	7.7	0.0	16.7	0.0
(Number of victims)[c]	23	36	26	3	12	11

[a] First victim.
[b] Combining up to three victims mentioned in a story.
[c] Number of victims, of total, when this type of harm is mentioned.

as a physical effect increases as crime stories move from the tertiary to the primary level. Conversely, less severe types of physical harm, such as sexual abuse and severe trauma (e.g., gunshot wounds), decrease in importance from the tertiary to the primary level. Death is an important part of all types of disaster stories. Automobile accidents and fires occur almost daily; they are generally presented in the news, however, only when death or large amounts of property destruction occur. Death provides important newsworthy emotion, and it is the type of news the media think people want to hear. In addition, having death in a story allows a reporter to include more information about the victim. The names of rape and child victims are usually withheld from news presentation. If children are murdered, however, their names are presented, providing the public with another element to which to relate. Similarly, the impact of murder is not confined to a deceased victim: It touches family members, friends, neighbors, and co-workers. Reporters can expand the interest in these types of stories by discussing the impact the murder has on these secondary victims. The victim can be referred to by additional characteristics such as "the father of four," "wife, and mother of two," or "a supervisor at an automobile factory," thereby expanding the relevance of the story to larger portions of the audience.

Other Aspects of Victims as News. Some reporters found it difficult to describe why they think one crime is more newsworthy than another. "It's a sixth sense. I just know a good story, and I am great with leads," described Brad Donovan, a thirty-five-year veteran with the *Tribune.* A number of factors that can raise the newsworthiness of crime are not only difficult to put into words but are also not easily captured by examining media content. Reporters build up a news sense over a period of years, and certain criteria of newsworthiness are particular to each reporter. As discussed in Chapter 2, factors such as whether the crime is dramatic, novel, or unusual are important in raising the newsworthiness of any type of crime (Chibnall 1977; Ericson, Baranek, and Chan 1987, 1991; Grabosky and Wilson 1989; Hartley 1982; Roshier 1981). On a number of occasions, the behavior of victims or their reactions provides this drama or novelty.

Misdemeanors or property offenses are not likely to become news unless a reporter notices a significant pattern (see Table 3.6). Whether these patterns are discovered is dependent on the skills of the individual reporter. When there is a pattern, the seriousness of these crimes increases because the reporter can attribute harm to a number of victims. It is difficult to distinguish these patterns because reporters' contact with most criminal justice sources is superficial. Yet some reporters are particularly adept at deciphering newsworthy patterns. One of the reporters who worked the police beat for the *Tribune,* Kyle Edwards, was a thirty-year veteran who possessed an uncanny ability to discover newsworthy patterns of crime when examining blotter reports. When leafing through police reports, he selected a host of different crimes not of interest to the other police beat reporters, then attempted to explain how and why certain crimes had occurred. Generally, the other police reporters chose homicides; Edwards, however, overlooked most homicides. He looked for repetition, patterns, and out-of-place circumstances that piqued his curiosity. On one particular day, he spotted a number of crimes involving the theft of copper wire and was keeping a file on these incidents. He thought the thefts possibly involved a ring of criminals who stole the wire, then melted it down and sold it in a different form. If such a ring were discovered, Edwards would have a jump on the competition because of the information he had compiled on these crimes.

The behavior of crime victims can add drama and emotion, raising the newsworthiness of a story. A murder might be raised to the level of primary story if a crime victim resisted the attacker in a heroic effort to avoid being victimized. Although instances in which the victim resisted are rarely mentioned in the news (less than 5 percent of the incident stories), when they are presented they raise the level of newsworthiness because of the drama they provide. Similarly, victims who show a particular tenacity for survival raise the newsworthiness of a story. Sexual assaults and shootings have the potential to become news stories. When a rape victim escapes her attacker by crawling under a car (under which the rapist could not fit) and screaming for help, these crimes become primary stories. Such stories provide adventure and drama that can be visualized by a consumer.

Characteristics of Defendants as Elements of News

Characteristics of defendants can also be influential in raising the level of newsworthiness of crime. Defendants, like victims, are outsiders to the newsmaking process. They will generally not be contacted by the media, and much of what is reported about them is taken directly from established source contacts and existing records. Even though defendants are not directly involved in the process, some of their characteristics indirectly influence the newsmaking process.

Defendants are important to crime stories because they can provide an element of evil. The news media capture evil by portraying defendants as violent predators preying upon public safety (Surette 1992). Defendants were mentioned in over 90 percent of the specific incident stories. The stories in which they were not mentioned were those in which a crime had just been discovered and the police had no leads regarding who had committed the crime. Such stories are lower-level ones that focus on the incident as well as on the victim if such information is available. Even though defendants are not mentioned in these stories, however, the stories still present what is important about the defendant. Since the defendant is at large, the public is at risk.

The same demographic information provided about victims is presented for defendants in Table 3.10. This table provides data on whether defendants are named in crime stories and whether their address, sex, race, age, occupation, prior record, and marital status are provided. Percentages are cited for the first defendant mentioned in each specific incident story. Column two combines data on up to three defendants mentioned in each story; column three provides data on the defendants in newspaper stories; and columns four through six provide tertiary, secondary, and primary newspaper results, respectively.

Demographic characteristics are generally not important parts of a crime story; thus information that is harder to collect, such as the occupation of the defendant, is less likely to be presented than is information that is easily obtained from a police report. The public is left to construct images of both victims and defendants, based on whatever stereotypes it might have, because little of this information is included in stories (Sheley and Ashkins 1981; Surette 1992).

Defendants are more likely than victims to be named within crime stories. If the police are simply investigating a crime or have a number of suspects but none has been charged, the media will not usually print a suspect's name. Once the police officially charge a suspect, however, the news media have no reason not to print the defendant's name and will do so, in contrast to their informal policy regarding the withholding of sexual assault and child victims' names. The decision to print a defendant's name is handled on a case-by-case basis. Defendants may be named prior to being charged if it is inevitable that they will be charged eventually or the crime that occurred is a significant news story. For example, Dahmer was not charged when news media started presenting the story. The Nightly broadcast his name. When I asked why, the managing editor responded: "The networks were airing it, newspapers were going to use it, and the Associated Press printed it."

Past research has shown that defendants are presented either as violent predators or as politicians and bureaucrats (Graber 1980: 57–58). The current research supports these results, indicating that young males are most likely to be presented as the predators in crime and that occupation, when given, is usually professional or politician. A defendant who is a politician or a professional influences whether crime becomes news and the level of newsworthiness that crime achieves. For example, the defendant's occupation in 5.8 percent of newspaper tertiary stories was politician. When primary newspaper stories were examined, over 14 percent of the defendants were identified as politicians. Politicians are generally well-known and have a direct responsibility to serve the public. Even when they commit less serious crimes that would usually not be considered news, their involvement raises the interest of the public. A *Tribune* reporter, for example, came across a case in which a county inspector was charged with theft in office because he was working another job when he was supposed to be working for the county. The defendant

TABLE 3.10 Defendant Characteristics

	Def[a] (in percentages)	All Defendants[b] (in percentages)	All Newspaper Defendants (in percentages)	Newspaper Tertiary (in percentages)	Newspaper Secondary (in percentages)	Newspaper Primary (in percentages)
Named						
Yes	14.2	18.1	15.4	17.9	13.2	16.4
No	85.8	81.9	84.6	82.1	86.8	83.6
Address						
None	63.7	65.3	64.0	58.3	63.3	70.0
Specific	6.6	6.8	7.2	12.6	6.7	3.3
General	6.4	6.3	7.1	8.3	6.9	6.2
City	21.0	19.7	19.8	19.0	20.9	19.0
Other[c]	2.3	2.0	1.8	1.8	2.3	1.4
Sex						
Male	85.1	79.9	81.1	76.8	81.8	83.8
Female	9.5	10.6	10.7	10.1	11.2	10.5
Other[d]	1.2	1.1	0.9	1.6	0.9	0.5
Unknown	4.2	8.4	7.3	11.5	6.2	5.3
Race						
White	17.6	13.4	9.4	2.7	7.3	18.3
Black	9.2	7.9	6.3	2.7	4.9	11.4
Other[e]	3.5	3.1	2.7	2.9	2.6	2.8
Unknown	69.6	75.5	81.6	91.7	85.2	67.5

(continues)

TABLE 3.10 (continued)

	Def¹ᵃ (in percentages)	All Defendantsᵇ (in percentages)	All Newspaper Defendants (in percentages)	Newspaper Tertiary (in percentages)	Newspaper Secondary (in percentages)	Newspaper Primary (in percentages)
<u>Age</u>						
Not identified	39.5	44.9	41.0	38.0	38.1	47.8
0 - 12 years	0.2	0.2	0.2	0.4	0.1	0.2
13 - 16 years	2.9	3.6	3.9	4.0	4.5	2.8
17 - 25 years	16.8	16.6	17.2	22.2	16.8	13.4
26 - 35 years	15.2	13.3	13.9	15.0	15.7	10.5
36 - 50 years	17.7	14.7	16.5	14.6	16.6	18.0
51 - 64 years	6.4	5.4	6.0	4.9	6.9	5.8
65 years and older	1.4	1.2	1.3	1.1	1.3	1.6
<u>Occupation</u>						
Professional	9.8	8.9	10.1	8.1	10.6	11.1
Politician	10.4	8.9	9.9	5.8	9.1	14.4
Criminal justice personnel	7.2	7.0	6.6	5.2	8.6	5.0
Service	0.6	0.6	0.7	0.5	0.6	0.8
Labor	2.7	2.3	2.5	0.7	2.8	3.6
Student	3.0	3.2	3.2	2.5	2.7	4.7
Unemployed	0.9	0.7	0.8	0.4	0.6	1.4
Other	0.7	0.9	1.1	1.3	0.9	1.2
Entertainer	2.7	2.0	1.8	2.3	1.8	1.2
Helping	5.0	3.9	4.1	4.1	3.8	4.5
Defendant	1.1	0.9	1.0	1.0	0.9	1.1
Not identified	55.9	60.6	58.3	67.9	57.6	50.9

(continues)

TABLE 3.10 *(continued)*

	Defl[a] (in percentages)	All Defendants[b] (in percentages)	All Newspaper Defendants (in percentages)	Newspaper Tertiary (in percentages)	Newspaper Secondary (in percentages)	Newspaper Primary (in percentages)
Prior Record						
No mention	92.2	93.5	93.7	94.5	93.7	93.0
Some	6.2	5.2	5.0	5.0	4.8	5.3
Substantial	1.1	0.8	0.8	0.0	1.0	1.4
Other	0.5	0.4	0.5	0.5	0.5	0.3
Marital Status						
Married	9.0	7.1	7.1	5.2	5.9	10.3
Divorced	1.3	1.1	1.0	0.2	0.9	1.9
Other	0.9	0.8	0.7	0.7	1.1	0.2
Unknown	88.9	91.1	91.3	93.9	92.2	87.7

[a] First defendant mentioned in specific incident stories.
[b] Total number of defendants mentioned in specific incident stories.
[c] Combines state and county results.
[d] Includes businesses, corporations, and the government.
[e] Includes Hispanics, Middle Easterners, and Asians.

plead guilty to a misdemeanor, and his sentence was suspended. It was not a very interesting story. Yet because the man was a public figure who violated the public's trust, the reporter produced a tertiary story and the organization presented it. Since certain crimes are not serious, they rarely become primary news. Politicians who commit misdemeanor drug offenses, however, might be presented as super primary stories, and lesser offenses such as bad-check writing are presented as primary stories. An examination of the presentation of occupation in less serious crime stories that were primary showed that occupation was not identified more than 40 percent of the time. When it was identified, politicians were presented as committing over 25 percent of those crimes. Thus, less serious crimes can become news if there is an additional element of interest to the public. Crimes committed by professionals within the criminal justice system and by helping professionals are also important predictors of which crimes become news.

According to Uniform Crime Report statistics, persons 17–24 years of age are those most likely to commit crimes. Content results for the defendants in the current analysis indicate that this age group is also the most likely to be presented in the news. Crime stories involving defendants who were between age 17 and age 24 decrease in importance, however, from the tertiary to the primary level. Table 3.10 indicates that crimes involving a defendant in this age group are most likely to be presented as tertiary news; therefore, the typical crimes committed by this group are defined by the news media as less newsworthy. Age was less likely to be identified in primary stories than in tertiary and secondary stories. The age of the victim was an important variable that increased the newsworthiness of the crime. The defendant's age, however, appears to affect the newsworthiness of crime infrequently.

The race of the victim and the defendant is generally not presented in the news, but the content results indicate that race is more likely to be identified in primary stories than in tertiary ones. This finding indicates that obtaining a picture is an important aspect of primary stories. Race could be easily identified for primary stories because a picture of either the defendant or the victim was in the news.

White victims and white defendants are more likely to be presented as primary news (see Table 3.8 and Table 3.10). Approximately 8 percent of the victims and 18.3 percent of the defendants mentioned in primary stories were white, compared with 5.9 percent and 11.4 percent of blacks, respectively. Differences in the presentation of victims and defendants by race are related to the way story importance can be influenced by the geographic area of a city in which a crime occurred. Crimes occurring in particular geographic regions of the city and involving certain victims and defendants were automatically assumed to be lower-level news stories, if they were covered at all. Since news space is limited and only a small percentage of all crimes that occur get into the news, some crimes are defined as ordinary, everyday, and therefore not newsworthy.

Part of the news formula in deciding what is presentable is whether the crime is unique and rare. The public and reporters are desensitized to crimes that occur in certain parts of the city because they are automatically assumed to be "normal." Black-on-black killings are an example of this thinking. Crimes that involve atypical victims (white, suburban) or atypical defendants (also white, suburban) are more likely to become primary stories because they occur less frequently, making them extraordinary.

Contrasting Images of Victims and Defendants

Each of the factors cited in the previous discussion of newsworthy victim and defendant characteristics can have an independent influence on which crimes become news. An examination of those that are emphasized and those that increase in importance provides some clues as to the types of characteristics on which the media rely for mass appeal. Most murder becomes news because it is a crime that is out of the ordinary. On a slow news day, the murder of an 18-year-old victim, killed in a drug deal that went bad, might be news because of the seriousness of the crime, although it would be a low-level story. Murders committed against or by specific individuals are considered more important because of their ability to invoke a variety of emotional reactions. On any news day, a police officer who murders a child is a primary story. Mawby and Brown's (1984) research highlighted the need to examine the contrasting images of victims and defendants in the news and described the way each element of a crime can combine with others to become an important determinant of news. Understanding how content images of victims contrast with images of defendants and the type of crime increases our understanding of what is newsworthy in crime stories.

One important variable is the relationship between the victim and the defendant. This relationship is not generally identified, either because it is unknown or because the crime is assumed to have been committed by a stranger. When the relationship is identified, crimes between acquaintances are the victim-offender relationship most likely to be presented in the news. If there is a casual relationship between the victim and the defendant, such as a crime committed by a neighbor or a friend, this information will be presented in the story because it may provide a simple explanation for why a particular crime occurred. These stories are generally not important news stories, however; most are presented as tertiary and secondary ones.

The importance of age is increased when certain characteristics of the defendant exist. Approximately 9 percent of all victims mentioned in specific incident stories were under 12 years old. When crimes committed by female defendants were examined, the percentage of victims that were under age 12 jumped to over 20 percent. Female defendants who victimize young children were important news stories, a finding consistent with past research (Mawby and Brown 1984). Crimes committed by parents were most likely to be presented as primary stories. Parents are responsible for protecting their children, and when this trust is violated the public reacts with repugnance. Violations of the family-as-protector image are viewed by the media as extreme and worthy of public consumption. Children and the elderly are viewed by the public as being the groups least likely to be able to protect themselves. Any parent who would victimize the helpless is thought to be truly evil, increasing the importance of the story.

Parents victimizing their children pose unique problems for the media in selecting these crimes as news. Age has been highlighted as being an important consideration in news selection. Often, however, stories involving children will not be produced and presented because of the nature of the crimes. Child-abuse cases are avoided. The media present a select group of child victimizations in order to protect the victims. The content results indicated that most crime stories involving parents were murder; less than 1 percent of all crimes from the content analysis were child-abuse cases. The news media avoid identifying child-abuse victims in a news story because they do not want to stigmatize them. When a parent is charged with child abuse, the news organization still cannot identify the defendant because the child victim would be identified by association. If the media cannot identify the defendant after charging, the story decreases in importance because the media would have to be vague in their presentation. These concerns about identification are no longer valid if a child is murdered.

Age of the victim increases in importance when the defendant's occupation is a helping profession. Any crimes committed by teachers, priests, or doctors have the potential to become news because of the public's ability to relate to each of these professionals. Crimes they commit become more important when children and students are the victims. Results from the content analysis indicated that the number of all victims in the news portrayed as students was over 5 percent (see Table 3.8). An examination of the interaction between the characteristics of victims and defendants showed that over 25 percent of victims mentioned when the defendant was a helping professional were students, and the type of crime most likely for these professionals to be cited as committing was crimes against special groups. The importance of the victim's age increases when individuals who are entrusted with children's care (females, teachers, and similar groups) violate this trust and victimize children.

Further evidence that some occupations can raise the newsworthiness of crimes traditionally thought not to be serious enough to be in the news can be seen by examining the interaction between the type of crime and occupation. Over 25 percent of all crimes presented were murder. For politicians and professionals, however, the murder figure was only 11 percent, the fourth largest category behind victimless crimes, white-collar offenses, and crimes against criminal justice.   Politicians and professionals are presented as victimizing helping and other professionals, and such cases can raise the newsworthiness of crime.   These crime stories are important because the public can easily relate to professionals and politicians.

Death of all kinds, not just murder, is an important newsworthy characteristic that can interact with other such characteristics to raise the level of newsworthiness of crime.   Crime stories about children who were murdered are important; such stories generally reach the primary news level.   Victimizations of helping professionals readily become news stories.   When helping professionals are badly beaten or burned, the story will usually be tertiary.   If they are killed, however, it is more likely to be a primary story.

Conclusion

Crime victims, defendants, and the type of crime are important elements of crime stories.   Particular victims, defendants, and crimes influence the level of newsworthiness crime achieves.   Serious crimes are generally more newsworthy than less serious crimes.   Both young and elderly victims raise the importance of crime stories, although young and elderly defendants have a less consistent effect on newsworthiness.   All elements of a crime can interact to increase how newsworthy a crime becomes, and the level of newsworthiness, in turn, affects the way a particular crime story is produced.

What is newsworthy and is presented to the public about each of these elements (crime, victim, defendant) results from the combined influence of different factors.   The preferences, constraints, and resources of reporters and organizations can limit or increase the newsworthiness of a particular crime.   Some stories can only be secondary stories because they occur close to a deadline and the reporter does not have enough time to flush out the importance of the story.   Stories about certain crimes, victims, and defendants can increase or decrease in newsworthiness over time, influenced by political and public pressures.   Taxicab driving is generally not a newsworthy occupation.   If, however, there is a sudden outburst of taxicab drivers being killed while on the job or an extremely heinous case that grabs the public's attention, taxi-driver stories increase in importance and will be followed for a brief period.   These concerns, because they help capture the attention of the audience, can interact with the media's generation of a newsworthy theme to affect what is presented about crime.

Notes

1. Pooling occurs when there is one cameraperson for all the television stations to videotape testimony. Each station has equal access to what is videotaped.

2. Every story within an entire newspaper or across a broadcast was placed in only one news category.

3. Government and political stories were broken down into domestic, foreign, and international affairs. Domestic affairs were defined as activities of local, state, and federal governments in the United States. Foreign affairs were the activities of a foreign country—for example, France's vote on the European unity treaty—and international affairs were those stories that discussed the activities of at least two different countries.

4. Reporter notices a particular pattern and reports on a number of crimes, e.g., a story on a number of burglaries that have occurred in a particular neighborhood.

5. Some newspapers, on occasion, will have a crime page on which all the crimes that appeared in the police blotter over a period of time would appear, but this is atypical.

6. Super primary stories could not be identified for this analysis. The story typology discussed in Chapter 2 was developed after the crime stories were coded. The analysis that compares across levels is based on the space given to stories, which is only one aspect of the different categories discussed. A distinguishing feature of super primary stories is that a number of similar stories are presented on the same day. No stories that met this criteria could be identified.

7. The types of crime mentioned in stories were coded in the following manner: If a reporter mentioned one, two, or three crimes in a story, those crimes were coded as crime1, crime2, and crime3, according to their order of appearance. For example, if a story was about a murder, a rape, and a robbery, mentioned in that order, then crime1 would be coded as murder, crime2 would be coded as rape, and the robbery would be coded as crime3. If a suspect was charged with more than three crimes, the three crimes most emphasized in the story were coded. If that was not apparent, the first three crimes in sequential order were counted. Results are presented from each category (crime1, crime2, crime3). In addition, the results for the crime1, crime2, and crime3 variables were computed into a single variable called all crime, which includes all of the crimes that were coded.

8. In a similar manner to the data collection for multiple crimes and sources, content data were collected for up to three victims mentioned in a story, as well as for up to three defendants. Data on any primary victim (i.e., the person directly affected by the crime) mentioned in the story were collected first. Then, if data were provided for any secondary victim, that information was coded. Table 3.7 presents information combining the results for both types of victims. It should be noted that an analysis was done that compared the ways primary and secondary victims were presented; it indicated no difference in the demographic characteristics of the two types of victim.

9. The high percentage of age not being provided is an inflated figure. In coding story content, age was only considered as being identified when the *exact* age was provided in the story. Thus, vague indicators of age, such as references to a victim as a "child" or a "juvenile," were coded as "not identified," even though the consumer would have some image of the age of the victim from what was provided.

4

How Crime Victims
Affect the Media

Crime victims, witnesses, and citizens are considered outsiders to the news–production process. They are not typically contacted by the news media and when they are, they are used as "vox pop." They provide flavor and reactions and authenticate the coverage given to events (Hartley 1982: 90). Crime victims satisfy vox pop needs by supplying the media with emotion. A crime victim who can supply good, newsworthy emotion results in a story's becoming higher level and influences when victims are contacted, how they are contacted, the types of questions that are asked, and what is presented about the victim. It is important to understand news organizations' use of crime victims because of the media's increasing reliance on vox pop journalism (Ericson, Baranek, and Chan 1989: 15).

Criminal justice professionals process cases as if the system were an assembly line (Cole 1992). As a group, they are directly responsible for the day-to-day processing of individuals involved in crime. Crime victims sit at the sidelines, participating only as interested bystanders as the police arrest, attorneys protect or convict, judges sentence, and guards correct. Victims are considered outsiders to this process, even though their participation is crucial to discovering, arresting, and prosecuting suspects.

The news media process crime news stories in a similar quick-fix fashion, establishing working relationships with criminal justice sources in order to generate a "going rate" of crime stories. Police and court sources are the primary definers of crime news because they provide the media with enough front-region access to easily satisfy daily story requirements yet protect their own interests by limiting access to back regions (Ericson, Baranek, and Chan 1989). In a similar manner to the way the victim's role has traditionally been construed in the criminal justice process, crime victims have not been considered important elements of the newsmaking process. The present research indicates, however, that crime victims can be influential in determining which crimes are selected, produced, and presented to the public.

This chapter examines the victim's role in the newsmaking process. First, I discuss how crime victims can influence crime story selection decisions. Second, I examine how victims are used in the production of crime stories by considering how crime news information varies depending on the type of story that is being presented (tertiary, secondary, primary, or super primary) as well as the type of information the source is asked to provide. This discussion also includes details of how victims are contacted and interviewed for a crime story. Finally, I examine the ways the victim's role in the news-production process varies according to the type of story being produced and how this process affects the presentation of victims in crime stories.

Crime Victims and Media Selection Decisions

Crime victims can influence whether a crime is selected as being *potentially* newsworthy. Police beat reporters search for newsworthy crimes by making telephone calls to a variety of criminal justice sources throughout the day. In addition, they examine police blotter reports and the arrest log, generally finding an overabundant supply of stories that can easily be translated into crime news. These initial story considerations are monitored and controlled by the police. The blotter reports perused by reporters provide brief descriptions of the crimes that went through central processing. Cursory information is presented that includes type of crime, basic demographic characteristics (name, race, sex, age) of the victim and the defendant, injury, location, weapon, and sometimes a brief narrative of the circumstances of the crime. Access to the blotter reports is virtually unrestricted. Based on their morning police calls and the perusal of these reports, police reporters seek additional information by requesting the full arrest report from the police mouthpiece, who decides which reports to provide. Similarly, court reporters leaf through piles of motion papers, appellate decisions, returned search warrants, and indictments in seeking potential news stories. Court reporters also have a listing of the cases on the docket, which provides the defendant's name, type of crime, and type of proceeding (motion, sentencing, and other proceedings).

Victims are important predictors of which crimes are selected and considered potentially newsworthy from these contacts. The characteristics discussed in Chapter 3 that help a reporter capture newsworthy emotion can determine which reports are pulled for follow-up. A reporter is more likely to request the full arrest report of crimes involving old or young victims, regardless of the type of crime listed. Diaz, the *Midwest Tribune* reporter who earlier stated that only homicides were news, had a tendency to expand his selection criteria when he came across an assault or rape that involved a child or an elderly victim.

Reports that list a recognizable name are high priority. Reporters try to gather additional information in order to discern the newsworthiness of a crime when the location provides some hint as to the occupation of the victim (or the defendant), such as crimes that occur in government buildings, schools, and day-care centers. Reporters are more likely to consider crimes when the impact noted in the injury column is death, severe trauma, or odd and heinous (e.g., a rape victim doused with drain cleaner), or the financial injury is significant.

A list of potential news stories is generated from these initial considerations. Additional hurdles have to be overcome by a reporter when contacting sources who provide the necessary details to determine whether a crime is newsworthy. Police reporters either obtain the full report, which provides further details about the circumstances of the crime, or officers involved in an investigation are contacted by telephone for an update. Court reporters contact bailiffs and attorneys or attend the proceedings thought to be newsworthy. A number of crimes selected as potential news stories are excluded because the police have no new information regarding a particular crime; others are excluded because the news organization does not have enough resources to follow up on every potential crime story or attend every court proceeding. "It's amazing how priorities change as other things come up," said an informant from the Midwest Nightly. In addition, a reporter might ask for the full report or clarification regarding a crime, but the police or court source may refuse to provide any information, particularly if such information reflects poorly on the performance of the source.

Characteristics of the victim can influence sources' decisions about whether to provide information to the news media. Some police officers think rape and child victims should not be in the news, so they do not provide information about crimes involving them. Although this does not eliminate a reporter's ability to cover these crimes, it does limit it, and a reporter risks losing access to sources if he or she decides to go against sources' wishes. Officers might be willing to provide information about an investigation but are protective of the victims, asking the reporter to avoid contacting them because doing so might jeopardize the investigation. At an afternoon editorial meeting at the Nightly, for example, a reporter asked the managing editor whether the station was going to do a story on an eight-month-old baby who had been raped. Gary Kundrat, the managing editor, said no, even though he described it as "an awful crime." This crime was not covered initially because the detective who was involved in the investigation asked that the media not contact the victim's mother, fearing this might discourage her from cooperating with the police and thereby jeopardize the investigation. A story was eventually done when the defendant was arraigned, but it was a lower-level news story because the detective still did not want the media bothering the victim's mother.

Crime Victims and the Production of News

In order to put a crime story together, reporters must contact various sources for additional information about each element of the crime. The sources used in crime stories have been neglected by researchers (Ericson, Baranek, and Chan 1989), but they are an important consideration because what is presented about crime is determined primarily by what is supplied by informants. The sources used and the number contacted vary according to the importance of a story. As the newsworthiness of a story increases, so does the media's reliance on sources outside of their established criminal justice contacts. The way the selected crimes are produced into news is discussed by examining who is contacted for story information and how the process changes according to the level of newsworthiness of a story.

Who Is Contacted

A source can be asked to provide information about the incident, the victim, or the defendant. For instance, a police officer might be asked to comment on the circumstances of the crime: where the crime occurred, what happened, and why. In addition, the officer might be asked to comment on who was involved and to describe various demographic characteristics, the relationship between the offender and victim, or the victim's condition. Past research has failed to consider how reliance on sources varies according to the type of information provided to the media. We would expect police officers to provide credible information about the crime incidents. It is, however, more difficult for the police to provide credible information about the impact of the crime on the victim because they were not directly affected by the crime. In order to obtain credible and newsworthy information about the impact, the media contact and interview crime victims or their families. Table 4.1 presents content results of the sources used for incident, victim, and defendant information.

The results indicate that the police were the primary source used for obtaining all types of information. Various local and federal law enforcement officers provided approximately 29 percent of the source information on the incidents, 32 percent of that on the victim, and 26 percent of that on the defendant in crime stories. Police officers are a primary source of information because they are easily contacted as sources, are available twenty-four hours a day and seven days a week, and are accustomed to the daily intrusions of the media asking about a crime. Moreover, a number of police personnel can provide the different types of information contained in a story. The reporter might rely on the police mouthpiece for incident information. If the mouthpiece is unavailable, the reporter can contact a captain in charge of the district in which the crime occurred, the investigating officers directly involved in the case, or any patrol officers who were at the scene.

TABLE 4.1 Incident, Victim, and Defendant Sources

Type of Source	Incident Information (in percentages)	Victim Information (in percentages)	Defendant Information (in percentages)
Police	29.4	32.6	26.3
Court	25.3	5.0	25.4
Politician	3.0	1.5	2.4
Defendant	8.9	4.0	10.4
Not specific[a]	6.9	3.7	4.4
Citizen	2.6	3.1	3.6
Victim acquaintance	3.7	16.7	2.4
Documents[b]	3.7	1.5	2.3
Victim	3.6	11.0	1.5
Other[c]	1.9	1.4	2.8
Witness/juror	3.6	1.2	1.6
Media	2.1	1.7	2.1
Expert	0.9	0.9	1.9
School/church	1.4	3.7	2.5
Corrections	0.8	0.8	2.9
Defendant acquaintance	1.3	1.1	5.6
Hospital[d]	0.9	10.2	2.0

[a] Source cited as "sources say," "officials say," "authorities say."
[b] Police or court documents.
[c] Highway spokesperson, community groups, weather service, and similar groups.
[d] Doctors cited, emergency medical service, and coroner.

Court informants are important sources of information regarding the crime incident and the defendant but are rarely used to obtain information about the victim. Prosecutors, defense attorneys, bailiffs, and judges were responsible for approximately 25 percent of the information on the incident and the defendant but only 5 percent of information on the victim. Such infrequent reliance occurs for two reasons. First, most court cases are resolved by plea bargaining. The news media cover these stories by focusing on the defendant, and court sources are used for information about the defendant's sentence and the incident. Crime victims are not usually contacted by prosecutors pleading a case; therefore, if the reporter asked, they would have no idea how the victim would react to the plea. The reporter could attempt to contact the victims for their reactions, but cases resolved by plea are not likely to be primary stories so the effort of contacting the victim would be unnecessarily burdensome.

Second, an important stage of the criminal justice process that is presented in the news is the trial. When victim information is needed for a court story, victims or their families are more accessible at the courthouse than they would be at home immediately after the crime. The court process affords the opportunity for reporters to establish a relationship with surviving family members with little burden on their resources. While at the Nightly, I spent a number of days with various reporters covering a story about a man who murdered his stepdaughter. The mother and grandfather were in the courtroom daily, as were print, broadcast, and radio news organizations. The mother knew most of the reporters by name and talked with each prior to the court proceedings or during recess. These interactions promote a feeling of trust between the victim and the reporter, increasing the victim's willingness to comment on camera. Moreover, much of the source information relied on in court stories can be provided when a witness testifies. Reporters can easily obtain pertinent victim information when victims, defendants, or witnesses testify instead of asking members of the courtroom workgroup.

Hospital staff, coroners, and emergency medical technicians are used for victim information but rarely for incident or defendant information. These sources provided over 10 percent of victim information used to inform the public about the condition of a victim or the cause of death in this study, and they can also provide extensive demographic information. Hospital-related staff are primary sources of victim information because they provide what is important about crime victims. These sources are a surrogate for the victim or the victim's family, providing the media with newsworthy emotion. In order to avoid intruding, the media will not contact the victim or the victim's family if a reporter is going to write only a tertiary story about the incident. Hospital staff and other medical professionals play a filtering role because they can easily provide the victim information that the news media need. Hospital sources, like police and court sources, serve a credibility function for the news media because they are well established as reliable sources for the type of information they are asked to provide.

Both primary and secondary victims are important sources of victim information for the news media. Past research has indicated that the media rarely rely on the victim for information about the incident (Ericson, Baranek, and Chan 1991; Voumvakis and Ericson 1984). Table 4.1, which combines the results from both primary and secondary victim attributions, indicates that victims or their family members constituted less than 8 percent of the sources that provided incident information and 4 percent of those for defendant information. Victims and family members did, however, account for over 25 percent of the sources who commented about the victim. When murder was excluded from the analysis, the media's reliance on the victim increased from 11 percent to over 15 percent of the sources used for victim information.

Finally, news media are less likely to provide information collected from sources familiar with the defendant's perspective. Reporters are not in a position to contact the defendant to discuss motivations, alternative explanations, or current living situations. The information provided about defendants is most likely to be from criminal justice sources. One reason for the exclusion of the defendant's perspective is the organizational time constraints that affect the production of a story. It is difficult to gain access to defendants who are in jail.

Reporters have easier access to defense attorneys, but because the majority of information for court stories is taken from testimony, defense attorneys are rarely asked to react to a judge's decision, verdict, or sentence unless the story is significant. Some of these same organizational constraints influence the amount of effort expended to provide the victim's perspective. If the story is not important and the crime victim does not answer the telephone, the story will simply present information obtained from criminal justice sources. The victim's perspective is, however, somewhat more likely to be presented than is the defendant's because of easier access.

Source Variation Across Levels of Newsworthiness

The news-production process expands to meet the demands of crimes that are more newsworthy. News organizations rely on sources other than criminal justice personnel for information as a crime story increases in importance level. Crime victims become key source contacts as a story moves from the tertiary to the primary level. A reporter's ability to contact a victim and the degree of cooperation the victim or the victim's family provides are key determinants of the presentation of a particular story.

Table 4.2 provides a more detailed analysis of the sources used for obtaining victim information. It provides the sources about the victim usually cited, source data when murder is excluded from the analysis, and the results of newspaper reliance of sources in tertiary, secondary and primary stories. Table 4.2 indicates how as a story increases in newsworthiness, the media rely on a greater range of sources, including those outside of the criminal justice system, to obtain additional story information.

Police and hospital sources are the primary ones—approximately 63 percent—used for victim information when a crime story is tertiary. These sources are easily accessible, they provide what little information is needed about the victim for a tertiary story, and they do so without question. If a crime is unimportant and is going to be used only as a filler to satisfy organizational needs, the victim or the victim's family will not be contacted directly, partly to avoid inconvenience and partly because reporters do not have space to present quotes from the victim.

The media's reliance on sources outside of their established source contacts increases as stories move from the tertiary to the primary level. Police sources provided over 45 percent of the victim information in tertiary stories but were cited less than 25 percent of the time in primary stories. This finding indicates that the news media expand their reliance on sources for victim information as a crime approaches the primary level. Reporters are much more thorough in preparing primary stories because such stories are thought to be important news. Reporters will contact a number of different sources for the same information to clarify or check its reliability. From the quotes available, they can select the

TABLE 4.2 Victim Source Information

Type of source	All Sources All Sources (in percentages)	Newspaper (excluding murder) (in percentages)	Newspaper Tertiary (in percentages)	Newspaper Secondary (in percentages)	Primary (in percentages)
Police	32.6	34.6	45.2	37.3	23.8
Court	5.0	4.7	5.8	7.3	3.6
Politician	1.5	1.3	0.0	0.9	2.4
Defendant	4.0	4.3	0.0	4.7	4.0
Not specific[a]	3.7	4.1	4.8	3.4	4.0
Citizen	3.1	2.8	1.0	2.1	4.4
Victim acquaintance	16.7	13.5	5.8	14.2	20.2
Documents[b]	1.5	1.7	2.9	1.7	0.8
Victim	11.0	15.0	8.7	12.4	11.1
Other[c]	1.4	1.7	1.8	0.4	2.0
Witness/juror	1.2	0.9	0.0	1.3	1.6
Media	1.7	1.9	1.0	1.7	2.4
Expert	0.9	0.6	1.0	0.9	1.2
School/church	3.7	2.8	1.0	5.2	4.0
Corrections	0.8	1.1	1.9	0.0	2.0
Defendant acquaintance	1.1	0.6	1.0	0.0	2.4
Hospital[d]	10.2	8.5	18.3	6.4	11.1

[a] Source cited as "sources say," "officials say," "authorities say."
[b] Police or court documents.
[c] Highway spokesperson, community groups, weather service, and similar groups.
[d] Doctors cited, emergency medical service, and coroner.

one that is most attractive as news. The information included within tertiary crime stories, on the other hand, is cursory and is generally provided by one or two sources. Contacting additional sources allows the reporter to expand on theperspectives provided in a story. Citizens might be asked to comment on the effect a crime has had on the community, neighbors to reflect on whether they are concerned about their safety, experts to reflect on what might have caused the crime, and victims or their families to discuss their reactions to the crime. Each of these additional contacts can contribute to the emotional appeal of a story.

Less than 9 percent of the sources who provided information about the victim in tertiary stories were victims, and less than 6 percent were family members. In primary stories, however, crime victims accounted for over 11 percent and family members for over 20 percent of the source information about the victim. Family members were the second most likely source to provide victim information in primary stories, close behind the police. Since murders are more likely to be primary news and the victims are not available for comment, the news media rely on secondary victims to provide the source information. The results in Table 4.2 also indicate that hospital staff and the coroner were important sources for the news media in primary stories when the victim was not available. Generally, these medical sources provide the impact information about the victim when the family is unavailable or unwilling to talk to the media, or else these sources supplement what the family members provide.

Crime Victims as Sources

Demographic characteristics of the victim and his or her interaction with the defendant can influence whether a murder is presented to the public as a tertiary, secondary, primary, or super primary story. Such interaction also increases the newsworthiness of less serious crimes. The effects of these characteristics on the importance of a story are not controlled by the victim but are defined by the media as newsworthy because they pique the public's interest. Primary and secondary victims have more control over the level of newsworthiness of a story when they are contacted as story sources. Victims are contacted to provide the extra emotion that might raise the level of newsworthiness of a story. If the victim cannot provide emotion through good quotes, refuses to give the media a picture, or is unwilling to talk to the media, the level of newsworthiness of a story is lower even though such a victim may belong to a newsworthy class of victims.

Crime victims are used so the public can visualize what it is like to be involved in a crime. This visualization is captured most effectively through emotional quotes or an actual picture. Because of limited resources and easy access to criminal justice sources, the majority of the media's coverage of crime is after-the-fact reporting, and stories are generally produced well after the crime occurred and the crime scene was cleared.   In order to obtain a personal view of the crime and its impact, news organizations must contact victims either at the hospital or at home as they work through their reactions to being victimized. The cooperation of the victim or the victim's family and the quality of information they provide are key factors that influence the type and amount of information presented about the victim in a crime story.   If the victim does not have a telephone or refuses to answer the telephone, other sources have to be relied on for victim information.   If the reporter is able to contact victims but they refuse to answer any questions, the reporter has to look elsewhere for victim information.   But if a reporter contacts an individual who is willing to talk and provide information to the news media, important emotional knowledge might be captured.   One of my informants discussed a situation that furnishes an example of how the quality of information provided by a source can change the presentation of a story.

> *Hess*: Recently, we were contacted by an irate mom who lived in what we would call a bad neighborhood. This was a black woman living in a black neighborhood, with lots of little kids, and her kid found a syringe with what looked like drugs. What we did was send a cameraperson out and we thought, at best, that we would get a picture of the syringe, and a little bit of sound with this lady. Well, this lady went off. What ended up happening was that her anger was so sincere about how bad the neighborhood was getting, that we decided to run it in its entirety: We ran about a 3-1/2-minute piece. It was like cinema verite: This lady popping off about she knows she is black and it is a bad neighborhood, that her kids deserve better than this, and we just let it go because it had poignancy. Normally, if a woman calls up and says this neighborhood is bad, would I send a camera crew? Probably not. When it happens in a spontaneous way, that is pretty interesting stuff.

> *Chermak:* That's a lot of air time.

> *Hess:* 3-1/2 minutes is unheard of in TV terms. One minute and 15 is my usual limit for a package [a primary story]. I made a decision to let this lady go because she wasn't repeating herself, and every point she made was a new point. It was well made. It was an unusual view of a very angry and frustrated woman caught up in a bad situation.

The media rely on certain sources to provide particular types of knowledge about the incident, the victim, and the defendant.   Examining the type of knowledge provided by each source for incident, victim, and defendant information helps to clarify why the media involve crime victims in the newsmaking process. Ericson, Baranek, and Chan (1991: 32) explained that sources can be asked to provide five different types of knowledge when contacted, including "*primary* (factual, asking 'What happened?'), *secondary* (explanatory, asking 'Why did it happen?'), *tertiary* (emotional, empathetic, asking 'What was it like to be involved in what happened?'), *evaluative* (moral, asking 'Was what happened good or bad?'), and involv[ing] *recommendations* (asking 'What should be done about what happened?') [emphasis in the original]."

Content results from this study indicate that the majority of knowledge provided by criminal justice sources is primary. Police and court sources are used by the media to describe what actually happened, when it happened, and who was involved. Eighty percent of the incident information, over 90 percent of the victim information, and 85 percent of the defendant information provided by police sources was primary knowledge. Similarly, 65 percent of the incident information, 59 percent of the victim information, and 45 percent of the defendant information provided by court sources was primary knowledge.

Reporters contact crime victims and their families for two types of knowledge. First, like criminal justice sources, they are contacted for primary information. Nearly 70 percent of the incident information, 59 percent of the victim information, and 43 percent of the defendant information provided by the victim was primary information. The media use victims for primary knowledge by asking them to clarify the circumstances of a crime; for example, crime victims explaining how they escaped from a suspect or were walking innocently down the street when attacked or describing the person who attacked them. Such crimes are more personal and effectively visualized when told by the victim than by an anonymous police source. Furthermore, crime victims are contacted for primary information other sources could not provide. For example, Kyle Edwards of the *Midwest Tribune* did a story about a woman and her child who were murdered in another state. The husband, who was the primary suspect, was arrested in a suburb near the *Midwest Tribune*. A police officer from the other state was able to provide most of the information about the crime, and the reporter was able to contact a journalist from one of the wire services to clarify what had happened. Neither of these sources, however, knew why the suspect was in a suburb eight hours away from where the crime occurred. The reporter had to contact the victim's family because at that time they were the only source who knew the suspect had relatives in that suburb.

Moreover, victims (either primary or secondary) are used as sources to provide primary descriptive information about the victim that is not known by criminal justice sources and that might be of interest to the public. Questions are asked about family relationships (e.g., whether the victims had children, were married, and similar points), occupation, awards, and plans for the future. Answers to these inquiries can provide additional newsworthy elements for a crime story. Learning, for example, that a woman who was murdered was the mother of two children increases the newsworthiness of a story. This type of information can generally only be gleaned from, and is most effectively said by, a victim or a family member who is willing to talk with the media.

Tertiary knowledge is emotional knowledge. Sources are used to provide tertiary knowledge when they are asked to comment on what it is like to be involved in an incident. A victim who was beaten by a police officer said, "I'm not a woman, but now I think I can understand how a woman feels when she has been raped. It made me feel unclean, humiliated, soiled. I didn't have any sense of self-worth" (*San Francisco Chronicle* May 30, 1990: A6). Crime victims are the primary providers of emotional tertiary information. The content analysis revealed that over 30 percent of victim information provided by a victim or a family member was tertiary. When reporters contact a victim, they are looking for emotion and reactions other sources could not or were unwilling to provide about the impact the crime had on the victim. Crime victims are important to crime stories because they personalize a story by bringing emotion and feeling to it. The public can at least try to relate to a victim's pain and loss. Steve Barber, a reporter for an affiliated television station, stressed how crimes can personalize a story: "I think victims are very important because they bring the human aspect: It makes the story real; just to see their pictures makes the stories real too. But to hear or see somebody who was a family member, that brings the story home because they are real, live human beings. It's not that cops are not, but that's their job. The victim is someone who is unlucky enough to be in the wrong place at the wrong time."

How Crime Victims Are Contacted

Reporters from the *Tribune* and the Nightly and those interviewed from other organizations admitted that contacting and interviewing crime victims is one of the most difficult aspects of their job. Hillary Mason of the Nightly described it as being terrible and said she would rather have another reporter do it. Mike Palivoda, a newspaper reporter for over twenty years, said, "It was the hardest thing I learned to do." Reporters have a hard time relating to crime victims and knowing what is appropriate. Manny Diaz from the *Tribune* said, "The toughest thing about it is you do not know what to say. I mean what are you supposed to say? Sorry? Well, that means shit to them." Although contacting crime victims is extremely difficult for reporters, they need to do so because of what the victim can contribute to a story.

Crime Victims in Tertiary Stories

Tertiary crime stories are covered to satisfy organizational needs because they fill news space. Since they are low-level news stories, reporters cover them as efficiently as possible, expending minimal resources. Reporters rely on their established relationships with attorneys, police officers, and bailiffs for tertiary source information. Low-level sources from criminal justice organizations provide the information in these stories, often cited as "police said," "court said," "authorities said," or "according to court records." A brief description of the incident and basic demographics of the individuals involved are presented. This information can be taken directly from a police report or a court jacket.

Crime victims and their families are generally not contacted when reporters are writing a tertiary crime story because of the additional burdens doing so would place on reporters' routines. Reporters would have to find victims' telephone numbers, contact them, and get them to agree to participate in a story that presents information that can be taken from an established contact. This inconvenience to both reporters and victims influences the decision to avoid making the contact.

Crime Victims in Secondary Stories

Secondary stories have the potential to become primary news stories. Reporters expend a considerable amount of energy and resources to put these stories together, but, for a number of different reasons, they remain lower level. Reporters might not have enough time to contact an adequate number of sources to make a story primary because it occurred close to a deadline; they might have enough time but be unable to contact the sources needed to comment on the story, or the sources may refuse to provide information; or they might arrive at a crime scene after newsworthy elements (such as the victim, a police car out front, or a crime scene boundary tape) have been cleared away.

Certain characteristics of the victim, as discussed previously (e.g., age and occupation), can promote a crime story to the primary level. Crime victims have the ability to make a story primary because of these characteristics, but they can also limit stories to the secondary level by refusing to participate. If crime victims exist, they will be contacted in a reporter's attempt to extract either a quote or a picture that can make a story primary. If victims are unwilling to talk to the media, this information cannot be presented, nor can a picture be provided. Only basic demographic information, taken from other sources, is provided in secondary stories.

The criminal justice sources who interact daily with the media develop an understanding of how the media operate, and the effective sources demonstrate a particular savvy for providing the media with self-serving newsworthy quotes. A television reporter from the Nightly commented one day as we left the police mouthpiece's office, "Don't you just love how the lieutenant provides us with our bites." Criminal justice sources who are unfamiliar with what makes important news and those who are unable to provide news in a sound bite are ineffective media sources and not utilized. Others become effective news sources, deciding what information to leak. A court reporter from the *Tribune* was upset with one of two district attorneys prosecuting a well-respected doctor and two pharmacists for drug crimes because his closing argument was boring and he did not give her anything she could include in the story. She explained later that other attorneys from the office asked her to get that particular attorney in the newspaper because he was just starting out. When we were leaving the courtroom before his closing was even finished, the other attorney prosecuting the case stopped her and told us to come back for his rebuttal to the defense. We heard some of the defense's closing and all of the closing by the other prosecutor. The latter, who was more accustomed to being a news source and knew what makes news, provided the reporter with a number of great quotes, including the lead for her story: "These three are nothing more than drug dealers in business suits."

Crime victims have no idea why the media contact them for story information because they are unfamiliar with the newsmaking process. Sometimes, even though victims are willing to talk to the media, they are unable to provide reporters with what they need, so the story becomes secondary. This is understandable considering that victims are contacted shortly after their victimization when they are experiencing shock, confusion, anger, disbelief, denial, and guilt and are attempting to cope with a sudden loss of equilibrium (Bard and Sangrey 1986). Some victims, just like some criminal justice sources, do not encapsulate their emotion in newsworthy sound bites. One of the informants was putting together what he thought might be a primary story because a woman had recently lost her husband in a car accident and her son in a boating accident. When they found her son's body, the reporter contacted the mother, who did not want to talk. "She is kind of freaked out right now," said the reporter. The victim's confusion is compounded by the criminal justice process: Police officers, detectives, and hospital personnel all ask a number of questions about an incident. Reporters add to an already confusing situation because they represent more people asking questions about the crime, another process victims become involved in, and more people who cannot completely understand what victims are going through.

Even though they might be willing to talk to the media and the information they provide to a reporter will generally be included in the story, some victims have difficulty expressing themselves or understanding what the reporter is looking for. If the reporter thinks a crime is an important story for a specific reason but the victim does not reflect on that reason, the story becomes less newsworthy. Thus, much of what victims say will not be presented in a story, or if they agree to go on camera, most of their reactions will be edited out of the story. For example, a police reporter from the *Tribune* covered a story about a murder suspect who called the police wanting to confess to a killing that had been unsolved for over eight months. The reporter thought this story could have been a primary news story, focusing on the mystery about why the suspect finally confessed after such a long period of time. After collecting the information about the incident and the defendant from the police, he called the victim's family to get their reactions. The police had not yet informed the family that a suspect had been arrested. The reporter tried to get the information he needed for the story, but the family member he talked to was in complete shock. He started with a question, "How do you feel that the individual came forward to confess?" The victim could only focus on the fact that she was upset with the police for not informing the family about the capture of the suspect. Although the problem the victim had with the police was presented in the story, the story remained secondary because the reporter thought its newsworthiness involved the fact that the suspect confessed after eight months. When the reporter called the editor to update her on the status of the story, he told her that "the only quote I can use is when she said she was in shock; the rest had to do with her being pissed off at the police."

Crime Victims in Primary Stories

Primary stories are interesting crime stories. A crime may become primary for a number of different reasons or a combination of reasons. These stories remain newsworthy over different stages of the criminal justice process. If a story is a primary police story that reports on the discovery of a crime, it is likely to be a primary story at each definitive stage of the court process, such as arraignment, opening and closing arguments, and sentencing. These stories will be in the news over a period of time as different witnesses testify while a case progresses through the system. If a trial spans several weeks or months, reporters will do stories across its length, although some witnesses might only be worthy of secondary coverage. Because of the media's continued involvement, reporters have the opportunity to establish a trusting relationship with the victim.

Victims are contacted by reporters when they think a crime could become primary. Victims are one of the key elements, in fact, that can ensure that a crime gets presented as a primary story. But reporters cannot predict the type of emotion they will encounter when they contact the victim. Sometimes reporters find more emotion than they asked for—emotion that contributes to a story's primary presentation. For example, Kyle Edwards of the *Tribune* discussed a story for which he contacted a rape victim to fill in some gaps for a secondary story. The story became primary, however, when he found out that the victim was upset with the response of a female police officer at the crime scene. Edwards explained what happened: "The victim had an eight- or nine-year-old car. When the woman police officer responded, she asked what she [the victim] was doing with such an old car [it did not start]. The officer angrily told the victim that she should have been raped. This changed the significance of the story dramatically."

A similar capturing of dramatic emotion that changed the level of importance of a story occurred while I was at the Nightly. One television reporter was generally sent to the courthouse each day to cover court activities. The managing editor of the Nightly told a reporter on a particular day to send the cameraperson to get some film on the sentencing of one of three defendants who had pleaded guilty to manslaughter, down from an aggravated murder charge. The editor thought it was going to be a short, tertiary note that might not make the evening news lineup. The reporter called back, however, explaining that the family of the victim was upset over the charge being reduced to manslaughter. The managing editor told the reporter to package it (make it a primary story) if she had enough emotion. When I asked him about the change, he explained that "the reporter has got a crying family and all that stuff on film."

Victims also serve as surrogates for the media in evaluating criminal justice performance. By using victims in this way, the media's dependence on criminal justice sources is not affected. A news director from an affiliated station thought victims who were abused by the system provided the additional emotion needed to elevate a crime that would not have been covered to a primary level.

> The situation last week in [Smithsville], where the nineteen-year-old who had been released from jail that morning shot his fifteen-year-old wife: I think the instance where we would go after a victim or a family of a victim is because they have something to say. The mother of this girl felt she had been abused and betrayed by the system. Her daughter's husband was in court this morning, and this afternoon he's released and murders her. A reporter simply telling a story like that does not have the same impact as hearing it from the people that were involved.

The victim's cooperation with the media changes the presentation of the story. It is difficult for reporters to contact victims and get them to agree to participate because they are in a state of crisis, fearful, and in need of support. If they refuse, the story will probably still be presented, but it will be a lower-level story. In order to increase the likelihood that a victim will answer questions, reporters use a number of techniques. These help reporters to establish a relationship that allows them to extract information from the victim, not unlike the relationship they try to build over time with police and other criminal justice sources. The techniques can be categorized as the slow notebook ploy, the information exchange, the passive receiver, and the do-whatever-it-takes phenomenon (which is discussed in the super primary section). The technique used varies according to the reporter as well as the importance of the story.

The Slow Notebook Ploy. One technique used by reporters who interview crime victims in person is the slow notebook ploy in which reporters start interviewing a victim with their notebooks in their back pockets. As the source becomes more comfortable with the questioning, reporters will slowly take out the notebook, then wait a few minutes before starting to write down quotes. "They often don't even know you're taking notes," said a Dallas newspaper editor (Sotomayer 1986: 14). This technique is used by reporters to overcome a victim's initial uncomfortableness, after which the victim is more likely to provide some newsworthy information. The slow notebook ploy is used by both newspaper and television reporters. A reporter only needs two or three good quotes from a source because of space constraints, so it is worth the effort to make a victim or source feel at ease when discussing the crime.

The Information Exchange. Most source contacts and interviews, especially in the newspaper business, are done over the telephone where the slow notebook ploy cannot be used. Here, the reporter tries to build a trusting relationship by offering an information exchange; that is, the reporter tries to provide victims with information they may not know. Reporters usually know more about the police investigation than the victim does because of their relationship with and access to the police, and they use this information to capture the victim's curiosity: "Did you know that they had a suspect?" Once the initial contact is made, the reporter tries to make the victim as comfortable as possible and may have to convince the victim that the coverage will be sensitive.

A story produced by Kyle Edwards helps to illustrate how reporters use the information exchange, how capturing newsworthy information often happens by chance, and how the different methods used by individual reporters can change what is presented in a news story. Edwards worked evenings on the police beat. He produced his stories in an old-fashioned manner, collecting information from various sources and then calling in the facts to another reporter who would write the story. Edwards never wrote a story, took a byline, or turned on a computer. Working evenings and weekends makes it somewhat more difficult to produce stories because the availability of sources is more limited. Thus, reporters who work these shifts have to rely on a wider variety of source contacts to meet their needs.

On my first day at the *Tribune*, Edwards picked up a stabbing that was broadcast on a police scanner. Minimal information was available because the crime had just happened. He was able to get the name, age, and address of the victim from the police dispatcher, but the source had not yet been given any other information by the responding officers. Edwards had to dig by contacting sources directly involved who might be able to provide more information. Nobody answered at the victim's home, so he was still without a story. He then used a reverse phone book[1] to contact neighbors to determine whether any of them knew anything. This is where the information exchange came into play. Edwards was able to get in touch with a few of the neighbors and started each conversation by saying, "I am sorry to be the person who brings this kind of information, but did you know that [victim's name] was stabbed tonight?" After explaining what he knew about what had happened and getting the source interested, he started asking questions about the victim and how the source knew the victim. By chance, one of the neighbors contacted was a former girlfriend of the man who had been stabbed, and Edwards was able to get some emotional quotes from her. Edwards closed the interview by offering to call back if he received any additional information. This sustained the relationship and assured that he had open access if he needed to call the woman back.

Passive Receiver. Sometimes victims will contact reporters, asking them to cover a story or asking why their story was not in the news. On one of my first days on the court beat at the *Tribune*, I observed a conversation between a victim and one of the court reporters. The woman's son had been murdered, and she wanted to know why the reporter had not done a story on the sentencing of the first of three defendants who were convicted in the case. The reporter explained to me later that she knew about the case but, because the three cases were being tried separately, was going to wait until the last of the three was sentenced. A similar instance occurred on the police beat. Greg Monroe wrote a tertiary story on a typical gang-related homicide in which both the victim and the defendant were thought to be gang members. After reading the story about the incident, the victim's father contacted Monroe to complain. The problem the father had with the story was that his son's relationship to the gang was tenuous at best, he had been steadily employed, he was still in school, and his family was proud of him. The reporter did another story, a secondary story, emphasizing the pain of the family and the positive things in which the victim was involved. Sometimes a victim's call does not translate into a story; however, the reporter takes down any information offered by the victim because of its potential to become news.

Victims' stories are extremely important and personal to them, which is the main reason they agree to participate or contact the media to ask them about potential coverage. Some crime victims want to talk about their victimization because doing so is therapeutic (Bard and Sangrey 1986). Others want to tell their story in the hope of preventing others from being victimized in a similar fashion or in the belief that their participation might help solve their case. When discussing why victims agree to participate, Ron Janus said, "A lot of times, if a crime is unsolved, the victim's family is sometimes hopeful that by going on the air, they can somehow be a part of helping the police solve it." Marilyn Tenko from the *Tribune* felt some crime victims provide information to the reporter because the story serves as a sort of public obituary for the person. Primary and secondary crime victims do not, however, understand that not all crimes can be in the news; each story is weighed against other potential stories when finalizing what eventually gets presented to the public, and quotes, comments, and reflections are often eliminated from a story or paraphrased because space is limited.

Once a relationship with a victim is established, the reporter tries to elicit emotional information worthy of primary coverage. If victims agree to participate, the reporter will ask the questions needed to fill gaps in what the other sources have provided. Questioning usually lasts approximately five minutes. A reporter's search for emotional reactions influences the type of questions asked. One of the first and most important questions reporters generally ask is "How do you feel?" Reporters then ask follow-up questions so that victims will clarify their reactions and provide different types of impact from which the reporter selects when writing the story. For example, a victim might respond to the initial question by saying, "I'm in shock right now." Then the reporter prods with such questions as "What did the doctor say?" or "Are you in much pain?" These questions attempt to extract information about the impact the crime had on the victim, and such information is most effectively provided by the person directly involved. Crime victims can increase the importance of a story by answering these questions with newsworthy quotes.

Good quotes capture the effect and emotion of the crime and help to raise its level of newsworthiness. They help the public visualize what it is like to be directly involved in the incident. In primary stories, victims are more likely to be directly quoted than paraphrased because their quotes are newsworthy. For example, the story mentioned earlier about the pregnant mother who lost her baby when hit in the stomach with a brick provides a good example of why the victim is contacted and what that contact can bring to a story. This was a primary story the reporter took a full day to produce. One of the last calls the reporter made was to the mother of the victim. I asked the reporter why he contacted the mother. He read off three quotes:

I was holding her when she died.

I had her baptized in case she died. I did not want her to die in sin.

The woman should be charged with murder because of the pain I'm feeling. . . . If she didn't give a damn, why should I?

When they read these quotes and see a picture of the mother on the front page still in her maternity clothes, people will be able to relate to the mother. After reading the quotes, the reporter said, "They provide the melodrama."

The public can visualize another mother, whose son was struck with a baseball bat at school, who vented her anger by saying, "The principal is covering his butt." This is best attributed directly to the source. Data were collected on whether and when victims were quoted directly in crime stories. These are quotes the reporter thought should not be paraphrased. In primary stories, crime victims were more likely to be given direct attribution than in any other type of story. Victims were quoted directly in 1 percent of the tertiary stories, 4.3 percent of the secondary stories, and 9.3 percent of the primary stories, illustrating the way information provided by crime sources can vary in news quality.

Another of the primary reasons the media contact crime victims is to obtain a photograph of the victim or the victim's family. "If there is no picture on the page, then it is scary to the reader," said an informer from the *Tribune*. Providing the public with a photograph of the victim is another way to capture emotion and make the story more appealing. Sometimes victims are contacted by the media *only* to see whether they would be willing to provide a picture or to go on camera in order to obtain the most up-to-date and newsworthy picture. Pictures give the story life and make it more real to the reader. A reporter described why he asks for pictures: "It makes the story more human. If the public can see the kid, a victim, it adds something. There is nothing to a name. When you see a picture, you see the life, the potential." Having a picture, especially a newsworthy one, can promote a crime to a higher level. Take, for example, the case mentioned earlier about the man who raped and murdered his stepdaughter. Many stories were done over a two-week period—some tertiary, some secondary, and some primary. Whether a story was promoted to the primary level on a particular day of coverage was influenced by the quality of the testimony provided by the witness and also by the picture available. When the grandfather of the girl started to cry on the stand, the story became primary and was the lead story on the news that evening. If victims are unwilling to go on camera or to provide the media with a picture, the story is less newsworthy; if they do so, the importance of the story is increased. The characteristics mentioned earlier that raise the newsworthiness of a crime story (age, occupation, and similar factors) are influential in determining the importance of a picture. Having a picture of a police officer in uniform who was murdered is more important (by newsworthy standards) than if he or she is not in uniform.

Crime Victims in Super Primary Stories

Few crime stories are super primary. When the news media contact and attempt to interview a crime victim for a lower-level story and the victim refuses to cooperate, the news media leave the victim alone, although this may prevent the story from becoming major. One of the informants interviewed said, "If, on the initial contact, they say 'leave us alone,' then that is it." When a story moves to the super primary level, however, the media's informal balancing of the public's right to know versus the individual's right to privacy is increasingly pushed toward the former. This is the final way news organizations get crime victims and other sources to participate. It can be categorized as the "do-whatever-it-takes" phenomenon. Competition between organizations becomes more intense as reporters search for different angles to keep a story alive that allow them to scoop other reporters. The ethical responsibilities of the journalist become more ambiguous as a crime story approaches the super primary level because of the belief that these stories are the most attractive.

Death-knock coverage, camping out on the victim's lawn, and coming onto a crime scene with cameras rolling rarely occur except when the coverage is super primary. The Jeffrey Dahmer case provides an example. Dahmer admitted that he had murdered his first victim as a youth in the town where he grew up, which was near the *Midwest Tribune* and the Nightly. After ten years of not knowing whether their son was dead or simply missing, the family, which still lived where the murder had occurred, found out that their son was the first in a chain of heinously killed murder victims. The fragments of their son's bones, smashed into small pieces with a sledgehammer, were spread throughout Dahmer's backyard. The reactions of the family members to the murder were an important element of the story as the police dug for the bones. The news media wanted to know "Did you ever give up hope?" and "How does it feel knowing that your son was Jeffrey Dahmer's first victim?"

Reporters descended upon this community like locusts. If a story is only primary, the victim's refusal to talk to the media might only result in turning away one or two newspaper reporters, three or four television reporters, and maybe a reporter covering news for a radio station. For a super primary story, such as the Jeffrey Dahmer story, however, family members might have to turn away over fifty reporters at their home every day for a number of days, avoid them while being followed in public, and ask them to leave the funeral of the victim. Most of the reporters assigned to cover the dig for the Dahmer victim's bones attempted to contact the family at various times during the day and night, which was extremely intrusive. The victim's family refused to talk to the media because of the constant badgering. One of the informants from the Nightly, reacting to the intrusiveness of other stations, said, "This is a perfect example of how the media can screw things up." After about a week, the family set up a formal news conference for a select group of news organizations and answered their questions in order to get the news media "off their backs."

Competition is stiff when the public becomes engaged by a story over a period of time. Some reporters resort to manipulation in order to scoop other reporters. Earlier, I mentioned the case in which a woman became involved with the media because her daughter had been kidnapped and was later found to have been murdered. This case was in the news for a number of months, and reporters were trying to scoop one another. The *Tribune* reporter explained:

Everybody was looking for a little angle that someone else did not have. . . . There were a couple of stories that I did that were nothing but rehash because there was nothing happening. It was a unique situation where everybody wanted to know the latest of what was going on. But since the cops were not saying anything, there was no new latest. We had to create—not create the news, but *create what we were going to present to people* [emphasis added]. . . . You start to get desperate, and you start to look real hard. I look back now and say, "Did I write this? Is this news?" But, hey, they put it on the front page, and people read it. It was one of the best-read stories in recent years.

The willingness of the mother to discuss the case with the media was part of the reason this story stayed in the news for such a long time and the community remained interested in it. In fact, she was more willing to update the news media on the investigation than the police were. When I discussed the case with her, I asked her why, even soon after they discovered her daughter had been murdered, she was willing to participate. The mother said she knew the media were using her, but at the same time she realized what the media could do and felt she effectively used them. She hoped that her appearing in the news might help solve the case and that somebody, somewhere would notice her daughter and return her home safely. After the daughter was found murdered, the mother felt her continued participation, or what she called her "continued exploitation," would keep the public interested enough to pressure the police to continue to investigate the case so the same thing would not happen to another mother.

For the majority of stories, most television reporters do not arrive at a crime scene or an interview with cameras rolling, pushing a microphone into the victim's face. To get the victim to feel comfortable, television reporters will first ask a few questions about the crime, not writing anything down, and then explain how the cameraperson is going to do the shot. Super primary stories, however, attract a larger range of organizations and reporters. The methods used in pursuit of these stories vary in intrusiveness according to the news organization and the individual. Some reporters have to be overbearing if they want to keep their jobs because management believes grieving victims attract viewers. Some reporters refuse to be intrusive. Barber, a television reporter in the business for about twelve years, explained why he refuses.

Many times I have people who say "I don't feel like talking," "Don't take my picture," I just won't do it against their wishes. There are other places that do it; that is the business. I have my own set [of] standards, and I never once had someone from here come and say "Why didn't you do this?" like the other station did. But I consider myself lucky. That's the way I feel. I put myself in the position of the victim, and a lot of times the victim or relatives of the victim talk a lot more than I would have. But that is the way it is: We are all different.

On the other hand, some reporters may be willing to do whatever it takes to produce a story, but organizational policy decisions constrain their behavior. News organizations do not operate in a vacuum, and editors pay attention to complaints from their readers. The most pressing complaint about the treatment of crime victims by news reporters has been the level of intrusiveness. Some news organizations have responded and have established policies, either informal or formal, that limit behavior. A super primary situation arose while I was at the *Tribune* in which a reporter was willing to do whatever it took to break the story; however, organizational policy limited the opportunity. A story occurred in which a woman was hospitalized after surviving a parachuting accident. This was an important news story because the woman's fall was captured on video. The story had caught the attention of national news media and the tabloid press, who were badgering the family. One of the police reporters wanted to see whether he could get past security and interview the woman. His editor, however, told him not to do so because "she thought they had some policy against doing this."

Conclusion

Although criminal justice sources are the main conduit of crime news, crime victims and other sources who might provide different perspectives play an important role in the media's generation of crime news because they often can provide the extra element needed to make a crime newsworthy or, at the least, raise its level of newsworthiness. These individuals can affect story selection decisions and the methods used by reporters to put stories together. Decisions by victims to agree to appear on camera might ensure that the victims' perspective is provided in the story. The importance of primary and secondary victims is highlighted when we consider the four different levels of crime stories. Crime victims increasingly are contacted and asked to comment on the crime story as it increases in importance, and the quality of information they provide ensures the presentation of a higher-level story. When victims refuse to comment, the presentation of victims is based on hearsay information provided by police, court, and hospital sources. Whether victims agree to become involved in the process and the quality of information they provide both contribute to what ultimately gets presented to the public about crime.

Notes

1. A reverse telephone book does not list telephone numbers by name but by address. Thus, as long as a reporter knows the victim's address, it is easy to contact his or her neighbors.

5

The Presentation of Crime
and Victims in Print
and in Electronic Media

Crime messages are conveyed to the public through numerous media. For example, the word *police,* painted within a red circle that has a slash through it and appearing on a highway bridge overpass, carries a distinct but superficial criminal justice message. Word of mouth, pamphlets, billboards, signs, and similar vehicles can all transport crime information to the public, although the message conveyed is influenced by the type of media used. Postman (1985: 6–7) makes this point.

> Consider the primitive technology of smoke signals. While I do not know exactly what content was once carried in the smoke signals of American Indians, I can safely guess that it did not include philosophical argument. Puffs of smoke are insufficiently complex to express ideas on the nature of existence, and even if they were not, a Cherokee philosopher would run short of either wood or blankets long before he reached his second axiom. You cannot use smoke to do philosophy. Its form excludes the content.

Different media are attractive to consumers for specific reasons, which include the news formats of a media organization (Altheide 1984; Ericson, Baranek, and Chan 1991). The public attends to news from a particular organization because that news fits its needs or interests. In order for a news organization to capture the largest percentage of the market share, it must produce and present news in a way that satisfies the reasons the audience invests time and money for the news product. Such formats influence decisions about the newsworthiness of events. Certain situations, circumstances, and—in the present study—crimes are selected because they are the most compatible with particular formats (Altheide 1984), and sources are more amenable to those news organizations whose formats are the most compatible with their message (Ericson, Baranek, and Chan 1989, 1991). According to Ericson, Baranek, and Chan (1991: 21), "Aspects of format fundamentally delimit and shape the news product: for example, the time available for a broadcast-news bulletin and the space available in a newspaper; the sequencing of broadcast-news items and the layout of a newspaper; the technologies associated with the medium; and the beats available as routine rounds for acquiring preselected material from sources that is itself formatted for the purposes of the reporter's medium." It would have been impossible for the person who put a slash through the word *police,* as mentioned earlier, to fully exhibit the rationale of this statement because of medium constraints. Space, time, and resources limited what could be said, as well as what could be attended to by the consumer, since only so much information can be processed when one is driving by at fifty-five miles per hour.

News organizations fulfill format requirements by structuring the news-production process in a way that emphasizes the organization's format strengths (Ericson, Baranek, and Chan 1991). These strengths are, in fact, what helps to sell news. Researchers argue that the presentation of news content should vary in television and newspaper media because of the distinct format differences (Altheide 1984; Ericson, Baranek, and Chan 1991); however, past research has been unable to establish consistent findings (Ericson, Baranek, and Chan 1987; Garafalo 1981). It has been argued that the deemed newsworthiness of a particular crime varies for the different media because television stations are primarily concerned with an appealing visual product, the stations are more likely to be in competition for audiences and advertising from other stations because cities often have a number of television stations but only one major newspaper, and time constraints affect television reporting more than newspaper reporting (Sheley and Ashkins 1981: 494; see also Ericson, Baranek, and Chan 1991; Surette 1992). Research examining New Orleans (Sheley and Ashkins 1981) and Toronto media (Ericson, Baranek, and Chan 1991) supports this hypothesis. Sheley and Ashkins's (1981: 499) results indicated that murder and rape account for twice as much of the crime news space in television reports as in newspaper reports. Others, however, have argued that crime news should be similar across news organizations because of the nature of source selection as well as the reliance of different media on each other for story selection decisions (Ericson, Baranek, and Chan 1989; Gordon and Heath 1981; Voumvakis and Ericson 1984).

Print and Electronic Media Formats

Television is a popular companion for many Americans because it is easily accessible and constantly available, and video consumers can be entertained with little effort. One of television's main strengths is that it has both visual and audio capacities, which "greatly enhances its connotative capacity [and] allows it to bind its messages to the context in which they were produced" (Ericson, Baranek, and Chan 1991: 23). Researchers have argued that the primary concern of television journalists is to obtain an appealing visual product (Epstein 1974). A television informant stated: "We are in a 'see and say' business. We want the pictures to go with the words. Sometimes it can't be avoided that you don't have the pictures, but that is the nature of business. If we didn't need pictures, then I would be writing for some newspaper." The more drama and action that are captured on film, the more important the story is to the organization. Conversely, the visual capacity of newspapers is limited. Still pictures, headlines, story placement, and the juxtaposition of stories help newspapers to convey some connotative meaning (Ericson, Baranek, and Chan 1991: 23, 24); however, the strength of that meaning is limited by the medium.

The television news-production process is structured in such a way as to fill visual format requirements. Accessibility to sources and their willingness to go on camera influence what can be presented about crime. Police and court sources who are able to provide newsworthy material in short, concise sound bites are more likely to be prominently displayed as story sources. Crime victims who refuse to comply with the visual format needs of television media can modify the scope of a story. For example, the managing editor of the Nightly was upset one Monday morning because the weekend staff had not done a story on a gun-shop owner who had been murdered at work. An affiliated station had done a "great" story that included emotional video of the victim's son. The managing editor asked Hillary Mason to produce a similar story for the broadcast that evening. She was able to get a police source to comment on camera and to use footage of the crime scene; however, the family of the victim was unavailable for comment. The story was presented as a secondary-level story because she could not get video of the family.

The pressure on television organizations to generate advertising revenues is great. These organizations compete directly and intensely with other stations for the local marketable audience. An informant from a small-market television station said, "My first role is to get young, affluent people watching our news. My second role is to uphold journalistic standards." This concern for marketable news, and the adoption of formats to satisfy this requirement, "leads to speculation that television crime news departs more widely from objective reality than does newspaper crime news" (Sheley and Ashkins 1981: 494). Print organizations have the space and flexibility to tailor parts of their newspapers to specific groups. Television stations have to make their product appealing to as many diverse groups as possible in order to attract the largest viewing audience (Kaniss 1991; Lee-Sammons 1989).

Changes that have occurred in the United States over the past ten years regarding the allowance of cameras in the courtroom have made court cases more appealing to broadcast news organizations because such cases can easily satisfy television news formats.   Court stories excluded from television presentation in the past are more likely to be covered now because of the ease with which testimony can be recorded.   A news director of a New York television station reacted to a legislative rule that excluded cameras from the courtroom after the station had been experimenting with cameras for two years: "We now think twice about going to a trial. On a slow day, with cameras in the courtroom, listening to the real-life drama of court going on, it made a story. Now, if the same case was occurring, but I can't get a camera in, then it is harder to tell the story. It is only a reporter standing there.   We are a visual animal.   It is more likely that we would not cover it or cover it in a much shorter way."   His comment illustrates television's need for visual material. Court stories are less important for television when cameras are excluded from courtrooms.

One of the format strengths of the *Midwest Tribune*, as well as most other newspapers, is that it has significantly more resources available to produce a wider range of crime stories than does television.   The *Tribune* had offices set up as beats in police headquarters and in the county and federal courthouses and had suburban news beats through which specific reporters covered crime outside the city.   If the crime staff was short, any of a number of general assignment reporters could be used to fill resource gaps for crime news production.   All of the reporters at the Midwest Nightly, however, were general assignment reporters, and no specific reporter was assigned to make daily police contacts. Daily crime calls were made by the managing editor, who often relegated this arduous chore to an intern.   The newspaper beat reporters interacted with the main sources of crime news on a routine, unofficial basis.   The Nightly contacted sources by telephone to see whether they would be willing to comment on camera.

When producing a story, the processes used at both the *Tribune* and the Nightly were affected differently by the time and space available.   Newspaper reporters, because of their print orientation, have the luxury of being able to contact, and include information from, a variety of sources by telephone.   Crime stories can be put together quickly, a larger number and more diverse range of sources can be contacted, and most of the contacts can be made from the beat offices.   Television reporters, however, rely on a much smaller number of sources for story information.

Time as a format strength for newspaper organizations has changed dramatically in the past decade.   Most newspapers have converted to electronic editing and pagination, "enabling some deadlines to be moved back and giving reporters more time to do their jobs" (Willis 1990: 169).   Having extra time can change what is presented in a story.   Manny Diaz of the *Tribune* wrote a story on a house fire from information collected by interviewing the fire chief, paramedics who tended to four injured firefighters, and the woman whose house had burned down.   Diaz had little time to write the story because the fire occurred late in the day.   His story reached the editor before his deadline, but it did not include any of the quotes from the woman who had lost her home. When he called the editor to see whether she had received the story, the editor told him she would not be able to read it for fifteen minutes.   This gave the reporter enough time to rework the story and incorporate the victim's quotes.

Editing for television stories is slow, cumbersome, and time-consuming. Reporters need much more time than do newspaper reporters to incorporate additional aspects of a story—a luxury they rarely have.   Reporters covering various types of crime stories for the Nightly could contact sources by telephone but had to interview sources in person to fulfill their visual format needs. Reporters had to contact sources, get them to agree to go on camera, drive to a location convenient for the source, and hope that what the source had to say would satisfy the requirements of newsworthiness.   Since television reporters need to locate and collect sound bites from each source in person, they often have to drive to different parts of the city to interview sources, then return to the station to write and edit the story.

Newspapers have significantly larger amounts of space to include a more diverse range of news stories and, if necessary, have the capability to expand that space to include extra stories.   According to Ericson, Baranek, and Chan (1991: 28), "The main evening television-news show typically contains fewer words than a single page of a broadsheet quality newspaper."   The average newscast time for Albany and Cleveland broadcasts in the present study, excluding commercials, was approximately twenty-two minutes.   Newspapers use their space advantage to provide a wider range of stories, to use a wider range of sources, to present longer and more complex stories, and to discuss them in greater detail.   The *Midwest Tribune* filled its extra space needs through its comprehensive access to police and court documents television stations generally ignore.   Television stations do not need the extra access to crime information because they present, on average, only three or four crime stories per broadcast.

The Presentation of Crime Compared to Other News Topics

Table 5.1 provides data on the number, percentage, and rank order of stories that are presented in newspaper and television media.   Significant differences across media were found in fifteen of the sixteen story categories.   Death and automobile accidents were among the categories that produced the largest differences.   These stories were the fifth and sixth most likely categories to be aired on television but were the eleventh and sixteenth most frequent newspaper story topics presented, respectively.   News format differences between print and broadcast news organizations, which affect their standards of newsworthiness,

TABLE 5.1 Presentation of Crime in Newspaper and Television Media

	Newspaper			Television		
	Number	Percent	Rank	Number	Percent	Rank
Sports	4,591	19.2	1	1,036	33.1[a]	1
General interest[b]	3,494	14.6	3	197	6.3[a]	4
Business technology	3,506	14.6	2	110	3.5[a]	8
Crime	2,331	9.7	5	548	17.5[a]	2
General stories[c]	2,654	11.1	4	95	3.0[a]	11
Domestic affairs	1,697	7.1	7	293	9.4[a]	3
Foreign affairs	1,848	7.7	6	118	3.8[a]	7
Science[d]	1,068	4.5	8	107	3.4[a]	9
Schools	833	3.5	9	56	1.8[a]	14
International affairs	662	2.8	10	62	2.0[a]	12
Death[e]	441	1.8	11	172	5.5[a]	5
Celebrations[f]	312	1.3	12	106	3.4[a]	10
Environment	284	1.2	13	26	.8[a]	15
Automobile accidents	37	.1	16	126	4.0[a]	6
Fires	79	.3	15	59	1.9[a]	13
Presidency[g]	113	.5	14	20	.6	16
	N = 23,950			N = 3,131		

[a] Indicates that comparisons between television and newspapers are significant at the .05 level.
[b] Stories about arts, entertainment, people, gardening, and similar topics.
[c] Stories about specific incidents such as chemical leaks, gas leaks, power outages, missing persons.
[d] Includes medical and health issues.
[e] Includes accidents, suicides, plane crashes, and deaths from natural disaster.
[f] Includes ceremonies and parades.
[g] Not political stories but stories about activities of the president, such as playing golf.

account for these significant variations. Television news broadcasts are limited to a few brief items in every newscast, whereas newspapers are more apt to rely on longer items (Ericson, Baranek, and Chan 1991: 28). Television stories on accidents and deaths can be easily produced and satisfy visual format needs. A cameraperson can be sent to collect video from the scene of a crash without being accompanied by a reporter. A reporter, assignment editor, or intern can call police and hospital sources from the television station to collect the information necessary to write the story. A brief twenty- or thirty-second television piece can be produced from this information.

Both newspaper and television news agencies reserve time and space for extensive coverage of a variety of sporting events. On average, between six and eight sports stories are broadcast in each television newscast. The results presented in Table 5.1 also indicate that newspapers provide some space to cover foreign, science, and school affairs. Foreign affairs are less frequently presented in television news because the focus of a locally affiliated station is on the immediate viewing audience and the broadcast organization must present events that are the most relevant to this audience. In addition, science and school stories are generally not visually appealing and are difficult for television reporters to put together because a number of sources have to be contacted and interviewed and the issues involved are generally too complex to be encapsulated into a thirty-second piece.

Crime was the fifth most likely category to be presented in newspapers, supplying approximately 10 percent of the total number of stories. It was the second most popular type of story in television news, accounting for over 17 percent of stories. Although crime is a popular topic used by both media to attract consumers, the results indicate a significant difference between the presentation of crime in print and electronic media. This difference can be attributed to the space advantage of newspapers, which allows them to cover a large range of different stories and dilutes the importance of crime as a story topic.

Crime stories that discussed police actions (arrest, investigation, and similar topics) and court actions (arraignment, trial, sentencing, and similar actions) were presented significantly differently in the two media. Television news organizations were most likely to present stories on police stages (56 percent of crime incident stories reported a police stage), whereas newspapers were most likely to cover court stages (46 percent of all crime incident stories). Television stations were almost twice as likely as newspapers to present a report when a crime was first discovered by the police. Similar to the reasons automobile accidents and fires are frequently reported, the discovery stage of the criminal justice system is disproportionately presented in television news because these stories can be produced at the convenience of a reporter. Police calls are made by television personnel throughout the day to discover any newsworthy crimes that have occurred. This reliance on the police gives these sources a considerable amount of control of the images of themselves that are presented in the news, more control than they have over newspaper coverage because television reporters are not given options from which to choose. Newspaper reporters examine a variety of documents provided to them by the police, which gives them a number of options.

Television reporters generally arrive at a crime scene long after the participants are gone. This does not inhibit reporters' ability to report these crimes, unlike the difficulties they would face in producing a story on a political news conference or a court proceeding they had missed. Just as they can shoot video of the remnants of a burned-out building or a smashed car, camerapeople can still shoot pictures of the crime scene, and the reporter might get one or two official sources to comment on camera. Although these stories would not be likely to be primary stories because the crime scene was cold, they will still be included because of the ease with which they can be put together. A story assembled by Nightly personnel illustrates how such stories become news. The managing editor of the Nightly changed his mind about covering a homicide not originally scheduled to be covered after he saw that the other local television stations did a story on the crime. The Nightly had little time to do the story but sent a cameraperson and an intern to collect video. They shot video of the outside of the home of the victim and of the district police station. A twenty-second voice-over was produced in about two hours, just in time for the evening newscast.

Newspaper and television reliance on different stages of the criminal justice system highlights disparities in the way each produces news. Historically, news coverage of courtroom activities has been dominated by print media because of the exclusion of electronic and audio equipment from the courtroom (Ericson, Baranek, and Chan 1989). Video of an artist's sketch is not visually appealing. Even with cameras now allowed in some U.S. courtrooms, courthouses are still dominated by newspaper reporters. The *Tribune*'s court beat reporters occupied an office on the first floor of the courthouse in a corner near a door past which all of the district attorneys had to walk. On numerous occasions, attorneys would stop in as they were leaving or arriving at the courthouse to discuss what they thought were newsworthy cases. Because of their convenient location, the court reporters had firmly established relationships with judges, bailiffs, and attorneys. Often, court reporters would simply stumble on a story while riding in an elevator with an attorney or waiting for a court session to start.

Tribune reporters had established access to courtrooms, courtroom workgroup personnel, and court documents. "We are part of the ecological system of the court," stated one of the *Tribune*'s court reporters. Their access allowed them to walk freely behind doors and counters, through courtrooms, and into the outer offices of the judge's chambers, providing them with another opportunity to mingle with bailiffs and attorneys as they waited to appear in court. Television reporters do not discover newsworthy court cases in the same fashion or have firmly established relationships with such a variety of courtroom personnel. They do not examine court documents, such as appellate decisions or filed motion papers, because any stories that might be found within these documents are too complex and too visually unappealing to fulfill television format requirements.

The morning assignment editor from the Nightly usually made court contacts by telephone from the news station. These were calls to follow up on stories that had been covered previously. A Nightly reporter was sent to the courthouse only when the station knew a newsworthy court case was occurring. Of course, at the courthouse reporters were able to mingle with attorneys and bailiffs to get information about other cases that might be considered. Because they were not a regular part of the courtroom workgroup, however, television reporters did not know as many attorneys and judges as newspaper reporters did.

The need for a visual component led to the Nightly's limited coverage of cases within the court system. *Tribune* reporters could simply pop in and out of courtrooms, often capturing tertiary news stories at random. Television reporters cannot rely on this same random capturing of news. Nightly reporters had to receive advance approval from the judge in order to record a session, and they needed time to set up equipment while court was not in session. If the station was unable to obtain permission to be in the courtroom before a court stage began, it would be unable to collect video and the story would not be produced. The Nightly relied more heavily on police stories that could be put together quickly with few barriers to production.

Types of Crimes Presented

The results shown in Table 5.2 indicate that some crimes are presented similarly by newspaper and television media because they are attractive to consumers of both types of news organization, whereas others are presented differently because of the format strengths of a particular medium. Table 5.2 presents comparison percentages for the first crime mentioned in each crime incident story and provides results from combining the crimes into the all crime variable. In addition, it shows whether there was a statistical difference in how print and electronic media displayed a particular category of crime. Chi-square results are provided to show whether there were differences between the first crime category (FC), local and national[1] first crime stories (LFC, NFC), the all crime category (AC), and local and national results for the all crime category (LAC, NAC).

Murder was the most popular crime presented, accounting for approximately 25 percent of the sampled crime stories regardless of the type of media considered. This equality in presentation holds when the stories considered cover both local and national murders. Reporters from both of the organizations observed looked for newsworthy homicides, and criminal justice sources

TABLE 5.2 Categories of Crimes Presented in Newspaper and Television Media

	Newspaper First Crime		Television First Crime		Newspaper All Crime		Television All Crime		Comparisons Across Media					
	Number	Percent	Number	Percent	Number	Percent	Number	Percent	First Crime	Local First Crime	National First Crime	All Crime	Local All Crime	National All Crime
Murders	429	27.5	114	27.0	760	23.7	158	25.6	N	N	N	N	N	N
Other violent crimes[a]	243	15.6	81	19.1	499	15.5	122	19.7	N	N	N	Y	N	N
Property offenses	113	7.2	20	4.7	222	6.9	39	6.3	N	N	N	N	N	N
Victimless crimes[b]	221	14.2	42	9.9	402	12.5	49	7.9	Y	N	N	Y	Y	N
White-collar crimes[c]	158	10.1	23	5.4	349	10.9	31	5.0	Y	N	Y	Y	N	Y
Special group crimes[d]	121	7.8	64	15.1	284	8.5	94	15.2	Y	Y	Y	Y	Y	Y
Misdemeanors	85	5.5	17	4.0	271	8.4	35	5.7	N	N	N	Y	Y	Y
Crimes against criminal justice[e]	133	8.5	28	6.6	335	10.4	43	7.0	N	N	N	Y	Y	Y
Does not specify	56	3.6	34	8.0	90	2.8	47	7.6	Y	Y	Y	Y	Y	Y

N = Not significant.
Y = Chi-square statistics significant at the 0.05 level.
a Robbery, shootings, assaults.
b Drugs, prostitution, gambling.
c Embezzlement, bribery, forgery, fraud, corporate crime, securities violations.
d Sexual assault, child, elderly, bias-related victimizations.
e Perjury, resisting arrest, obstruction of justice, tampering with evidence, intimidating witness/victims.

supplied whatever information they had on murders that had occurred. There seems to be a shared understanding across media that murders have the potential to become important news stories and are the crime of greatest interest to consumers. At the same time, murder stories fulfill organizational format considerations. More information can be given about the victim, and criminal justice sources are more willing to provide necessary information because doing so cannot further endanger the victim. Police often request that the media withhold the name when they think the victim might be missing rather than dead because of the unwarranted grief publicizing the name could cause or the danger in which giving the name might put the person.

A recently completed analysis of Canadian media examined the ways print and electronic media present crime. Ericson, Baranek, and Chan (1991: 244–245) presented violent crime as a combined category that included murder and other violent crimes. Their tests of significance compared results across popular and quality media and made statistical comparisons with radio content. In their study, violent crimes accounted for 35 percent of popular newspaper news stories and for over 40 percent of popular television news stories (1991: 245). This is similar to the present findings when murders are combined with the other violent crime category. The present findings are not, however, consistent with other research that made comparisons across media. Sheley and Ashkins (1981: 499–500) reported that close to 70 percent of the newspaper crime stories and over 85 percent of television crime stories in their analysis involved violent crime. One possible explanation for the differences observed in the presentation of violent crime is that their study focused on only seven index crimes; thus, the presentation of violent crimes was amplified because less serious crimes that could undercut their salience were not considered. The present research indicates that any crime can become news, depending upon the circumstances surrounding the event.

Crimes against special groups of victims was the only category of crime that produced significant differences across all of the comparisons considered. These crimes were almost twice as likely to be presented as television crime stories. Moreover, when compared with other television stories focusing on a crime that occurred outside of the station's state, these crimes were the second largest crime category cited in television broadcasts, accounting for over 20 percent of the national stories. Broadcast organizations' heavy reliance on these stories results from space, visual, and time formats. As already mentioned, space is severely limited in television newscasts. In order to attract the widest audience possible, television stations must rely on groups—such as children—that are easily identifiable by, and emotionally relevant to, a diverse range of viewers. Newspapers provide a broader range of crimes, watering down the importance of special victim stories. Television stations do not have that luxury and must rely on what will attract the most people.

Crimes committed against special groups were most likely to be presented as tertiary or secondary stories in both television and newspaper news, mainly because of the difficulties involved in producing these stories. Reporters rarely contact either rape or child victims, and police sources are generally more protective of information about these victims. Reporters and news and source organizations are aware of the stigma attached to these crimes and the difficulties involved in prosecuting them. Thus, stories on special victims focus on the defendant, using police and citizens as the main sources, thereby limiting their newsworthiness.

The results presented in Table 5.2 also reveal some significant differences in the presentation of white collar crime across media. White-collar offenses were the fourth most likely stories to be reported in newspapers, accounting for approximately 11 percent of the total number of crime stories. Interestingly, they were the least likely story to be reported as television crime news. These findings are consistent with the results presented by Ericson, Baranek, and Chan (1991: 247), who also found that white-collar crimes were more likely to be presented in newspapers. Although these crimes have become increasingly newsworthy because of public-opinion shifts about their seriousness, they are not important television stories because of their complexity, which can be more easily analyzed in a long newspaper script. An example from my observations illustrates the difficulties television media have in making a white-collar story appealing because of format constraints. A primary white-collar story covered in the *Tribune* over a number of days concerned a complex welfare scam that involved employees at different hierarchical levels within the Health and Human Services Department. This story was neglected by the television stations because in the space provided, only newspaper reporters could capture the intricacies involved and give readers the opportunity to fully grasp the different aspects of the story. White-collar crimes rarely satisfy the visual format needs of television because there is rarely a specific crime scene or a victim on which to focus.[2] In addition, white-collar crime is generally not a threat to the immediate safety of the audience. When a serial rapist strikes, the news report serves as an easily visualized warning. In television it is difficult to warn people about white-collar victimization because too much explanation is needed.

Even though white-collar offenses are less likely to meet the format needs of television media, it is interesting that the local presentation of these offenses was not significantly different across the media. We might expect that crimes against the local business community would be of general public interest and something on which newspapers would capitalize. The results, however, indicate that both types of media used local white-collar offenses to the same extent. These offenses accounted for approximately 7 percent of the print and television stories; all white-collar stories accounted for nearly 17 percent of the national newspaper stories but less than 8 percent of the television stories. Three reasons can explain these results. First, television news is focused primarily on events that affect the immediate viewing audience. Television news does not waste time describing a complex national white-collar crime but appears willing to provide the space for a local offense. Crimes that affect the local business community are of strong interest to the consumer. Second, newspapers generally have a designated section for business news, providing extra space for more white-collar offenses. Finally, it should be mentioned that these findings can also be partially explained by the sample period. Various junk-bond cases, including that of Michael Milkin, occurred during the newspaper sample period and sparked national interest. Although Ivan Boesky's case had been completed, he was constantly in the news testifying against others and was released to a halfway house during the sample period.

As we might expect, less serious crimes, such as property offenses, were more likely to be reported when they were local rather than national. Both types of organization were most likely to present misdemeanors and crimes against the criminal justice system as tertiary crime news, and these crimes were more likely to be of local origin. On the whole, these offenses were not considered serious enough to influence either medium to expend space on stories unless they involved a famous person or some noteworthy occupation (e.g., university president). No significant differences were found across the media for misdemeanors and crimes committed against the criminal justice system with respect to first crime comparisons. There were significant differences, however, when comparing results across the all crime variable. Misdemeanors and crimes against the criminal justice system are rarely news. Differences in their presentation in the first crime and all crime variables can be attributed to the fact that newspapers have the format space to list other crimes with which a defendant was charged, whereas these crimes are not generally mentioned on the air.

The large number of insignificant differences between the media is surprising considering their distinct format differences. Murder, other violent crimes, and property offenses are rarely presented differently. Murder and violent crime stories are important because of the tendency of the news media to think these are the crimes the public wants to see and that less serious crimes are generally of no interest. The sources used to obtain information about crime stories are the same across media organizations, which influences the similarities in presentation. Reporters at both the *Tribune* and the Nightly, for example, relied primarily on the police mouthpiece for information. Moreover, the similarities found in the presentation of some crimes result from each popular medium attending closely to the news presented in other media (Ericson, Baranek, and Chan 1989; Gordon and Heath 1981). The police beat reporters from the *Tribune* had a television set in their office so they could view news. The managing editor of the Nightly read numerous city newspapers first thing in the morning and added potential stories to the daily story list if he thought one could meet the format needs. If a story is missed by either a print or a broadcast organization, it can be redone, but it is presented differently because of media format differences so it does not appear to the public as old news.

Sources Used for the Presentation of Crime

News media are structured to produce crime stories efficiently, which influences who is relied upon to produce a story, the number of sources that are cited, and the sources presented within a story. Content results revealed significant differences between the news-item sources cited in newspaper news and those in television news. Television stations rely disproportionately on in-house reporters to present crime news material, whereas print media are more likely to supplement the stories written by their reporters with news from wire services or to borrow an interesting crime story from another newspaper. Ericson, Baranek, and Chan (1991: 155) found similar intermedia differences and credited them to television stations' use of both wire-service and newspaper information without attribution. The differences in the news-item sources used by each of the two media are compounded by the fact that newspapers have larger amounts of space in which to present a diverse range of crime stories. Newspapers rely on newsworthy stories either from wire services or from other papers to fill the space they have available.

The content results indicate that television stories contain fewer source attributions within crime stories than do newspaper stories. Over 60 percent of the television stories cited no source or only one source within a story, illustrating the fact that television journalists provide crime information without attributing it to a source (Ericson, Baranek, and Chan 1989, 1991). Only 6 percent of the total number of televised crime stories cited more than five sources. Television reporters do not have the time to collect story information from a large number of sources because many sources have to be interviewed in person. If reporters did collect this information, they would be wasting their time because the space available for television crime stories is limited. In addition, it would be confusing to the viewer if reporters jumped around to a large number of different sources. The number of sources used in newspaper stories was far higher. Approximately 55 percent of the newspaper stories cited over five sources, and only 6 percent cited no source or one source. Newspaper reporters do obtain the facts for a story from a large number of sources because the information can be collected over the telephone and is more easily incorporated into the story because of the amount of space available.

Table 5.3 presents data on the type of sources used for incident, victim, and defendant information, comparing percentages across the media. The results, surprisingly, indicate few significant differences across media considering the large discrepancy in the number of sources cited. We would expect that newspaper reporters would be more likely to use a larger range of sources because of their format advantage. The content results indicate, however, that neither television nor newspaper stories cited a wide range of sources except for individuals with a direct interest in the crime (criminal justice sources, victims, and defendants). Thus, although the number of sources used is different across media, the types of sources used are not. There were no significant differences in the use of school or church officials, witnesses, and politicians. Experts were not used for television stories in this analysis and only rarely provided information for newspapers. The results suggest that these sources are not important to either medium in obtaining crime story input. During the observational periods, source contacts reached by telephone or in person were generally someone directly involved in the incident or a criminal justice source who could give the story credibility.[3]

One source used differently across media is citizens. The fairly significant difference between media in the use of citizens as incident and defendant sources can be explained by two factors. The first is organizational convenience. Police beat reporters from the *Tribune* contacted many sources for a story by telephone, whereas television reporters had to go to the scene to collect video. Crime scenes and television cameras tend to attract crowds; therefore, it is convenient for a television reporter to ask a curious onlooker for reactions. The second reason citizens are used more frequently by television reporters is that they are a source of last resort. If television reporters cannot get a police source or other direct participants to go on camera, they rely on citizens to fill their video gaps. While I was at the Nightly, I went with an informant to cover a story on a series of rapes. The police were not talking because they did not want to create panic among the public, and no victims were available for comment. The reporter filled the visual needs of the medium by taking video of the community in which the crimes had occurred and randomly selecting citizens to voice their concerns about the danger.

Police personnel are the main source of information for both types of media, both of which have established relationships with criminal justice sources. *Tribune* police beat reporters interacted frequently with the police spokesperson each day, requesting reports or information about newsworthy incidents. Similarly, the managing editor of the Nightly was in contact with the same spokesperson throughout the day, and reporters requested interviews with him whenever they needed sound bites.

The content results indicate that police and court sources are used similarly by print and electronic media for providing victim and defendant information. There was a significant difference, however, in the way the two media used these sources for incident information. Television stations relied more heavily on police sources for incident information than did newspapers, whereas newspapers were more than four times as likely as television reporters to use court sources. These results can be explained by the differences in coverage of criminal justice stages. Television news focused on the discovery stage, when

TABLE 5.3 Source Comparison in Newspaper and Television Media

	Victim		Incident		Defendant	
	Newspaper (in percentages)	Television (in percentages)	Newspaper (in percentages)	Television (in percentages)	Newspaper (in percentages)	Television (in percentages)
Police	33.0	29.2	28.7	40.7[a]	25.9	33.8
Court	5.4	1.5	27.3	6.2[a]	25.7	22.5
Politician	1.4	3.1	3.0	3.1	2.4	2.8
Defendant	3.7	6.2	8.6	11.1	10.3	7.0
Not specific	3.9	1.5	7.2	4.6	4.8	0.0[b]
Citizen	2.9	4.6	2.2	6.8[a]	3.3	8.5[a]
Victim acquaintance	15.3	29.2[a]	3.4	6.5[a]	2.1	7.0[a]
Documents	1.5	1.5	3.7	4.3	2.5	0.0[b]
Victim	11.1	9.2	3.1	8.3[a]	1.4	2.8
Other	1.4	1.5	1.9	1.5	2.8	2.8
Witness/juror	1.2	1.5	3.5	4.0	1.6	1.4
Media	1.9	0.0[b]	2.1	1.5	2.2	1.4
Expert	1.0	0.0[b]	1.0	0.0[b]	2.0	0.0[b]
School/church	3.9	1.5	1.5	0.3	2.4	4.2
Corrections	1.4	0.0[b]	0.9	0.3	3.1	0.0[b]
Defendant acquaintance	1.0	1.5	1.4	0.3	5.7	2.8
Hospital	10.5	7.7	0.9	0.3	2.0	3.0

[a] Indicates comparisons that show significant differences at the .05 level.
[b] Comparisons impossible because one of the cells has a quantity of zero.

court personnel are not yet involved and the police are the most effective source of incident information. As cases move into the court system, television stations rely on cameras in the courtroom to satisfy their visual format needs. A picture of the defendant in the courtroom can be shown as the anchor presents the story without attributing the information to any particular court source. This holds especially for tertiary and secondary court stories. For example, video of the defendant, the defendant's attorney, and a court reporter was shown while the anchor read the following: "Murder suspect [Dave Beardon] was in a Common Pleas Court today. [Beardon] is wanted for the murder of his wife and five-month-old son in West Virginia on Mother's Day. Today, he waived extradition and is on his way back home to stand trial. [Beardon] was arrested in [Pleasantville] yesterday on a public drunkenness charge. Police said 'that they discovered that he was wanted in West Virginia when they did a search on a National Crime Computer.'" Television stations can produce court stories without having to talk to participants in the case because they can simply show testimony. If a court story were primary, however, reporters would try to obtain an attorney's or a participant's reaction. Court stages were the most frequent activities reported by newspapers, who generally have court beat reporters to cover a variety of courthouse activities, thereby increasing their presentation of court stories.

Print and electronic use of surviving family members as news sources was significantly different regardless of whether those victims were asked to provide victim, incident, or defendant information. In fact, in television stories secondary victims, such as the mother or father of a homicide victim, were as likely to be used for commentary about the victim as were police sources. These sources are used less often in newspaper crime stories. The willingness of family members to be interviewed on camera provides the type of emotion reporters need to satisfy the video format requirements of television news. The public can relate to, and is disheartened by, seeing a parent or a wife describing the loss of a loved one. The use of family members to describe reactions to victimization sends a powerful and visually appealing message that is more difficult to capture in print.

Newspaper reporters will rarely contact surviving family members for tertiary and secondary stories because they do not have space to include such information. However, these sources will be contacted when the story is important. The quality of quotes provided by these sources determines how prominently they are placed in a newspaper story. Tertiary and secondary stories are less likely to be presented as television news because of time constraints. Family members are contacted more frequently for television stories because reporters need to capitalize on their emotion in order for a story to be presented.

Another example of the use of victim acquaintances for emotional impact is television's use of the victimization of special groups. Such incidents are among the more frequent topics on television news stations. The problem with producing these stories is that television reporters rarely put a child or a female rape victim on camera because of the added trauma doing so could cause. Thus, if reporters determine that it is necessary to have video of a direct participant, they will collect victim source information from either parents or siblings rather than the actual victim.

Crime victims as sources are used fairly similarly across news organizations. Both media are most likely to use them for victim information and least likely to use them for defendant information. There was a significant difference, however, in how the media rely on victims for incident information. In television stories, actual victims were the third most likely category to comment about the incident, ranking far behind the police. Victims are presented for the same emotional reasons their families are. The difference across media in retrieving incident information is the result of the limited number of sources used by television. Television sources are asked to provide as much information about the incident, victim, and defendant as possible because of the time constraints in producing stories. Newspaper reporters, however, can get two or three different police officers to comment on an incident and can concentrate on using a larger variety of sources for other types of information.

Medical sources are another important source of victim information for media. Hospital staff, coroners, and emergency medical technicians are used equally by television and print media. These sources are convenient when direct participants are unwilling to comment or when the story is lower level.

Presentation of Victims and Defendants

Table 5.4 provides victim and defendant demographic characteristics presented in print and electronic media. Most characteristics collected for the content analysis were infrequently provided in either medium. The age of victim was presented in 50 percent of the newspaper stories and 34.5 percent of the television stories; the address of either the victim or the defendant was provided in just over 35 percent of newspaper stories and approximately 29 percent of television stories; and the location where the victim lived was provided in approximately 8 percent of newspaper stories and approximately 13 percent of television stories.

Basic participant identifiers, such as the name and address of the victim or defendant, were provided differently in the two media. Over 60 percent of the victims mentioned in newspaper stories were named, compared with only 42 percent in television stories. Two reasons can be identified as contributing to this difference. First, crimes against special groups are used more frequently in television broadcasts than in newspapers. Reporters avoid naming a child or female victim because of the nature of their victimization. Second, television

TABLE 5.4 Victim and Defendant Demographic Characteristics in Newspaper and Television Media

	Victim		Defendant	
	Newspaper (in percentages)	Television (in percentages)	Newspaper (in percentages)	Television (in percentages)
Named				
Yes	63.4	42.2	84.5	66.4
No	36.6	57.8[a]	15.5	33.6[a]
Address				
None	63.6	71.3[a]	63.9	72.4[a]
Specific	4.5	2.0[a]	7.3	4.7
General	9.7	2.0[a]	7.1	1.6[a]
City	20.7	22.7	19.9	18.9
Other[b]	1.5	2.0	1.8	2.4
Location				
City	3.2	9.8[a]	X	X
Suburb	4.0	3.4	X	X
Rural	0.6	0.0	X	X
Not identified	92.2	86.9[a]	X	X
Sex				
Male	46.1	41.9	81.1	73.5[a]
Female	33.0	36.4	10.6	10.0
Other[c]	7.2	2.5[a]	0.9	1.8
Unknown	13.7	19.2[a]	7.4	14.7[a]
Race				
White	4.6	20.1[a]	9.4	35.6[a]
Black	3.9	13.4[a]	6.3	17.2[a]
Other[d]	2.2	2.1	2.7	5.2[a]
Unknown	89.2	64.4[a]	81.5	42.0[a]
Age				
0–12 years	9.2	9.5	0.2	0.5
13–16 years	5.3	2.6[a]	3.9	2.4
17–25 years	10.8	8.5	17.2	13.5
26–35 years	10.8	6.7[a]	13.8	10.0
36–50 years	7.9	4.9	16.5	4.5[a]
51–64 years	3.1	1.3	6.0	1.8[a]
65 years and older	2.9	1.0	1.2	0.8
Not identified	50.0	65.5	47.1	66.5[a]

(continues)

TABLE 5.4 *(continued)*

	Victim		Defendant	
	Newspaper	Television	Newspaper	Television
Occupation				
Professional	4.5	5.7	10.2	2.4[a]
Politician	1.8	3.4	10.1	2.9[a]
Criminal justice	7.3	5.9	6.6	9.0
Helping	5.0	0.3[a]	4.1	3.2
Student	5.3	5.7	3.3	1.3
Labor	1.3	0.8	2.5	3.2
Service	2.7	0.8[a]	0.9	0.3
Criminal	1.9	0.8	0.9	0.5
Entertainer	0.9	0.0[b]	1.8	3.4
Unemployed	0.3	0.0[b]	0.8	0.0[b]
Other	0.1	1.0[a]	0.8	0.0[b]
Not identified	68.7	75.8[a]	58.2	73.6
Victim-offender relationship				
Stranger	8.4	26.5[a]	X	X
Spouse	4.0	4.2	X	X
Parent	4.8	3.9	X	X
Other relative	1.4	1.6	X	X
Child	0.7	1.0	X	X
Acquaintance	15.6	18.6	X	X
Unknown	65.0	44.1[a]	X	X

X = Not available

[a] Indicates comparisons that show significant differences at the .05 level.
[b] Combines state and county results.
[c] Includes business, corporations, and the government.
[d] Includes Hispanics, Middle Easterners, and Asians.
[e] Comparisons impossible because one of the cells has a quantity of zero.

relies heavily on the discovery stage of the criminal justice system. The victim's or defendant's name might not yet be known, so, of course, it cannot be provided. In addition, the addresses of the victim and defendant are provided more frequently in newspaper stories because of space availability. Newspapers are significantly more likely to provide both specific and general addresses because of their ability to tailor a story to audience concerns in particular neighborhoods or sections of the city. Television stations tend only to mention the city in which the victim and defendant lived because of their need to make the story appeal to larger segments of the public.

Victims who reside in the city are significantly more likely to be presented in television crime stories than in newspaper stories. As already mentioned, the resources and mobility of television stations are limited. These stations are usually located in the heart of the city, so it is easier to cover victimizations that occur nearby. Television will cover crimes that occur outside of the city when they are thought to be important enough, but the coverage of late-breaking news must occur nearby to allow that story to be produced. Like the *Tribune*, many city newspapers are increasingly using suburban news bureaus to collect crime information in different parts of the city and surrounding areas because they have the space to include both city and suburban stories (Kaniss 1991). Newspaper reporters need only to make contacts over the telephone in order to produce the story, giving newspapers a distinct advantage in covering crimes that occur outside the immediate city.

The results provided in Table 5.4 indicate that age is provided in approximately half of newspaper stories and 35 percent of television stories. The age of the victim can, however, be an important variable that determines whether a crime is presented or promoted to a higher newsworthy level. Certain age categories have a similar level of newsworthiness across organizations. Victims under age twelve were the most likely category to be cited in television stories and the third most likely category to be cited in newspaper crime stories. Victimizations of children were viewed as being among the most newsworthy by reporters in the two media. In comparing tertiary, secondary, and primary stories across media, it was found that a young age for victims often promoted lower-level crimes, such as aggravated assaults, to the tertiary level and frequently promoted murders to the primary level regardless of medium. When a young age is provided, both types of medium think a crime becomes more engaging to a large percentage of the public. Most people, including reporters, are genuinely appalled when they hear that someone has victimized a child.

Occupation was not usually identified in either medium, but it was less likely to be identified in television news. This difference exists because newspapers give their reporters the space to mention the occupation in passing. When occupation was mentioned in crime stories, most of the types of occupations considered were presented similarly in the two types of media. Often the occupation of the victim or defendant determines what crime gets presented in the news. Some occupations influence crime story selection regardless of the news organization because of the public's ability to identify with certain occupation types. Criminal justice personnel, professionals, politicians, and students were among the most popular occupations cited for victims and defendants regardless of the medium examined. Print or broadcast media think consumers are interested in these types of occupations. Moreover, the occupations that are the most frequently cited in Table 5.4 also increased in frequency as stories moved from the tertiary to the primary level in both media, indicating that both types of media consider crimes committed by certain occupational groups to be important stories.

Professional and political defendants were presented differently in the two media. These findings are reflective of some of the format differences across media described earlier. Professionals and politicians are generally portrayed as committing white-collar crimes, whose complexity makes them more amenable to newspaper presentation. Another factor contributing to the differences is the fact that local and national crimes by politicians were commonplace during the newspaper sample period studied. In addition to the extensive presentation of Marion Barry in all of the newspapers in the analysis, the *San Francisco Chronicle* had a local super primary story involving state politicians that was frequently in the news.

Males and females were presented similarly across media. Although male victims were more likely than females to be presented in the news, females were a fairly close second, and were overrepresented in comparison with the actual amount of crime that occurs against them. Society thinks females, like children, are more vulnerable and feels crimes committed against them are more newsworthy.

Race, however, was presented differently between print and electronic media, a fact that is illustrative of the visual display of victims and defendants in television stories. The race of either participant was rarely provided in newspaper stories unless it helped to explain why the crime had occurred. The higher percentage of race presented in television crime stories occurs because of the need to broadcast pictures of the individuals involved. Thus, the frequency of race was easily captured by content coding television crime stories.

Table 5.5 compares how television and print media present the level of harm crime had on the victims. Overall, there were few significant differences in the presentation of financial, property, psychological, and physical harm. Property and psychological harm were rarely provided in either medium, and if they were, neither specified the amount or type of loss. A wider range of stories in which the victim suffered some sort of property damage can be provided in the extra space of a newspaper, or this information might simply be mentioned as an afterthought to the physical harm. Property and financial losses rarely satisfy the visual needs of television crime stories.

Most of the physical harm mentioned in crime stories is presented similarly in print and electronic media. Death is by far the most newsworthy type of harm victims suffer. Seventy percent of the instances of physical harm mentioned in both media involved death. Severe trauma, broken bones, cuts, and minor injuries were all presented comparably across media, but bumps and the physical beating of victims were presented differently. The power of a videotaped beating and its effect on the victim was illuminated by the Rodney King incident. A home video of Los Angeles police officers beating King made America wince. This was a more important television news story than newspaper story because the beating satisfied the video format needs of television. The follow-up video of King's swollen eyes, cuts, and scars directly illustrated the beating that had occurred. Overall, a victim who remains alive after a severe beating and who is willing to go on camera provides good video,

TABLE 5.5 Type of Harm Reported by Newspaper and Television Media[a]

	Victim	
	Newspaper (in percentages)	Television (in percentages)
Financial amount ($)		
0–100	11.1	20.0
101–1,000	12.8	40.0
1,001–35,000	20.5	20.0
35,001–100,000	11.1	0.0[c]
100,001–999,999	5.1	0.0[c]
Above 1 million	10.3	0.0[c]
Does not specify	29.1	20.0
Property amount ($)		
0–1,000 3.8	0.0[c]	
1,001–10,000	9.0	0.0[c]
10,001–50,000	2.3	4.8
50,001–999,999	3.0	0.0[c]
1,000,000–6,000,000	5.3	0.0[c]
Home destroyed	5.3	0.0[c]
Does not specify	69.2	95.2[b]
Physical harm		
Death	70.0	69.9
Broken bones	1.6	0.8
Cuts	3.3	3.1
Bumps	0.2	1.5[b]
Severe trauma	8.6	9.3
None/minor	1.9	2.7
Beaten	4.3	7.7[b]
Sexually abused	7.5	0.4[b]
Other	0.2	0.4
Does not specify	2.3	4.6
Psychological harm		
Fear	30.4	30.0
Shock	8.7	20.0
Denial	13.0	0.0[c]
Anger	4.3	30.0[b]
Mood shifts	13.0	0.0[c]
Shaken up	21.7	20.0
Other	4.3	0.0[c]
Does not specify	4.3	0.0[c]

[a] Data presented only for those stories in which a type of harm is mentioned.

[b] Indicates comparisons that show significant differences at the .05 level.

[c] Comparisons impossible because one of the cells has a quantity of zero.

raising the newsworthiness of assaults and aggravated assaults as television crime stories.

Conclusion

Similarities and differences exist in the presentation of crime in popular print and electronic media. Some of the crimes presented, the types of sources used for crime information, and the individuals presented in stories are displayed similarly, even though crime stories account for a larger proportion of television news than of newspaper news. However, media format differences of print and electronic news organizations contribute to crime presentation differences. Although these two types of media rely on similar criminal justice sources for story ideas, media format differences have an impact on judgments of newsworthiness and on how crime news is produced. Certain crimes are more likely to be presented when they emphasize a medium's strength. Specific types of crime (such as crimes against special groups and white-collar crimes), the use of specific types of sources (secondary victims, citizens), and the total number of sources cited differ across organizations because of format needs. The reliance of news media on similar criminal justice sources gives those sources the opportunity to control the crime images presented in the news; however, if these sources do not provide stories in a way that satisfies the format strengths of a news organization, their news access is eliminated.

Notes

1. National stories for this analysis were those crimes that were committed somewhere outside of the state in which the news organization was located. Local crimes were those committed in the immediate area around the media organization.

2. It should be noted, however, that the presentation of white-collar crimes did increase in frequency from the tertiary to the primary level in television news. These levels were determined by the length of time devoted to a story. The results indicate that white-collar crimes are covered in television stories when they are worthy of primary coverage. The additional space devoted to primary television stories allows the reporter to capture some of the inherent complexities of these crimes.

3. The present analysis might not capture the full range of sources that are used in newspapers. The total number of sources used per story was counted. For data manageability, of the total sources cited in both television and newspaper stories, nine possible sources were coded (three incident, three victim, and three defendant). When there were more than nine sources in a story, source information was collected from the first, third, and fifth source for each type of information. Perhaps a wider range of significantly different sources would be found if the total number of sources from a story were included.

6

The Presentation of Crime and Victims in Different-Sized Cities

What happens to the presentation of crime and crime victims when the amount of available crime is significantly different across cities? The seriousness of a crime is an important variable that influences whether a crime is presented to the public. The types of local crime available that satisfy this criterion, however, are unequally distributed across media located in different cities. Media in some cities, such as New York or Washington, D.C., have an almost daily inventory of new murders from which to choose. Media in other cities, such as the *Kalamazoo Gazette* in Kalamazoo, Michigan, have on average only one murder per month to present. Do cities that have distinct crime rates present significantly different pictures of crime? Do they rely on alternative item sources, such as wire services, to maintain a comparable level of violent crime stories? Are victims presented differently?

The presentation of crime and crime victims across different-sized cities has been neglected in past content research. Only six of the large number of existing content studies have made comparisons across cities (Cohen 1975; Graber 1980; Lotz 1991; Marsh 1988; Skogan and Maxfield 1981; Windhauser, Seiter, and Winfree 1990).[1] The studies by Cohen (1975) and Skogan and Maxfield (1981) made comparisons across large cities that had some variation in crime rate. Cohen (1975) compared the presentation of crime in Detroit and Houston, and Skogan and Maxfield (1981) examined eight newspapers from San Francisco, Philadelphia, and Chicago. Although some minor differences were found across cities, the newspapers were fairly consistent in their presentation of crime, emphasizing violent crime disproportionately (Cohen 1975: 729; Skogan and Maxfield 1981: 134). Skogan and Maxfield (1981: 133), for example, found that murders and attempted murders accounted for half of the crimes mentioned.

The studies by Graber (1980) and Marsh (1988) measured the presentation of crime in cities with dissimilar crime rates. Graber (1980) examined presentation in Indianapolis, Indiana, Evanston, Illinois, and Lebanon, New Hampshire; Marsh (1988) examined six Texas newspapers: two Houston papers and one paper each from Dallas, Austin, Conroe, and Huntsville. These two studies indicated that the presentation of crime varied according to the violent crime rate in each city. Marsh (1988: 53) found that 44.6 percent of the crimes presented in the *Houston Chronicle* were murders. The *Huntsville Item*, which had access to far fewer local murders, presented these stories as only 16.3 percent of the total number of crimes.

The cities examined here were chosen to build upon and clarify those findings. Cities were selected for the present study in a way that allowed for a larger variation in city size and crime rate than has typically been employed in past research. Presentation data from Dallas, Detroit, Cleveland, San Francisco, Buffalo, and Albany were collected in order to make these comparisons. Table 6.1 presents index crime data for these six cities, illustrating the large differences in the amount and types of local crimes from which media in the various cities can draw. For example, the *Detroit News* could have presented nearly 600 Detroit homicides, whereas news media in Albany had only nine Albany murders to present in 1990. Access to wire services, national news reports, and stories in other newspapers guarantees that each medium has a variety of serious crimes it could present. The news media considered in this study, however, attend to an audience that is local. Advertisers buy time or space from these media to attract local consumers. Local issues and crimes are of primary concern because of the relevance to that audience. Although it is not expected that the media in the present study can or should be able to accurately reflect the crimes that are known to the police, content comparisons across cities will reveal whether the presentation of crime is consistent across media in cities with different crime rates.

Overall Presentation of Stories in Different Media

Table 6.2 presents the number of crime stories compared with other story topics in each medium. Crime was among the five most likely categories presented across the nine different media organizations, regardless of crime rate. In every city, crimes help to satisfy a medium's economic needs: They are interesting; they are easy to report because of access to police and court sources; and they are ongoing, so that reporters can follow newsworthy stories through the criminal justice process, thereby producing numerous stories.

Each of the broadcast stations was more likely to present crime as a story topic that was any of the newspapers. Crime was the second most popular topic presented by the three broadcast stations. Approximately 15 percent of the total number of stories presented in Albany, 20 percent in Cleveland, and 18 percent in Dallas were crime stories. The broadcast presentation of crime in Texas was

TABLE 6.1 Number of Index Offenses Known to the Police

Offenses Known	Albany (pop. 101,082)	Buffalo (pop. 328,123)	Cleveland (pop. 505,616)	San Francisco (pop. 723,959)	Dallas (pop. 1,006,877)	Detroit (pop. 1,027,901)
Crime index total	6,695	29,864	46,984	70,370	159,822	126,631
Murder	9	37	168	101	447	582
Rape	82	355	846	419	1,344	1,657
Robbery	386	2,172	4,917	7,053	10,565	13,010
Aggravated assault	575	2,711	3,259	4,815	12,194	12,498
Burglary	1,884	8,163	10,198	10,618	32,975	26,063
Larceny theft	3,264	12,203	15,289	35,583	74,229	41,139
Motor vehicle theft	435	3,540	11,408	11,361	24,513	30,376
Arson	60	683	899	420	1,555	1,306

Source: U.S. Department of Justice, Federal Bureau of Investigation, *Crime in the United States, 1990* (Washington, D.C.: United States Government Printing Office, 1990).

TABLE 6.2 Type of News Story in Nine Media Organizations

News Media

Type of Story	Albany Broadcast (in percentages)	Cleveland Broadcast (in percentages)	Dallas Broadcast (in percentages)	Albany Print (in percentages)	Buffalo Print (in percentages)	Cleveland Print (in percentages)	San Francisco Print (in percentages)	Dallas Print (in percentages)	Detroit Print (in percentages)
Sports	37.7	30.1	30.8	15.9	20.4	18.4	14.5	25.1	24.0
General interest[a]	4.5	6.3	8.5	13.8	13.3	14.3	20.0	9.7	17.0
Business technology	1.9	4.5	4.4	12.0	13.0	15.6	16.3	19.3	11.9
Crime	15.4	19.8	17.8	10.5	10.1	10.1	7.5	10.4	9.4
General stories[b]	6.4	1.0	1.1	11.8	12.6	11.5	9.3	9.7	12.0
Domestic affairs	10.5	5.5	11.7	10.0	6.5	6.9	6.2	5.9	4.5
Foreign affairs	4.3	3.7	3.2	8.2	7.3	8.3	11.1	6.8	4.6
Science[c]	3.5	2.9	3.8	4.8	5.4	3.8	5.2	3.0	4.2
Schools	1.5	1.4	2.6	5.0	3.1	3.4	2.2	3.1	4.1
International affairs	2.0	2.0	2.0	2.6	2.5	2.5	3.0	2.2	3.2
Death[d]	4.4	7.5	4.8	1.7	1.8	2.1	1.9	2.1	1.3
Celebrations[e]	2.7	4.3	3.3	1.6	1.7	1.1	0.9	0.9	1.4
Environment	0.9	1.5	0.2	1.6	1.1	1.0	1.0	0.9	1.5
Automobile accidents	1.5	6.9	4.2	0.3	0.1	1.0	0.1	0.1	0.1
Fires	2.0	2.9	0.8	0.3	0.4	0.3	0.2	0.4	0.4
Presidency[f]	1.0	0.0	0.9	0.1	0.8	0.5	0.6	0.6	0.4

[a] Includes stories about arts, entertainment, people, gardening, and similar topics.
[b] Stories about specific incidents such as chemical leaks, gas leaks, power outages, missing persons.
[c] Includes medical and health issues.
[d] Includes accidents, suicides, plane crashes, and deaths from natural disasters.
[e] Includes ceremonies and parades.
[f] Not political stories, but stories about activities of the president, such as playing golf.

not significantly different from its presentation in either Albany or Cleveland; however, the amount of time devoted to crime stories was different. On average, crime stories in Dallas were 55 seconds long, Cleveland's were 44 seconds, and Albany's were 38 seconds.

Discrepancies in the amount of time spent on a crime story are further illustrated in the presentation of tertiary, secondary, and primary crime stories shown in Table 6.3. Albany broadcast news presented the highest percentage of tertiary stories (stories under twenty seconds long) compared with the other two broadcast cities. Forty-two percent of the Albany broadcast crime stories were tertiary. Only 5 percent of the Dallas broadcast news stories were tertiary crime stories; here these stories were the most likely to be primary (over sixty seconds long). Primary crime stories in both Albany and Cleveland accounted for less than 15 percent of the total number of crime stories in each city, whereas Dallas presented them 24 percent of the time. Crime is an important news topic in the broadcast cities considered. Although a similar percentage of crime stories is provided, the space and type of crimes available that could be given primary coverage are different, as reflected in the discrepancies in the time devoted to broadcast crime stories.

Each of the six newspapers presented a similar number of crime stories. Over 10 percent of the total number of stories presented in four of the six papers were crime related. The Albany newspaper presented the most and the San Francisco paper the fewest crime stories. When the number of tertiary, secondary, and primary stories presented in each newspaper is considered, the findings are similar to those for the television comparisons. Newspapers from the smaller cities (Albany, Buffalo) were the most likely to present either tertiary or secondary stories and the least likely to present primary stories. The other newspapers were most likely to present either secondary or primary stories. Nearly 40 percent of the crime stories in the *Detroit News* were

TABLE 6.3 Level of Crime Story in Nine Media Organizations

News Media	Tertiary (in percentages)	Secondary (in percentages)	Primary (in percentages)
Albany broadcast	42.2	42.9	14.9
Cleveland broadcast	20.9	63.5	14.2
Dallas broadcast	5.0	71.1	24.0
Albany print	40.6	40.3	19.1
Buffalo print	31.9	44.1	23.5
Cleveland print	23.7	50.2	26.1
San Francisco print	25.3	39.2	35.5
Dallas print	25.2	42.7	32.0
Detroit print	20.7	40.9	37.8

primary, whereas 40 percent of those in the *Albany Times-Union* were tertiary and fewer than 20 percent were primary. The actual number of crime stories presented in each of the cities is fairly similar, whereas the amount of space given to crime stories differs substantially. Space differences are reflective of the degree to which news organizations depend on advertising revenue for survival. The amount of revenue generated through advertising has a direct influence on the amount of "real" news space available (Pasqua et al. 1990). Newspapers in major cities, therefore, have more space to cover stories. The extraordinary amounts of crime that occur in such cities make it easy for reporters to satisfy space requirements with newsworthy crime stories.

Overall, comparisons within print and television categories indicate similarities across cities. Each of the television stations relied heavily on sports, crime, and domestic affairs to fill nightly newscasts. Television stations in Dallas and Albany were significantly more likely than those in Cleveland to present "domestic political affairs," a category that includes political activities at the local, state, and national levels. These differences can be explained by reasons that are particular to each city. First, Albany is a state capital. Part of the broadcast sample period included the end of a legislative session, when domestic political news was of strong local interest. The high presentation of domestic affairs in Dallas news can be attributed to a political topic that was of significant interest to the local viewing audience during the sample period. Two military bases in cities surrounding Dallas were among those threatened to be closed because of cutbacks in military spending. The political maneuvering by the local community and its Washington representatives and the government's eventual decision to shut down the bases were of salient economic interest to the local broadcast audience.

Sports, general interest, business, crime, and foreign news stories were among the most popular in the newspapers examined, accounting for similar percentages of the total number of stories in all except the *San Francisco Chronicle*. The unique focus of the *Chronicle* can be attributed to its concentration on more nationally and internationally focused news. Foreign affairs were significantly more likely to be presented in this newspaper than in any other of those studied. Moreover, the *Chronicle's* concern with national and international news is reflected by the locations of the crime stories presented. It presented the highest percentage of national and international crime stories and the lowest percentage (23 percent) of local crime stories. Local crime stories accounted for at least 50 percent of the total number of crime stories in each of the other newspapers and at each of the broadcast stations. The emphasis of the San Francisco newspaper on crimes that occurred outside of the city was found in an earlier study that examined the same newspaper (Skogan and Maxfield 1981: 135). It is difficult to provide an explanation for this emphasis because of the methodological limitations of content analysis. One explanation could be the fact that San Francisco is a two-paper city. We might speculate that the

Chronicle attends to more national and international news in order to attract a proportion of readers that is neglected by the other newspaper. Skogan and Maxfield's study (1981: 135), however, found that both newspapers in San Francisco were most concerned with crimes that occurred outside of the city. Another plausible explanation for the difference is that this newspaper has limited resources available to collect local crime information. Taking news stories from wire reports is easy and consumes little time. We would expect, however, that the newspapers located in the smaller cities would have as few or fewer resources than those in San Francisco. The focus of the smaller cities is much more like that of the major cities than like that of San Francisco. A final, more plausible explanation is that this newspaper is providing a product that is most appealing to its audience. Media organizations survey the audience and know its interests. Advertisers pay for space according to circulation and number of the audience. The national and international focus of the *Chronicle* may simply be what attracts the largest possible audience in San Francisco.

Comparisons of news topics across types of media indicate findings that parallel the results presented in Chapter 5. Certain topics, such as crime, death, automobile accidents, and celebrations, are more likely to be presented in television news than in newspaper news, regardless of the city. These topics are more popular with television news because they satisfy visual format needs. Newspapers, because of their space advantage, are able to present a larger range of stories that cater to specific audience segments. This is evidenced by each newspaper's reliance on topics such as business and technology, schools, science, medical, and gardening—all of which are included to attract specific readers.

Types of Crime Presented in Each City

Table 6.4 provides the percentage breakdown of the types of crime presented in all nine organizations. Table 6.5 collapses the cities into categories of medium, large, and extra large. The Albany broadcast results were combined with the Albany and Buffalo print results to form the medium category. The findings from Cleveland broadcast, Cleveland print, and San Francisco print are presented as large-city results. The extra-large category includes findings from Dallas broadcast and Dallas and Detroit print. These categories were created in order to make some statistical comparisons, which are also presented in Table 6.5. The table reveals instances of significant differences between the medium cities and the large, medium and extra-large, and large and extra-large.

Murders are among the most popular crime topics regardless of the medium considered. Media in all cities demonstrated a willingness to present whatever local murders were available. There was some variation across cities, however, in the amount and type of murders presented—a finding consistent with past

TABLE 6.4 Types of Crimes Presented in Nine Media Organizations

Crime	Television			Newspaper					
	Albany (in percentages)	Cleveland (in percentages)	Dallas (in percentages)	Albany (in percentages)	Buffalo (in percentages)	Cleveland (in percentages)	San Francisco (in percentages)	Dallas (in percentages)	Detroit (in percentages)
Murder	12.6	27.7	38.3	15.3	17.3	27.6	24.9	25.9	30.4
Other violent crimes[a]	17.7	21.4	20.2	16.3	20.4	12.8	12.6	18.1	16.1
Victimless crimes[b]	9.8	10.5	2.7	14.6	14.6	12.0	12.8	10.3	10.2
Special group crimes[c]	17.2	10.9	18.0	7.3	6.7	12.6	4.5	11.5	6.9
White-collar crimes[d]	3.3	5.0	7.1	9.2	7.2	10.4	13.7	10.8	15.6
Crime against criminal justice[e]	11.6	5.0	3.8	11.9	12.6	9.5	14.8	6.8	6.6
Misdemeanors	10.7	4.5	1.1	10.7	14.8	6.5	8.7	5.1	5.4
Property offenses	9.8	5.5	3.3	11.5	4.7	7.2	3.4	6.4	6.4
Does not specify	7.4	9.5	5.5	3.2	1.6	1.4	4.7	5.1	2.3

[a] Robbery, shootings, assaults.
[b] Drugs, prostitution, gambling.
[c] Sexual assault, child, elderly, bias-related victimizations.
[d] Embezzlement, bribery, forgery, fraud, corporate crime, securities violations.
[e] Perjury, resisting arrest, obstruction of justice, tampering with evidence, intimidating witness/victims.

TABLE 6.5 Types of Crimes Presented in Combined Media Categories

	Medium (Albany-Buffalo) (in percentages)	Large (Cleveland-San Francisco) (in percentages)	Extra Large (Dallas-Detroit) (in percentages)
Murder	15.5[a]	26.8	30.0
Other violent crimes	18.0[b]	13.9[c]	17.7
Victimless crimes	13.8[d]	12.0[c]	8.9
Special group crimes	8.8	10.1	10.9
White-collar crimes	7.4[a]	10.6	12.0
Crimes against criminal justice	12.1[d]	10.4[c]	6.2
Misdemeanors	12.2[a]	6.9[c]	4.5
Property offenses	8.8[a]	5.9	5.8
Does not specify	3.4	3.4	4.1

[a] Significant differences comparing medium with large and medium with extra large (.05).
[b] Significant differences comparing medium with large (.05).
[c] Significant differences comparing large with extra large (.05).
[d] Significant differences comparing medium with extra large (.05).

research that made comparisons across different-sized cities (Graber 1980; Marsh 1988). News organizations that had access to the lowest rates of officially known murders (Albany, Buffalo) were significantly less likely to present a murder story compared with media in either the large or the extra-large cities. For example, 12.6 percent of the total number of broadcast stories and 15.3 percent of the print stories from Albany covered murders. However, nearly 40 percent of the crimes mentioned in Dallas broadcast news and 25.9 percent of those in Dallas print news were murder. The results presented in Table 6.5 indicate that the medium-sized cities had the lowest percentage of reported murder stories, the large cities were in the middle, and the extra-large cities had the highest percentage—paralleling the hierarchical distribution of officially reported murders.

The presentation of murder in large and extra-large cities was not significantly different despite the fact that two to three times as many murders occurred in the extra-large cities. Print and television news organizations in every city have a limited amount of news space in which to present crime stories. The similarities between media in large and extra-large cities indicate that there is a saturation point for the number of murders that can be presented. Reporters who work in extra-large cities, such as Dallas, Detroit, New York City, and Los Angeles, have new murders occurring regularly as well as ongoing murder cases available from the court or correctional system. Reporters in these cities, therefore, have the luxury of choosing the most newsworthy murders to fill the amount of news space available. The criteria adopted by these media in determining what constitutes an extraordinary and interesting murder are different and more stringent than those for smaller cities. An eighteen-year-old killed in a drug deal that went bad is not as newsworthy as it would be in smaller cities because such crimes are "normal" occurrences in the extra-large cities. Media in large cities reach a comparable amount of presented murders through compensating for the lower occurrence of the crime by covering a greater percentage of those crimes in some detail and following them through each stage of the criminal justice process. An informant from the *Tribune* (a newspaper that is considered large), who had worked at one time for a New York City newspaper, reflected on differences in the types of homicides covered in cities of various sizes.

> When homicides occur in New York City, because it happens everyday, it is only newsworthy when there is some drama attached. I did a murder story on a guy who used to cut records for Smokey Robinson. He was knifed in the studio but was able to crawl out and flag down a cab. He wrote a letter to his wife in the cab on the way to the hospital. It was really a touching letter. Around here [near the *Midwest Tribune*] almost all homicides are covered, and they are more likely to be followed across a number of days because there are not as many to rely on.

Table 6.5 indicates that media in medium-sized cities were somewhat more likely to present other violent crimes and drug crimes than were the media in the large and extra-large cities. This highlights the fact that the seriousness of the crime is an important variable in newsworthiness. The reliance of Albany and Buffalo media on such crimes is illustrative of their tendency to present the most serious types of crime available. Murders are not regularly available in low-crime cities. Although a particular amount of space is not set aside to present crime news, it is a topic of considerable interest to the public and the news organization. News media in cities with lower crime rates simply do not have the continual supply of local murders to present, so reporters cover crimes that are less serious than homicide. A managing editor from a medium-sized city mentioned the way he searches for the most serious crime available: "What we seek is the highest level we can get to of crime. If there is not a murder, then we sink down a notch. If a rape happens, suddenly it becomes newsworthy. If there is no rape, a mugging might fill the [news] hole."

In addition, medium-sized cities try to compensate for a limited number of local murders by presenting a higher percentage of murders of state and national origin. The content results indicate that cities that had significantly fewer murders compensated by presenting either state or national murders, thereby increasing their ability to bombard their audiences with death. Only 50 percent of Albany broadcast stories, 50 percent of Buffalo print stories, and 30 percent of Albany print media stories concerned murders of local origin. In contrast, over 80 percent of Dallas broadcast stories and approximately 70 percent of both

Dallas and Detroit print stories reported homicides of local origin. These results make it clear that both print and electronic organizations think the public wants to hear about murder. When murders are not available locally, they present cases from different cities and states.

The results in Table 6.5 indicate that the presentation of misdemeanors and property offenses in the media in medium-sized cities is significantly different from the presentation of these offenses in either the large or the extra-large cities. The medium-sized cities were significantly more likely to depend on crimes of a less serious nature, and media in extra-large cities were the least likely to present property crimes and misdemeanors. For example, 4.5 percent of the total number of stories presented in Detroit print, Dallas print, and Dallas broadcast media were misdemeanors such as harassment or trespassing. This finding is significantly different from the 12.2 percent of stories that are misdemeanors presented in Albany broadcast, Albany print, and Buffalo print media. Crimes that are not serious are less likely to be filtered out of the presentational decisionmaking process in cities with the lowest amounts of crime. Media in the largest cities concentrate on selecting the most newsworthy murder to present, whereas those in smaller cities have to choose the most newsworthy crime.

Less serious crimes are more likely to be covered in the cities with lower crime rates. But such crimes are rarely given primary coverage, regardless of the city; they are usually presented as tertiary or secondary stories. This finding helps to highlight the results, discussed earlier, that showed that primary crimes are less likely to be presented in cities with lower crime rates and that certain crimes rarely have primary appeal. Although less serious crimes are more likely to be presented in the media of cities with low crime rates, they are not significantly more likely to be given primary coverage. Regardless of the type of crime available in a city, certain crimes will not be promoted to a primary level merely to fill available news space because news media still do not think these crimes are of primary interest to their audience.

The television media in each of the cities examined were less likely to present misdemeanors and property offenses than were their print counterparts. The frequency of presentation of these crimes is even lower for the media in extra-large cities. Only 1 percent of the total number of crimes presented in Dallas broadcast news were misdemeanors, and 3 percent were property offenses. Each of these crimes was presented as over 5 percent of the total for print media in extra-large cities. This finding points to the format requirements of each medium. Broadcast media have less space in which to display crimes, so they rarely present these types of visually unappealing crimes.

News-Item Sources Used for the Presentation of Crime

News media have to rely on either the local crimes that are conveniently available or on alternative news items in order to present an attractive daily crime portrait. The results discussed earlier illustrate that cities with the lowest amount of serious crime present a somewhat different picture of crime, but they attempt to standardize the seriousness of crimes presented by relying more on murders of national origin. We would expect that the reliance of media on news-item sources (reporter, wire, and similar sources) would be different across cities because of the need for lower-ranking crime cities to use crimes occurring in other cities. For some types of crime, these cities are seemingly more likely to present crimes taken from wire services or from other newspapers.

Content comparisons of news-item sources are presented in Table 6.6. Except for the unique focus of the *Chronicle*, the differences in the use of news-item sources are fairly small. The San Francisco newspaper was significantly less likely to present a crime story written by one of its own reporters, significantly more likely to present a story from another newspaper, and most likely to use a crime story from a wire service than all of the other newspapers. As mentioned, the news focus of the *Chronicle* is on issues of national and international concern, which increases its reliance on these alternative sources. All of the other newspapers were most likely to present crime stories written by their own reporters covering local crimes. Similarly, wire services and stories presented in other newspapers were used because of their convenient availability and their contribution to creating a large pool of crimes from which to select those considered newsworthy.

The news-item sources used for murder stories, however, were significantly different for medium-sized cities in comparison with large and extra-large ones. Media in medium-sized cities used the easily accessible wire services to increase the number of murders presented. The use of wire services for murder stories was not significantly different between the large and the extra-large cities, which have access to enough new or ongoing homicide cases of local origin to present the most serious available.

Comparisons across the television organizations indicated no significant difference regarding the use of news-item sources. Crime stories in each of the stations were overwhelmingly (over 90 percent) told by a reporter or anchor without attribution. Such high use of the stations' own reporters can be partially explained by the frequent presentation of crimes of interest to the local audience. Approximately 70 percent of the stories presented by each of the television stations were local. Television media are more likely to present local crime stories than are newspapers because of the limited amount of space available in a thirty-minute broadcast, the desire to provide stories most relevant to the

TABLE 6.6 News-Item Sources in Newspapers

	Albany (in percentages)	Buffalo (in percentages)	San Francisco (in percentages)	Cleveland (in percentages)	Dallas (in percentages)	Detroit (in percentages)
Reporter	56.1	64.3	35.0	61.1	61.7	70.5
Editor[a]	0.7	0.5	0.0	0.0	0.5	0.0
Wire service[b]	34.5	26.8	36.4	25.7	31.6	23.8
Affiliated reporter	0.4	0.0	0.5	0.2	0.5	0.0
Another newspaper	7.2	5.2	25.8	7.3	5.3	5.2
Unknown[c]	1.1	3.2	2.3	5.8	0.5	0.5

[a] Includes those stories for which it was clear that the story had been written by an editor.

[b] Includes AP, UPI, Reuters, Cox, Newhouse, McCatchy, Gannett, and stories for which no specific wire organization was specified.

[c] Stories that did not have a source attribution.

viewing audience, and the knowledge that national and international stories will be covered by the national network news broadcast.

Sources Used Within Crime Stories

The assumed credibility of informants used within crime stories was the same across cities. Individuals directly involved or criminal justice sources were the most logical choices for story information, regardless of the city. Furthermore, organizational sources such as the police in different cities are motivated and constrained by similar factors; thus, the amount and type of information provided to the news media should be consistent across cities unless some extenuating circumstances exist. The content results should indicate similar use of sources for incident, victim, and defendant information within crime stories.

Tables 6.7, 6.8, and 6.9 provide the sources used for all types of information in each of the medium, large, and extra-large city categories. Significant differences among the different-sized cities in each of the sources cited are also shown. The information provided in these tables concerns the sources used in the presentation of *local* crimes; state, national, and international stories taken from wire reports and other newspapers were excluded. This analysis represents a comparison of the sources used by local reporters, controlling for the influence of the informants used in wire-report stories, which would be more likely to be the same across cities.

The results indicate that similar sources were used across cities. Criminal justice professionals and the individuals involved in a crime—the most knowledgeable sources available—were the primary providers of crime information. Other sources—such as politicians, citizens, experts, and school or church officials—were infrequently used for crime information, regardless of the city.

Police officers were the primary conduits of crime information, regardless of the city. This finding influences the type of information that can be provided in a story. In every city, police officers are conveniently available, accessible, and motivated to maintain a positive image. The news media from the medium-sized cities, however, were somewhat more likely to use police sources for all types of information. Two related organizational explanations exist for the small differences found. First, the media in the medium-sized cities have fewer personnel resources available. The *Tribune* (in a large city) had different reporters to cover police, court, and suburban activities; the paper also had a large number of general assignment reporters available to cover additional stories that could not be handled when the other reporters became overloaded. Reporters interviewed from smaller cities discussed the limited resources available to cover crime news, commenting that they are asked to be like utility

TABLE 6.7   Incident Sources Cited in Crime Stories in Combined Media Categories

	Medium (Albany-Buffalo) (in percentages)	Large (Cleveland-San Francisco) (in percentages)	Extra Large (Dallas-Detroit) (in percentages)
Police	43.3[a]	34.0	39.2
Court	23.7[b]	29.2[c]	15.9
Politician	1.4	2.5	3.7
Defendant	7.2	7.9	7.2
Not specific[d]	6.9[a]	4.1	1.2
Citizen	2.3	1.3[c]	3.5
Victim acquaintance	2.7[e]	3.5[c]	7.2
Documents[f]	2.5	3.9	1.0
Victim	2.3[a]	4.6	7.0
Other[g]	1.4[e]	2.2[c]	1.6
Witness/juror	2.1	1.3	5.8
Media	0.4	1.3	0.4
Expert	0.9	0.3	0.6
School/church	1.1	1.7	1.2
Corrections	1.4	0.0[h]	0.4
Defendant acquaintance	0.5	1.6	1.6
Hospital[i]	1.1	0.6	0.6

[a] Significant differences comparing medium with large and medium with extra large (.05).
[b] Significant differences comparing medium with large (.050).
[c] Significant differences comparing large with extra large (.05).
[d] Source cited as "sources say," "officials say," "authorities say."
[e] Significant differences comparing medium with extra large (.05).
[f] Police or court documents.
[g] Highway spokesperson, community groups, weather service.
[h] Comparisons impossible because one of the cells has a quantity of zero.
[i] Includes doctors, emergency medical service, and coroner.

infielders and cover a diverse range of story topics. In order to complete their task, reporters in smaller cities have to rely more often on the most convenientand credible source available. A police source can easily be reached by telephone.

Second, media in the medium-sized cities need to find the most serious crime available, a requirement that often requires expansion into a larger geographic region. The content results indicate that media in the medium-sized cities were significantly more likely to cover suburban and rural crimes than were media in the two larger-city categories. In the larger cities, homicides can be important news whenever they occur. In suburban and rural areas, however, most other crimes that occur rarely satisfy the criterion of newsworthiness as they could in medium-sized cities. Easy access to police sources makes it convenient for the

TABLE 6.8 Victim Sources Cited in Crime Stories in Combined Media Categories

	Medium (Albany-Buffalo) (in percentages)	Large (Cleveland-San Francisco) (in percentages)	Extra Large (Dallas-Detroit) (in percentages)
Police	44.7[a]	31.6	36.2
Court	7.1[b]	8.4[c]	2.0
Politician	0.0[d]	0.5	0.0[d]
Defendant	2.4[a]	11.1[c]	0.7
Not specific[e]	3.5	1.1	0.7
Citizen	2.4	4.2	3.4
Victim acquaintance	10.6[b]	16.3	24.2
Documents[f]	1.2	1.6	2.7
Victim	11.8	6.3	10.7
Other[g]	2.7	1.6	0.0[d]
Witness/juror	1.2	1.6	0.7
Media	2.4	0.0[d]	0.7
Expert	1.2	0.5	0.7
School/church	3.5	4.2	4.0
Corrections	0.0[d]	0.0[d]	0.7
Defendant acquaintance	2.4	0.0[d]	2.7
Hospital[h]	3.5[a]	11.1	10.1

[a] Significant differences comparing medium with large (.05).
[b] Significant differences comparing medium with extra large (.05).
[c] Significant differences comparing large with extra large (.05).
[d] Comparisons impossible because one of the cells has a quantity of zero.
[e] Source cited as "sources say," "officials say," "authorities say."
[f] Police or court documents.
[g] Highway spokesperson, community groups, weather service.
[h] Includes doctors, emergency medical service, and coroner.

media in medium-sized cities to cover the larger geographic area, despite their limited number of personnel.

Across all city size categories, court sources were more likely to be used for defendant and incident information than for victim information. Reporters have easier access to other sources of victim information (victims, family members) that can be cited. When making comparisons across cities, no significant differences were found in the use of court sources for defendant information. Court sources were, however, significantly less likely to be used by reporters for both victim and incident information in the extra-large cities compared with those in either the large or medium-sized cities. This variation can be explained by differences in coverage of specific stages of the criminal justice system. Media in the extra-large cities were significantly more likely to present the in these cities have new crimes happening daily that satisfy the criterion of newsworthiness, whereas media in the other cities have to be more concerned

TABLE 6.9 Defendant Sources Cited in Crime Stories in Combined Media Categories

	Medium (Albany-Buffalo) (in percentages)	Large (Cleveland-San Francisco) (in percentages)	Extra Large (Dallas-Detroit) (in percentages)
Police	32.9	29.3	31.6
Court	28.7	30.1	23.0
Politician	2.3	1.6	0.6
Defendant	6.4	6.5	8.0
Not specific[a]	7.5[b]	2.8	2.9
Citizen	4.0	3.7	3.4
Victim acquaintance	0.6[c]	3.3	5.2
Documents[d]	1.2	2.4	1.1
Victim	0.6[c]	1.6[e]	5.2
Other[f]	2.9	1.6	2.9
Witness/juror	0.0[g]	1.2	2.3
Media	1.7	0.0[g]	1.1
Expert	2.9	1.6	0.0[g]
School/church	3.5	4.5	2.9
Corrections	0.6	1.6	0.6
Defendant acquaintance	2.3[h]	6.9	5.7
Hospital[i]	2.3	1.2	3.4

[a] Source cited as "sources say," "officials say," "authorities say."
[b] Significant differences comparing medium with large and medium with extra large (.05).
[c] Significant differences comparing medium with extra large (.05).
[d] Police or court documents.
[e] Significant differences comparing large with extra large (.05).
[f] Highway spokesperson, community groups, weather service.
[g] Significant differences comparing medium with large (.05).
[h] Includes doctors, emergency medical service, and coroner.

with following newsworthy crimes across a number of different stages. Police sources and the individuals involved in crime have to be used at the discovery stage because these stories are not yet part of the court system.

Family members of crime victims were significantly more likely to be cited in stories from the media in extra-large cities than in those in the media of medium-sized cities. Almost 25 percent of the victim information provided in extra-large cities came from acquaintances of the crime victim. Family members were used for victim information in only approximately 11 percent of the sources cited in medium-sized cities. Moreover, victim acquaintances were significantly more likely to be cited for incident information in the media of extra-large cities compared with those of both large and medium-sized cities. The media in the extra-large cities have the additional resources and personnel to allow them to contact a broader range of sources and collect information from them. Since media in the medium-sized cities have fewer resources and cover a broader local area in presenting crimes, these media are more likely to rely on police sources to fill their needs.

This finding does not, however, fully explain the differences between the media in large and extra-large cities indicated in an examination of incident information. That is, the resources used to produce crime stories should not be as different as they turn out to be. Therefore, another part of the explanation of the differences is that the acquaintances of crime victims can provide the type of information reporters need and use in the extra-large cities to raise a certain crime, especially murder, to a newsworthy level. An emotionally charged surviving family member can promote what would have been considered an ordinary homicide to a level that is worthy of public presentation. Surviving family members do not need to be used as frequently for this purpose in the media of either the medium-sized or the large cities because they do not have as high a standard regarding the seriousness of the crimes that become newsworthy; thus, ordinary murders can satisfy the criteria for presentation.

Victims were not used for victim information in a significantly different manner across the three categories considered. In each city, victims were important sources of information, used to discuss the harm caused by crime. Victims were most likely to be used as sources of victim information in the medium-sized cities because of the tendency of the media in these cities to rely on less serious crimes that do not have a deceased victim. Victims were, however, used differently for information about the incident and the defendant. The results indicate that victims were significantly more likely to be used for both defendant and incident information in media of the extra-large cities compared with those of the medium-sized cities. This result is surprising and difficult to explain, considering the consistencies in the use of victims for victim information. Perhaps the additional space used to present stories in the extra-large cities increases the likelihood of using and presenting the same source for all types of crime information. That is, a victim might be asked to comment on the crime, the harm, and the defendant, all of which information is then put into the story. The more limited space available in the media of medium-sized cities may contribute to the use of victims only for emotional information. Another explanation might be that victims may be used more casually in the media of the medium-sized cities. Stories in which the victim is still alive in extra-large cities have to compete against a host of murder stories in deciding what will be presented. Thus, the actual victim is what promoted these crimes to consideration, a circumstance that is focused on in the story. The other media may not need the high-powered emotion in order for a similar crime to be presented.

Medical sources such as doctors and coroners are often relied on by news media for victim information. The use of hospital sources was rare for incident and defendant information in the cities studied but was frequent for victim information in large and extra-large cities. Hospital sources accounted for less than 4 percent of the total number of victim sources in medium-sized cities but were used in over 11 percent of cases in both large and extra-large cities. The differences across cities can be explained by each medium's focus on certain crimes. The frequent presentation of murders in large and extra-large cities contributes to the heavy reliance of their media on medical sources. Coroners are a conveniently available, credible source of information about the victim when little is available elsewhere.

Presentation of Victims and Defendants Across Cities

Crime victims can play a substantial role in determining whether certain crimes are presented to the public. Some demographic characteristics, the type of harm experienced, victims' willingness to answer questions, and their ability to provide newsworthy quotes can all influence which crimes get presented and which are filtered out, as well as the level of newsworthiness a story achieves. News media in extra-large cities are more likely to select and find crimes that deviate from what is statistically normal. As the volume of a particular type of crime increases or achieves some saturation point, a reporter has to search for crimes that are out of the ordinary in order to maintain audience interest. A self-perpetuating cycle is triggered as extraordinary news becomes ordinary, inducing reporters to search for the new or the renewed extraordinary. An informant noted how being saturated with a large amount of certain crimes affects what gets presented: "We have gotten jaded at this point. We hear at least three or four times a week about child molestations. We can't report all of them, so other things come into play, such as whether there was something unusual about it, or incredible; was it heinous? We look for, if there was a shooting or murder, what kind of neighborhood did it happen in, and how did it happen—in other words, was it during a drug sale, or was it a secretary walking down the street? That influences our thinking."

Certain victim characteristics are important to media in every city. The murder of a prominent community member would be an ongoing primary story in every city. Crime saturation levels are, however, different across cities. Since the amount and type of crimes that are traditionally thought to be the most newsworthy vary significantly across cities, victim characteristics are more likely to play a role in crime presentation decisions and be available in cities with the highest amounts of crime. Accordingly, public perceptions of what are thought to be ordinary crimes, especially in the largest cities, are influenced by those that are defined by the media as being the most extraordinary.

It is hypothesized that the characteristics of crime victims and defendants highlighted in earlier chapters as being primary story determinants are more salient in larger cities because such cities have a significantly larger amount of varying types of crime and therefore need something extra in order to sell the story.   Content analysis of the local crimes presented in these cities showed which victim and offender characteristics were the most newsworthy.   In addition, victim and defendant characteristics are provided for the crimes taken from wire services and other newspapers that feature crimes of state, national, and international origin.   It is hypothesized that these characteristics would deviate more widely across cities in the case of local crimes because of the luxury of having a larger assortment of local crimes from which to choose in the extra-large cities.   For crimes of nonlocal origin, the influence of victim and defendant characteristics should be more similar because of access to homogeneous news-item sources.

Content results comparing the presentation of murders illustrate how victim characteristics interact differently with the type of crime depending on the total amount of crime available.   Local murders in extra-large cities need additional newsworthy characteristics beyond the seriousness of the crime in order to make them interesting to media consumers.   "In New York City, it is not whether you should go cover a murder.   But if there are not at least three victims, then you don't bother, unless it is a child or an elderly victim," commented one of the informants interviewed.   These other influences are important in media located in smaller cities, but the absence of additional factors does not preclude the presentation of a murder in cities in which murder occurs less frequently.   This leads to the presentation of different types of murders across cities.   For example, content analysis revealed that media in extra-large cities were the least likely to present murders that had only one or two victims.   Approximately 40 percent of the local Detroit and Dallas murders had only one or two victims. In contrast, 87.5 percent of the local murders presented in Albany and 60 percent of those presented in Buffalo had one or two victims.   No pictures were provided to supplement local murder stories in Albany, and a picture was provided only 20 percent of the time in Buffalo.   In contrast, pictures were provided in over 40 percent of the murder stories in both Detroit and Dallas print media.   Occupation of the victim was provided in approximately 12 percent of the local murder stories in Albany and 20 percent in Buffalo.   Forty percent of the stories in Detroit and 30 percent of the stories in Dallas mentioned what is considered a newsworthy occupation, such as a criminal justice professional or a politician.

Victim considerations affect whether certain murders are promoted to a higher level of newsworthiness, as well as the location in the newspaper at which they are presented (e.g., front page, section).   We might expect that murders occurring in the smaller cities would be more likely to receive primary coverage because they are rare.   An examination of local murders did not, however, support this hypothesis.   Most local murders in cities such as Albany or Buffalo were likely to get some coverage, regardless of the individuals involved or the circumstances of the crime.   Murders that occurred in these smaller cities were, however, most likely to be given only secondary coverage and generally appeared in the second section of a newspaper. For example, all of the murders that occurred in Albany and over 60 percent of those in Buffalo were presented in the second section. Murders that occurred in Dallas and Detroit were most likely to be given primary coverage and to be placed on the front page or on the first page of the second section. Forty percent of the local murder stories in Dallas and nearly 60 percent of those from Detroit were given primary coverage.

There are two possible explanations for the differences in the presentation of murder. First, since the classification of stories as tertiary, secondary, and primary was determined by the amount of space given to them, the big-city newspapers may simply provide a lot of space and good placement. Advertising revenue and the local economy drive the amount of story space provided, and the bigger cities may be able to present more in that space. A second explanation might be that reporters in the larger cities have regular access to a number of murders and are more likely to find one worthy of primary coverage. A shared consensus exists as to what constitutes a primary story, and reporters from media in smaller cities have less local access to murders that would be worthy of primary coverage. Since the bigger cities can pick and choose, they are more likely to find a circumstance in some murder that would raise it to the primary level.

Tables 6.10, 6.11, and 6.12 provide results about differences in the presentation of victim and defendant characteristics across cities. Table 6.10 presents selected demographic characteristics of crime victims across the three categories of city size for crimes of both local and nonlocal origin. In addition, simple descriptive indicators, such as whether the victim was named, are provided and then discussed to highlight the ways news production processes and the coverage of different criminal justice stages vary across cities, thereby influencing what gets presented. Table 6.11 presents the defendant characteristics most likely to be cited in media for each of the combined categories, and Table 6.12 compares the harm to victims as presented across cities for local and nonlocal crimes. Finally, although the data are not provided in the tables, these analyses on victim and defendant characteristics were completed for the eight categories of crime (murder, other violent crimes, victimless crimes, special group crimes, white-collar crimes, crimes against criminal justice, misdemeanors, and property offenses), in order to examine whether the characteristics presented deviated by the type of crime considered.

Both victims and defendants were significantly less likely to be named in local crime stories by media in the extra-large cities compared with media in the medium-sized ones. This difference can be attributed to the tendency of the media in extra-large cities to rely more heavily on the discovery stage of the criminal justice process; further, media in these cities were more likely to present crimes with a larger number of victims and defendants. Crimes were coded as being at the discovery stage when a crime reported had just occurred

TABLE 6.10 Local and Nonlocal Victim Characteristics in Crime Stories in Combined Media Categories

	Local Crime			Nonlocal Crime		
	Medium (in percentages)	Large (in percentages)	Extra Large (in percentages)	Medium (in percentages)	Large (in percentages)	Extra Large (in percentages)
Named						
Yes	65.9[a]	65.9[b]	58.7	55.3[a]	57.2	56.6[b]
No	34.1	34.1	41.3	44.7	42.8	43.4
Address						
None	50.9[a]	56.2[b]	66.3	84.2[c]	66.4[b]	81.1
Specific	20.5[d]	1.1	0.9	0.4	0.3	0.5
General	10.8	17.4	8.0	1.2	3.4	1.0
City	17.0[d]	24.9	24.1	13.4[c]	25.2[b]	14.3
Other	0.9	0.4	0.7	0.5[c]	4.7	3.1
Sex						
Male	46.6	48.1	42.4	47.8[a]	47.0[b]	36.7
Female	27.6[a]	38.8[b]	43.4	24.9	30.2	28.6
Other[e]	15.3[d]	5.2	3.7	2.8[a]	4.2	7.1
Unknown	10.5[a]	7.9[b]	10.6	24.5	18.6[b]	27.6
Race						
White	4.7	6.5	10.7	6.9	8.8	6.0
Black	3.7[d]	5.9	5.5	8.9	5.5	6.6
Other[g]	1.0[d]	0.7	1.0	4.0	3.0[b]	6.6
Unknown	89.6	86.9	82.9	80.2	82.7	80.9

(continues)

TABLE 6.10 (continued)

	Local Crime			Nonlocal Crime		
	Medium (in percentages)	Large (in percentages)	Extra Large (in percentages)	Medium (in percentages)	Large (in percentages)	Extra Large (in percentages)
Victim-offender relationship						
Stranger	12.2	12.4	14.1	16.1[d]	10.4[b]	4.5
Spouse	4.2	2.1	3.7	4.5	5.6	5.1
Parent	3.1[a]	4.7	6.5	2.9	5.3	3.9
Other relative	2.4	2.6	1.5	0.0[f]	0.8	0.0[f]
Child	0.7	2.3[b]	0.5	0.0[f]	0.3	0.0[f]
Acquaintance	14.6[c]	26.2[b]	18.4	11.2[a]	12.0[b]	5.6
Unknown	62.8[d]	49.8	55.3	65.3[a]	65.5[b]	80.9
Age						
0–12 years	8.0[a]	10.6	14.0	6.9	6.3	6.6
13–16 years	4.3	6.8	5.5	6.1[d]	2.7	1.6
17–25 years	13.7	11.7	13.8	4.0[c]	9.9[b]	3.3
26–35 years	12.4[c]	7.9	10.2	10.5	10.1	9.3
36–50 years	9.0	9.2	7.1	6.9	5.5	4.4
51–64 years	3.7	2.9	3.1	2.8	2.2	1.1
65 years and over	3.0[b]	4.5	1.7	0.4[c]	2.7	1.1
Not identified	45.8	46.4	44.7	62.3[a]	60.5[b]	72.7

(continues)

TABLE 6.10 (continued)

Occupation	Local Crime			Nonlocal Crime		
	Medium (in percentages)	Large (in percentages)	Extra Large (in percentages)	Medium (in percentages)	Large (in percentages)	Extra Large (in percentages)
Professional	3.0[a]	3.8[b]	7.6	4.0	5.2	3.3
Politician	1.3	1.1	0.5	3.2	4.1	3.8
Criminal justice	7.4[c]	3.8	6.4	10.9	8.5	7.1
Helping	0.3[d]	2.0	2.4	6.5	9.0	6.0
Student	3.3[d]	6.8	7.8	3.6	5.8	1.6
Labor	1.0	1.8	1.9	0.0[f]	0.8	1.1
Service	4.0[e]	1.6	2.6	1.6[a]	0.8[b]	4.9
Criminal	0.3	0.7	0.7	2.8	3.3	2.8
Entertainer	0.0[f]	0.5	0.5	1.2	0.5[b]	2.7
Unemployed	0.0[f]	0.5	0.5	0.0[f]	0.3	0.0[f]
Other	0.0[f]	0.0[e]	0.2	1.6	0.3	0.0[f]
Not identified	79.3[a]	77.5[b]	68.9	64.4	61.4	65.6

[a] Significant differences comparing medium with extra large (.05).

[b] Significant differences comparing large with extra large (.05).

[c] Significant differences comparing medium with large (.05).

[d] Significant differences comparing medium with large and medium with extra large (.05).

[e] Includes business, corporations, and the government.

[f] Comparisons impossible because the quantity of one cell equals zero.

[g] Includes Hispanics, Middle Easterners, and Asians.

TABLE 6.11 Local and Nonlocal Defendant Characteristics in Crime Stories in Combined Media Categories

	Local Crime			Nonlocal Crime		
	Medium (in percentages)	Large (in percentages)	Extra Large (in percentages)	Medium (in percentages)	Large (in percentages)	Extra Large (in percentages)
Named						
Yes	86.5[a]	76.4	73.1	83.1	87.3	83.9
No	13.5	23.6	26.9	16.9	12.7	16.1
Address						
None	31.9[a]	58.7	71.8	79.5[a]	75.0[b]	85.0
Specific	34.1[a]	2.1	0.8	1.1	0.2	0.0[c]
General	13.9[d]	14.1[b]	3.1	1.4	0.9	0.0[c]
City	19.5	23.8	23.8	16.4	18.9[b]	12.6
Other	0.7	1.2	0.5	1.6[e]	5.0	2.0
Sex						
Male	83.6[e]	74.6[b]	83.6	77.0	81.5	79.5
Female	8.2[e]	15.7[b]	9.9	9.3	8.8	10.6
Other[d]	0.2	0.8	0.8	1.6	1.8	1.2
Unknown	8.0	8.9	5.7	12.0[e]	7.9	8.7
Race						
White	9.1[d]	12.6	15.7	15.8	12.7	17.5
Black	3.8[a]	8.2	11.5	10.0	6.9	9.1
Other[f]	1.6[d]	2.1	3.9	5.5	3.0	3.6
Unknown	85.6-	77.0[b]	68.9	68.7[e]	77.4[b]	69.8

(continues)

TABLE 6.11 *(continued)*

	Local Crime			Nonlocal Crime		
	Medium (in percentages)	Large (in percentages)	Extra Large (in percentages)	Medium (in percentages)	Large (in percentages)	Extra Large (in percentages)
Age						
0–12 years	0.2	0.6	0.0[c]	0.3	0.2	0.0[c]
13–16 years	3.3[d]	2.5[b]	8.6	1.9	3.6	1.6
17–25 years	30.2[a]	20.0	22.5	9.4[d]	8.4	4.8
26–35 years	22.4[a]	12.8	14.4	10.0	10.3	7.1
36–50 years	14.2	14.2	13.3	13.0	16.1	17.9
51–64 years	3.5	4.5	3.4	9.1[d]	7.3	4.4
65 and over	1.3	0.8	0.5	0.8	2.2	0.8
Not identified	24.8[a]	44.6[b]	37.3	55.4[d]	52.0[b]	63.5
Occupation						
Professional	5.1[c]	8.4[b]	5.5	9.7	13.1	13.1
Politician	2.7	3.1[b]	1.0	13.3[c]	18.7	17.5
Criminal justice	9.3	6.6	7.0	6.1	6.5	5.2
Helping	3.1[c]	6.6[b]	1.0	3.9[d]	4.1[b]	1.2
Student	4.7	3.1	5.0	1.9	3.0	0.8
Labor	2.9	1.6	1.6	1.7	3.0	3.6
Service	0.4	1.0	1.0	1.4	0.6	0.0[c]
Criminal	1.1	0.2	0.3	1.4	0.9	1.6

158

TABLE 6.11 *(continued)*

Entertainer	0.2	0.4	0.8	3.6	3.4	5.6
Unemployed	0.4	1.2	0.3	0.0[c]	1.3	0.4
Other	0.0[c]	0.8	0.0[c]	1.7	1.3	0.0[c]
Not identified	70.1	67.1[b]	74.7	55.4[e]	44.1	51.2

[a] Significant differences comparing medium with large and medium with extra large (.05).
[b] Significant differences comparing large with extra large (.05).
[c] Comparisons impossible because the quantity of one cell equals zero.
[d] Significant differences comparing medium with extra large (.05).
[e] Significant differences comparing medium with large (.05).
[f] Includes Hispanics, Middle Easterners, and Asians.

TABLE 6.12 Local and Nonlocal Types of Harm in Crime Stories in Combined Media Categories

	Local Crime			Nonlocal Crime		
	Medium (in percentages)	Large (in percentages)	Extra Large (in percentages)	Medium (in percentages)	Large (in percentages)	Extra Large (in percentages)
Financial amount ($)						
0–100	9.5	22.2	9.1	12.5	7.1	0.0[a]
101–1,000	28.6	0.0[a]	13.6	12.5	7.1	0.0[a]
1,001–35,000	21.4	29.6	22.7	12.5	14.3	0.0[a]
35,001–100,000	7.1	18.5	4.5	0.0[a]	14.3	22.2
100,001–999,999	7.1	3.7	0.0[a]	12.5	7.1	0.0[a]
Above 1 million	0.0[a]	7.4	0.0[a]	37.5	28.6	33.3
Does not specify	26.2	18.5[b]	50.0	12.5	21.4	44.4
Property amount ($)						
0–1,000	2.0	0.0[a]	2.9	0.0[a]	14.3	7.7
1,001–10,000	10.2	2.7	11.4	0.0[a]	7.1	7.7
10,001–50,000	0.0[a]	8.1	0.0[a]	0.0[a]	7.1	0.0[a]
50,001–999,999	4.1	5.4	0.0[a]	0.0[a]	0.0[a]	0.0
1,000,000–6,000,000	0.0[a]	5.4[a]	2.9	16.7	21.4	0.0[a]
Home destroyed	0.0[a]	0.0[a]	5.7	16.7	0.0[a]	30.8
Hundreds of millions	0.0[a]	0.0[a]	5.7	0.0[a]	0.0[a]	7.7
Does not specify	83.7	78.4	71.4	66.7	50.0	46.2
Physical harm						
Death	51.7[c]	66.8	72.0	74.0	79.1	73.8
Broken bones	1.0	2.4	0.6	2.5	1.0	1.5

(continues)

TABLE 6.12 *(continued)*

Cuts	6.9	3.5	1.5	1.0[b]	3.8
Bumps	0.5	0.6	0.0[a]	1.3	0.0[a]
Severe trauma	8.4	8.4	9.3[d]	4.9[b]	10.0
None/minor	10.3[c]	0.3	0.5	1.3	0.0[a]
Beaten	7.4[c]	3.2	6.4	5.2	5.4
Sexually abused	5.9	9.6	1.5[d]	5.6	4.6
Other	0.5	0.3	0.5	0.0[a]	0.0[a]
Does not specify	7.4[c]	1.3	3.9[d]	0.7	0.8
<u>Psychological harm</u>					
Fear	66.7	30.0	0.0[a]	0.0[a]	0.0[a]
Shock	0.0[a]	10.0	0.0[a]	50.0	0.0[a]
Denial	0.0[a]	0.0[a]	0.0[a]	0.0[a]	0.0[a]
Anger	33.3	10.0	0.0[a]	0.0[a]	0.0[a]
Mood shifts	0.0[a]	20.0	0.0[a]	0.0[a]	100.0
Shaken up	0.0[a]	20.0	100.0	0.0[a]	0.0[a]
Other	0.0[a]	10.0	0.0[a]	0.0[a]	0.0[a]
Does not specify	0.0[a]	0.0[a]	0.0[a]	50.0	0.0[a]

[a] Comparisons impossible because one of the cells has a quantity of zero.

[b] Significant differences comparing large with extra large (.05).

[c] Significant differences comparing medium with large and medium with extra large (.05).

[d] Significant differences comparing medium with large (.05).

and no suspects had been charged. News media will generally not present defendants' names until after they have been charged with a crime. Since the discovery stage is overrepresented in crime stories presented in the media of the extra-large cities, defendants' names are more likely to be withheld. Also, these media's likelihood to print stories with a larger number of defendants increases their tendency not to name those defendants. The lower frequency of presentation of the names of crime victims in these cities occurs because names may not be known at the discovery stage, or the police may choose to withhold names until a suspect has been formally charged in order to protect victims from intimidation so they are not discouraged from getting involved in the process.

The content results in Tables 6.10 and 6.11 indicate that some differences exist in the presentation of demographic variables for local crimes, supporting the notion that the media in the extra-large cities are more likely to present those victims who can make a crime extraordinary. Demographic characteristics highlighted earlier as influencing primary presentation are more important in cities with significantly more crimes to choose from. For example, the media in the extra-large cities were significantly more likely to present victims who were female, under twelve years old, or members of a newsworthy occupation including business professionals, helping professionals, and students.

For local crimes, female victims were significantly more likely to be presented in the media of extra-large cities compared with those of large and medium-sized cities. They were also the most likely type of victim to be cited in the media of the extra-large cities, being presented approximately 43 percent of the time. In contrast, female victims accounted for less than 30 percent of the victims in the medium-sized news organizations. Regarding the presentation of victims in local murder and other violent crime stories, females were also significantly more likely to be presented in the media of both of large and extra-large cities. Since victimizations and particularly murders of females are more rare, news media in cities with enough crime, especially serious crime, present these victimizations as news. Generally, seriousness combined with local origin constitute sufficient criteria to qualify a crime for news presentation in the smaller cities.

For nonlocal crimes, no significant differences exist in the way females were presented across cities. This finding supports the notion that characteristics influencing nonlocal presentation decisions are more similar in cities of all sizes. Males, statistically the most victimized sex, were significantly less likely to be presented in the media of the extra-large cities than in those in other cities. For nonlocal stories, the "other" category—consisting of victimizations of small businesses, institutions, or the government[2]—was more likely to be presented in the media of the extra-large cities compared with those in the medium-sized cities. For local stories, however, this category was significantly more likely to be presented in the medium-sized cities. These differences provide further evidence that the media in the extra-large cities select different types of crimes.

Local burglaries and other property offenses are much more likely to be cited in the media of the medium-sized cities compared with the media of other cities, in which small businesses are generally presented as victims. The vast majority (10.2 percent) of the "other" local category cited in the media of the medium-sized cities mentioned a small business being victimized because property offenses are more likely to be newsworthy in these cities. The media in the extra-large cities used the "other" category far differently when presenting nonlocal crimes. The victimizations of small businesses were rarely presented, and the majority that made up the "other" category for the media of the extra-large cities were crimes against institutions (cemeteries, churches) or the government (Housing and Urban Development, Medicaid). These latter types of crime can successfully compete for media presentation with the different types of serious local crimes that occur in these cities.

Most of the age categories were represented fairly similarly across cities. Victimization of young children, however, was significantly more likely to be presented in the media of the extra-large cities compared with those of the medium-sized ones. When age was mentioned in the extra-large cities, children under twelve were presented in 14 percent of the stories—nearly double the 8 percent presented in the medium-sized cities. Victimizations of children are more repulsive to the public than other victimizations and are likely to be covered in a city of any size. Since the media in extra-large cities are more likely to need extraordinary crimes to tempt consumers, victimizations of children are more likely to be reported. Although there was no difference in the presentation of children under twelve in murder stories, this age victim was the most likely to be cited in victimizations of special groups and other violent crimes, illustrating the ability of this age group to raise less serious crimes to a newsworthy level in extra-large cities. For similar reasons, the media in the extra-large cities were significantly more likely to present victimizations committed by parents compared with the media in medium-sized cities.

Table 6.10 indicates that the occupation of the victim was significantly more likely to be presented in the media of the extra-large cities compared with those in both medium-sized and large cities. This result remained consistent across each category of crime. The differences increased for those categories, such as property or other violent crimes, that are less serious because these crimes are unlikely to have achieved newsworthiness from the seriousness of the crime alone. For example, the media in the medium-sized cities presented the occupation of the victim in only 10 percent of property crime stories. In contrast, the media in the extra-large cities presented the occupation of the victim in over 50 percent of such stories.

Newsworthy occupations such as business professionals, politicians, criminal justice professionals, and helping professionals can promote a crime to a newsworthy level in any medium, but they are more frequently required in order for media in the extra-large cities to consider a particular crime for presentation.

The content results indicate that business professionals were over twice as likely to be cited in local crime stories in the media of the extra-large cities compared with those in both the medium-sized and large cities and were approximately ten times as likely to be cited as being victimized by murder in the extra-large cities than in the medium-sized ones. Other important occupations that were more likely to be used by the media of large and extra-large cities compared with the medium-sized ones included helping professionals, such as teachers or priests, and students.

Some of the occupation content results are not completely supportive of what was expected. Crimes committed against politicians were rarely presented differently across the city categories. Politicians were rarely portrayed as being victimized in any of the cities, and when they were, similar percentages were presented. One of the cities in the medium-sized category was a capital city, which might have contributed to equal access for politicians who were victimized. Victimizations of criminal justice professionals were significantly more likely to be presented in the medium-sized cities than in large ones. Victimization of individuals responsible for protecting the public became news to the same extent in the cities considered. Media in each city consider the victimizations of criminal justice professionals to be important news because of the ease with which the public identifies with them.

Occupation is an important victim characteristic that is provided by the news media when they consider it to be newsworthy. This is indicated by the results, which show that fairly similar occupations were used within crime stories across cities and that few significant differences in the presentation of occupation across cities were found for nonlocal crimes. Since the media in the extra-large cities have increased access to a larger number of victimizations and have greater access to particular occupations such as business professionals, these media have the opportunity to present more newsworthy occupations.

Occupation of the defendant was rarely presented differently across cities. When differences are indicated, the results are not consistent with what was hypothesized. For example, media in the extra-large cities were least likely to present an occupation for local crimes and were significantly less likely to present professionals, politicians, and helping professionals than were the media in the large cities. These findings are problematic, considering that we would expect that the higher occurrence of certain types of crime, such as white-collar crimes, would make it more likely for the media in the largest cities to present crimes committed by business professionals. An examination of this category of crime does not support this hypotheses. Business professionals were, however, significantly more likely to be presented as committing the less serious property crimes and misdemeanors in the extra-large cities, again demonstrating the ability of certain demographics to raise crimes not usually considered newsworthy to such a level.

Regarding the types of harm that are presented, the results shown in Table

6.12 indicate that physical harm was the only type commonly cited in crime stories. Property and psychological costs were rarely provided by the media of all cities. In fact, each of these types of harm was provided in less than 3 percent of the stories across each of the city categories considered. Even when other harms besides physical are provided, they are generally mentioned as an afterthought. For example, in discussing psychological harm, a reporter will simply mention in passing that the victim was "shaken up." In both local and nonlocal stories each of these types of harm was provided infrequently and was not presented differently because such harm is generally not of interest to consumers or compatible with the types of crime reported in the news.

The physical impact of crime, the only type of harm mentioned frequently in crime stories, was described in some detail. Such harm is the most newsworthy because of the ease with which the public can relate to it. The local content results indicate that death was the most likely physical harm to be presented in all cities. Since the media in the large and extra-large cities have access to and present more murders, death was significantly more likely to be presented there. Furthermore, the media in the medium-sized cities were significantly more likely to describe their victims as having been badly beaten or having no or only minor injuries; they also may have been unable to specify the type of physical harm experienced by the victim.

The results presented in Table 6.12 indicate that most of the categories of physical harm considered were presented similarly across cities. It is interesting to note that the media in the medium-sized cities compensated for the lack of local deaths by presenting national and international deaths, resulting in a similar proportion of deaths being covered across any of the combined city categories. The significant difference found in the use of sexual abuse could be attributed to the different types of nonlocal crime selected for presentation. Since murders were rare in the medium-sized cities, media in those cities were more likely to search for newsworthy nonlocal murders or to include stories about victims who experienced severe trauma (for example, a gun shot wound). In contrast, media in the larger cities had an ample amount of local murders available to allow them to present a wide range. This may contribute to the media in these cities being somewhat more likely to search for and present other types of physical harm, such as sexual abuse, when selecting their daily crime agenda.

Conclusion

The news media considered in this study are responsible for attracting an audience that is locally situated and must do so by presenting local crimes. News media in different cities have access to different types of local crime, which constrains what ultimately gets presented to the public about crimes that happen in the local community. For example, news media in cities with large amounts of serious crime are most likely to present murder, and a different type of murder, than those in other cities. The results about the sources used indicate that similar criminal justice sources were used across cities because of the relationships the media need to build with them, although police are used somewhat more frequently in the medium-sized cities because of organizational constraints. Family members of victims were used more frequently in the media of the extra-large cities because of their ability to promote crimes to a newsworthy level when a large array of different crimes exists for selection. These results also indicate some support for the hypothesis that certain victim characteristics can promote particular crime types for presentation. Sex, age, and occupation were used more frequently by the media in the extra-large cities. There were, however, inconsistencies in the use of both victim and defendant characteristics for both local and nonlocal crimes, which highlights the fact that these characteristics are evaluated as being worthy of news coverage to the same extent by media across the different cities considered. What gets presented about crime and the amount of news space given to a story are not determined by one single characteristic. The importance of a crime story is determined by an evolving process in which the type of crime interacts with characteristics of the persons involved, the amount of time a reporter has to produce a story, a reporter's interest in a story, the willingness of sources to provide information, and the quality of the information provided.

Notes

1. Although they examine the presentation of crime across different cities, the studies by Windhauser, Seiter, and Winfree (1990) and Lotz (1991) cannot be compared with the findings presented in the current analysis. Windhauser, Seiter, and Winfree (1990) examined the way the presentation of crime in twenty-two Louisiana cities changed over a five-year period, neglecting the type of crime, sources, and victims presented in these cities. It is difficult to compare Lotz's (1991) study because he performed a *word* content analysis that compared the number of times a word such as "murder" is mentioned in a story with that of other words such as "drugs" or "died" (see pp. 106–110). The frequency of each word was then compared across cities. The content analysis used in the current study and the other studies mentioned in the introduction to this chapter relied on analysis of the themes presented in the stories.

2. For example, a crime story might report that a gas station was robbed. These types of stories were content coded as "small-business" victim. "Institution" was coded when a story discussed a school or church being vandalized. "Government" victim stories were those in which a person defrauded the government, such as in a Medicaid scam. Each of these victimizations was collapsed into the "other" category.

7

The News Media in Society

The founding fathers tried to negotiate a fair balance between individual liberties and government authority when framing the Constitution. Wearied by governmental oppression, they restricted their own authority to safeguard democracy, providing constitutional protections to guarantee a free and independent press. The expectation was that the news media would be an intermediary force between these two competing interests—one of the more important mechanisms through which the public could question the legitimacy of government institutions, using its First Amendment protections to ensure an open discussion of diverse opinions. The news media were to be removed from political influence and police organizational life and were to report violations of the public trust. When their role in society has been described, the news media have been referred to variously as a watchdog, a fourth estate or fourth branch of the government, the voice of a democratic society, an agent of power, and an agent of social control (Altschull 1984, Ericson, Baranek, and Chan 1987; Hulteng and Nelson 1971; Lasswell 1948).

The news media play a significant role in society because they have the power to decide what issues are worthy of public consumption. Of the significantly large number of events that occur each day, the news media have the discretion to decide which events should be transformed into news. What they decide to provide satisfies a number of important functions for society. The news media inform the public about the events they present, allowing it to digest at least a portion of what occurs.

The Powers of the Watchdog

Crime is an important topic in society and in the news media. The content results indicated that crime was among the most popular of all news topics in each city considered, regardless of the type of media. The public knows violent crime is a serious problem. The ability of the news media to inform is significant because the majority of the public has no personal exposure to the types of crimes that are presented in the news. The presentation of crime in the news media helps define the boundaries of society, contributing to social stability by revealing what is acceptable behavior (Ericson, Baranek, and Chan 1987).

Even though the news media are closely linked to source organizations because of their heavy reliance on the information these organizations provide, reporters are willing to present transgressions committed by even the most frequently used sources, thus sacrificing this relationship. When thirty police officers were arrested for various drug and gambling violations, for example, both the *Tribune* and the Nightly covered this crime as a super primary story, thereby damaging public perceptions of the police. Moreover, the constant reliance on criminal justice sources allows the news media to serve a watchdog function, overseeing the performance of those institutions with which they interact daily. The mere existence of a relationship between a news organization and a source contributes to self-policing by the source organization in order to reduce the likelihood of negative publicity. At the same time, the news media give these organizations credibility by deciding that they are the legitimate providers of knowledge about crime and criminal justice (Ericson, Baranek, and Chan 1991).

The news media are a source through which individual citizens can question the legitimacy of government, lodging complaints about their treatment by the system. When an individual citizen approaches the media with a potential story, there is no guarantee that it will get covered or even be considered worthy of coverage, but a reporter will at least listen and do some follow-up to see whether it is newsworthy. Individual citizens' complaints about the length of a sentence meted out to a defendant, police performance in solving a case, or a district attorney's accessibility are among the more newsworthy quotes that can be provided by sources.

The news media are most likely to provide stories on those crimes that are defined as the most serious by the public. This research found that the type of crime was an important variable in determining what gets presented in the news. Serious crime, especially murder, is the crime of choice for news media. Murder has predominated in the news over time and remains the most likely crime to be presented in both print and electronic media. Some variations exist because of the number of murders available to a particular news media, but organizations with the least amount of local access attempt to compensate by presenting murders that occurred elsewhere. Murders are the most likely crimes to be presented, to receive primary or super primary presentation, and to be followed across a number of stages of the criminal justice system. Is there value in presenting a large amount of violent crime? Hulteng and Nelson (1971) argued that presenting murder is a legitimate part of news because of the need for the public to be informed that this type of crime is being committed. Since a large number of murders are presented, the threat of that crime is not taken lightly, and its presentation may cause members of the public to take precautions because they fear becoming victims (Heath 1984).

In addition to informing society about murder, the news media on occasion run special segments, articles, or investigative reports about specific issues or innovations implemented within the system even though these stories are time-consuming and costly to produce. For example, one of the police reporters from the *Tribune* spent some time with the police helicopter division for a story about the responsibilities of the unit, the pros and cons of such a unit, and what it costs to maintain it. Print and television media provide additional information about crimes that are of high interest to the public beyond the actual incident. A well-publicized super primary case can bring a problem to the attention of the public. In order to explore the topic, reporters exhaust the sources who are knowledgeable about the crime, who provide information about the significance of the problem and its development. Eventually, stories that more fully analyze the problem, editorials, and citizen opinion segments appear in the news, offering a diverse range of viewpoints.

Interest in the welfare of crime victims has been stimulated by victims' presentation in the news media. The news media have heightened public awareness and informed the public about various aspects of victimization. The public has been made aware of some of the pains of victimization, problems encountered in the criminal justice system, and changes that have been made to try to assist victims more effectively. This information has altered the way crime victims are treated by professionals in the criminal justice system.

Although the seriousness of the crime is an important triggering characteristic that influences the news-production process, other factors, such as the age of the victim, can determine how a crime story is presented. Demographic characteristics, the type of harm experienced, or the victim's willingness to be used as an informant can affect reporter selection and production decisions. Certain victims are more likely to be considered worthy of presentation than others because they can increase the salience of a story.

The content analysis revealed that specific demographic characteristics of crime victims—something over which the victim has no control—are salient influences on whether certain crimes get presented. Age, occupation, and sex were the most important of these characteristics. These same factors were highlighted by ethnographic observation as influencing reporter selection decisions, methods used to produce a story, number of source contacts made, and the amount of space given to a story. The news media have firmly established the fact that crimes against certain victims are more newsworthy and deserving of more news coverage than others. Since news personnel think the public can easily relate to a child or an elderly victim, these stories are more likely to be portrayed as primary and super primary. Occupations are rarely provided in the news. The likelihood of presentation increases when certain occupations, such as police officers, lawyers, teachers, students, priests, and government employees, are victimized. Crimes such as burglary are far less likely to be presented than are more serious crimes. However, when the victim has a newsworthy characteristic, the story is more likely to be in the news, at least as a tertiary story, thus expanding the crime images that are made available to the public.

News media provide specific harms that increase the appeal of the news product. Physical harms predominate in the news, followed by property and financial losses. Psychological harms and problems experienced as a result of becoming involved in the criminal justice system are rarely provided. These findings are related to the types of crimes that are portrayed in the news. Victims affected by the most serious crime are in the news, affecting what harms get presented to the public. Death is the harm most likely to be presented to the public because of the media's presentation of murder. In these cases, family members of victims become extremely important providers of victim information because the actual victim is unavailable.

The political vitality of special groups of crime victims has flourished because of prolific media campaigns. National concern for crime victims has been influenced by the large number of victim service organizations that have emerged across the country. The majority of these groups are designed to attend to the needs of certain types of victims, such as rape, domestic violence, and child-abuse groups. These groups have been vocal about the treatment of victims and have used the news media effectively, criticizing the political and criminal justice response. Their political activities have increased the newsworthiness of crimes committed against these victims and brought attention to their needs. The unique problems of these special groups are more familiar and understood by media consumers than are those of other groups because of their presentation.

Muzzling the Watchdog

The news media's portrait of the crime problem in society is narrow and distorted because of the way news is constructed. The majority of events that occur are excluded from public preview. The media may not find out about particular crimes, they may be exposed to crimes they do not consider newsworthy, or time limitations may preclude or limit their presentation of crime. What ultimately gets presented in the news is determined by a filtering process. The need to satisfy organizational objectives and the interrelationships between news and source organizations determine which crimes are considered for presentation, which survive the newsmaking process, and how much space is given to a story.

The news media are forced to rely on certain sources, such as officials from the criminal justice system, because they are easily available and are willing to satisfy story needs. This research indicated that the primary sources used by the news media for all types of story information are police and court sources. Medical sources, such as coroners, are used frequently for victim information because of their willingness to provide this information quickly over the telephone. The news media structure their activities so they have routine contacts with these sources. Because they have their own organizational agenda to consider when providing information, such sources provide a specialized image of crime that furthers their own interests. Criminal justice professionals use the news media to justify decisions made and to promote their innovative ideas in the news. Other sources that could provide alternative explanations (e.g., experts, defendants, victims) are used less frequently because of the burden these contacts add to the daily routines of reporters.

The media's heavy reliance on criminal justice sources limits what is presented about crime victims. The majority of victims presented in the news are those who report to the police and are involved in the system. Yet statistics indicate that a large percentage of individuals do not report their victimization to official sources. The media's presentation of victims is not reflective of these crime victims, and the ineffectiveness of the criminal justice system to do anything about this situation is not cited in the media as a reason that victims fail to report. Moreover, the sources relied upon for information present the plight of victims in a way that furthers their own interests. Viano (1987: 443) discussed the way increased national concern for crime victims resulted from support of conservative ideological objectives. He stated, "The importance and popularity that victim-related issues enjoy today is due in part not so much to a reawakening of compassion, decency, and concern for fellow human beings but rather to the prevalence of conservative ideology in the 1980s." Conservatives have used crime victims to further their own objectives, requesting stricter punishments for crimes committed against certain types of victims and limiting the rights of defendants.

Although criminal justice sources have control of the selection of crimes for presentation and are able to accent their own authority by being cited within stories, news media have organizational concerns that influence their decisionmaking and that limit a source's ability to dominate public crime images. Of the crimes made available to them for presentation, the news media select those that are the most entertaining and the most likely to sell. Even though crime is a popular news topic, each day it has to compete with a range of other potential topics. The primary objective of the news media, at least those media considered in this study, is to provide a product that sells. The news media attempt to provide a product that will appeal to the largest percentage of a diverse audience. This, in turn, makes the news organization attractive to advertisers. In order to improve their marketability, media organizations gauge their audience and attempt to provide what the public is interested in by highlighting current trends and discussing crimes that are popular and that entertain. For example, when William Kennedy Smith and Mike Tyson were accused of committing rape, interest in other date rapes—which generally do not meet standards of newsworthiness—was stimulated. Similarly, interest in police brutality grew after the Rodney King beating. Crime stories become less important when other news topics are of concern to the audience. News consumers were less interested in crime stories during the Gulf War, for example. Although crime stories were still presented, they were relegated to the back pages of newspapers as tertiary and secondary stories.

The commercial interests of selling news and attracting advertisers contribute to the heavy presentation of violent crimes in the news. The public can easily identify with the victims and defendants of violent crime. Stories about these individuals are simple and understandable (the individuals involved can be visualized), and they grab the attention of the audience (Jamieson and Campbell 1983). Discussions of the causes of crime or hypotheses about the ineffectiveness of the police in solving crimes are much more difficult and time-consuming to try to understand.

The news media's desire to attract an audience is intertwined with, and affected by, organizational concerns about presenting the news product in an efficient, economical manner. Financial, time, and space factors constrain the news media's picture of crime. Decisions about access and presentation, as well as formal policies, can all affect the media's relationship with sources and the quality of information provided to the public. For example, the *Tribune* used only one reporter to staff the police beat in the evening and on weekends. This decision severely limited the paper's ability to produce stories about crime during these periods. If a late-breaking crime occurred in the evening, the reporter would gather whatever information he or she could and produce a low-level story or simply give the information to a daytime reporter. Similarly, the ability to produce stories about a particular type of crime may be eliminated or severely limited by a policy that restricts media access.

The time available to produce a story influences the methods used by reporters to construct that story. Source information is obtained through interviews, but those who are asked to provide information may not necessarily be representative of community consensus regarding a particular issue or crime. Existing research indicates that crime victims are rarely used as story informants (Ericson, Baranek, and Chan 1991; Sherizen 1978; Voumvakis and Ericson 1984). The present research attempted to expand the understanding of the sources used by news organizations by examining the ways sources are asked to provide different types of information. This research indicates that crime victims or family members are used frequently to comment specifically on victim information, although they are used to provide a specific type of knowledge. Primary and secondary victims are used to make the story more emotional and pertinent to the reader. Reporters try to get victims to agree to participate by developing a trusting relationship with them, using a variety of techniques. The content and ethnographic results indicate that decisions by the news media to contact victims, agreement by the victim or the family to answer questions, and the quality of information these sources provide can determine the images the public receives about victimization.

Newspapers and television news are among the most popular forms of mass communication that transmit ideas about crime. Each type of media is attractive to consumers for different reasons related to the formats adhered to when producing news. Individuals and organizations attempt to take advantage of format strengths in order to make their news product appealing. Distinct format differences require that each type of media present crime and victims in a way that accentuates what is advantageous to it. That is, each news organization must tailor its product to satisfy the reasons members of the public are using that product. Newspapers have significantly larger amounts of space that can be expanded to include late-breaking news, to cover a broader range of topics, and to cover larger amounts of a specific type of story. Reporters use the space flexibility to provide more detailed analysis within a story. Broadcast stations have a limited amount of space but compensate for the lack of it by conveying messages through video.

The results using the combined content and ethnographic methodologies indicate that format differences contribute to some variation in the images presented. Although crime is among the most popular topics for both types of media, crime stories account for a larger percentage of the total number of television stories because newspapers include sections, inserts, and stories covering a broader range of assorted topics, which depletes the salience of crime stories. Additionally, certain types of crime were found to be more amenable to either print or electronic media depending on format advantages. White–collar crimes, for example, were more likely to be presented within print media because of the availability of extra space, thereby allowing the complexities of these crimes to be explored. Moreover, these stories are not typically appealing to the video format needs of television news.

News stories are produced in such a way as to satisfy and highlight format strengths. Television news relies on video images, so reporters have to interview sources in person on camera, whereas the majority of contacts of newspaper reporters are made over the telephone. Thus, a larger number of sources can be contacted and included within a newspaper crime story. Television reporters rely on one or two sources directly knowledgeable about a crime because of time constraints and size limitations. In order to effectively satisfy these needs, television reporters are significantly more likely to use the family members of crime victims as sources because of the emotion that can be captured when seeing them describe their reaction on video.

Although there were some differences in the presentation of crime across media, there were also numerous similarities. Murders were the crimes most prominently displayed regardless of the media considered. Crime victims were presented similarly across organizations. Certain characteristics of victims, such as age and occupation, were equally appealing to both types of organization when determining which crimes were presented and the level of newsworthiness achieved. Additionally, both predominantly presented physical harm, neglecting other types of harm that could be done to a victim.

Tertiary, secondary, primary, and super primary stories were defined as such similarly across the various media, and each organization structured its newsmaking process to allow it to produce these stories. Tertiary and secondary stories were considered low-level news stories by each organization. Fewer resources were expended for these stories, and, if need be, they could be eliminated. The process used to generate these stories was much simpler, and the time it took to put them together was slight. The amount of information provided about the crime incident, victim, and defendant was superficial and the number of sources cited were few because neither organization considered these stories to be important. Tertiary stories were somewhat less likely to be found as television news because of space constraints.

Primary stories are important for both types of organization. Print and electronic media provide additional space so reporters can fully develop these stories. Both newspaper and television organizations increase the amount of resources used to produce primary stories. During a television editorial meeting, for example, it is decided which stories are worth primary coverage. These stories are put together by having a reporter make a number of source contacts to set up interviews, and the end product will run between one and two minutes. Factors that influence whether crimes are promoted to a primary level are consistent across organizations. The seriousness of the crime and certain characteristics of the victim can raise the level of news story for either type of media.

Organizations have similar criteria for crimes that receive super primary coverage. These stories are so unique and rare, compared to crimes that occur daily, that they receive extra coverage in both types of organization. These stories are what the public is most interested in, and each type of organization realizes that it needs to take advantage of the story. Regardless of the amount of resources available, organizations expend as many people as possible to cover different aspects of super primary stories. Each will cover them in a way that emphasizes their respective format parameters, but both consider them a first priority.

The two types of media considered in this study share the same audience, which contributes to the several consistencies that were found in the presentation of crime and victims. This finding is exacerbated by the fact that reporters in both types of media rely on similar criminal justice sources to discover which crimes are available. These sources are likely to react similarly to reporters from either type of media when deciding what information to provide. The public relations spokesperson withheld or provided information to either organization without discriminating, but the number of requests made by each were different because of space requirements. Another major source for both types of media is other media organizations (Ericson, Baranek, and Chan 1989; Gordon and Heath 1981; Voumvakis and Ericson 1984). *Tribune* reporters would tune in to the six o' clock news and could at least write a tertiary or secondary story if a broadcast organization covered a story they had missed. Television stations attend closely to many area newspapers, wire services, and news presented by other stations, and this material assists them when writing their story, further ensuring that the picture presented across media is nearly identical.

Reporters working for media organizations in various-sized cities have access to very different types of local newsworthy crime. Each of the media organizations considered in this study presented a specific image of crime, although variations in the availability of certain types of crime resulted in presentation differences across cities. In each city, serious crimes were preferred over other types of crime for presentation and primary presentation. When the availability of murders was scarce, the smaller news organizations compensated by presenting state and national murders in order to increase the level of seriousness achieved. Even though seriousness was illustrated as being an important newsworthy factor in the cities, those with access to a number of murders or serious crimes had the luxury of searching for the most newsworthy stories available. The crimes that become news in cities with large amounts of crime would be news in any city, but differences exist because the sheer volume increases the likelihood that an extraordinary crime will be discovered. The images provided by media in the larger cities such as Dallas and Detroit are actually more limited than those in smaller cities because extraordinary murders or other serious crimes are presented primarily because ordinary homicides have little appeal.

Certain characteristics of crime victims were highlighted as being able to promote crimes in these cities to a newsworthy level. Age, occupation, victim behavior, or reactions to the crime increased the likelihood of the presentation of a particular crime. These factors are more likely to be important in cities with the largest amounts of crime because of the need to select crimes that are extraordinary. This research indicated that a number of characteristics were more likely to be displayed in the extra-large cities in response to this need. Murders affecting numerous victims, special groups of victims, or victims of a newsworthy occupation were important factors in cities such as Dallas or Detroit because of access to numerous murders. Similar factors were illustrated as promoting other types of local crime to a newsworthy level in the large and extra-large cities, as well as elevating national crimes in all city size categories.

The Costs of Crime News Production

The news media present a limited portrait of crime, victims, and defendants. The production of news eliminates the vast majority of crimes that occur from consideration, and those that remain are presented as they are defined by criminal justice sources and are used to entertain consumers rather than enlighten them. What gets presented about crime does benefit society in some ways. At the same time, however, the news media reproduce and support a specific ideology because of the nature of the news-production process.

Any function the presentation of crime in the media serves is mediated by the fact that certain issues have to be selected over others. Whatever is presented in the media is distorted in some sense because of the media's inability to capture reality (Shoemaker and Reese 1991: 2). For example, the public rarely gets media exposure to less violent crimes, even though these are the crimes people are most likely to experience. Other types of crime are less newsworthy because they lack an easily identifiable individual. Corporations charged with committing environmental crimes, for example, are rarely in the news because it is difficult to specifically identify a victim and get access to the information required to make such an event newsworthy. The news media's deciding what is important by emphasizing certain types of crime at the expense of others constitutes ideology (Gans 1979; Humphries 1981; Jamieson and Campbell 1983). The selection of certain events over others illustrates the hegemonic model of public communication, in which news organizations are spokespersons for dominant groups and their ideology (Gitlin 1980; Iyengar 1991). Events in the news are primarily about the powerful; furthermore, reporters rely on those in power to interpret these events. Since some crimes are systematically excluded, what is presented constitutes a picture that legitimizes the status quo, confirming the present structure of society and assisting in the social control of individuals (Ericson, Baranek, and Chan 1987; Fishman 1980; Tuchman 1978). Groups not presented in the media are thought to be less important.

Most crime incidents are presented in the news as episodic events (Iyengar 1991). They are constructed as separate events, unrelated to previous crimes or to the causes of crime. The content results indicated that criminal justice source institutions were rarely criticized or evaluated. Treating each crime as a separate event supports the notion that newsmaking is a procedure not to know (Fishman 1980). According to Ericson, Baranek, and Chan (1987: 9), "The very act of discovering and construing events in the world in journalistic terms blinds the journalist and consumers of his product to other ways of seeing." The presentation of crime in this episodic way diverts attention from underlying causes of the problem and shields politicians and criminal justice professionals from responsibility.

Moreover, exposure to a limited range of crimes and the treatment of instances as episodic events assist criminal justice organizations in their pursuit of their program and resource goals. The news media present crime in such a way as to give the consumer the impression that the criminal justice system works. The discovery stage of the process was found to be the most frequently reported. The presentation of discovered crimes enforces the notion that crime is an important problem and that the police and the public are vulnerable to victimization. Crimes that are reported when discovered are followed as they progress through the system, such as when the police make an arrest, when the suspect is arraigned, and if the defendant pleads guilty. Stories rarely criticize the police for their inability to make an arrest, or a story will simply highlight the fact that the police investigation is continuing. The dismissal of a court case or a finding of not guilty is considered a less important news story and is less frequently presented. Such events are neglected because the organization fills daily news requirements by placing its reporters in a location that gives them exposure to new crimes.

Occasionally, news media will present similar events around a specific theme, resulting in a moral panic by the public. In a recent anthology examining issues in newsmaking criminology, Gregg Barak (1994: 13) stated that "sometimes the media follow social trends and the dictates of their audiences; sometimes they are out in front of their audiences, creating social trends." I observed media coverage of a moral panic when I first started at the *Tribune*. A number of stories were covered of instances in which rocks were tossed over a bridge overpass, damaging passing vehicles. The public's interest in this type of crime was piqued because of one serious instance in which a large rock was thrown over a bridge, killing a mother in a car as her husband and children looked on. This case was in the news from its occurrence through the sentencing of the defendant. A number of similar crime instances were presented because of public interest, even though harm in those other instances was not nearly as serious. Researchers who have examined moral panics have argued that they are driven by ideology (Fishman 1980; Hall et. al 1978). The public receives a narrow view of the problem and may believe it is more significant than it actually is. The media turn to those in power for an explanation of these events, allowing the "deviance-defining elite" to interpret them in a way that furthers its own political cause (Ericson, Baranek, and Chan 1987: 35). The focus of these moral panics is on the need for additional criminal justice resources and the implementation of legislation to address the heightened concerns, not on the limitations of organizations in responding effectively to the crimes in question. Once the theme runs its course, the public is led to believe that the problem was solved by the response.

Politicians and criminal justice professionals use information provided in the news to make decisions. Stories that are presented as super primary are more likely to stir public opinion and stimulate a reaction from these decisionmakers. These same individuals use the media to justify decisions and promote their ideas within the news. If the news media were to scrutinize these ideas and provide information clearly identifying the problems of the system, this would assist politicians and professionals in making more informed decisions and give the public an opportunity to consider different sides of a particular issue.

The news media are not immune to outside influences, and the pressure from various victims' groups, which has increased over the past thirty years, has caused professionals who work for news organizations to reevaluate what is presented about crime victims. Informal and formal organizational policies regarding what should be presented about victims and how they should be used as story sources help to determine the portrait of victims that is presented. News media have specific policies about providing the names and addresses of victims. Child and rape victims are not named unless they are murder victims, the story is extraordinarily important, or the victim agrees to be named. General addresses are provided for most victims so they are not put in additional danger. News media adopted these policies in direct response to criticisms voiced by various groups.

Pressure has also been exerted about how and when reporters question tragedy victims. The victim's involvement in the news-production process has been neglected in past research. The stereotypical scenario, based primarily on anecdotal accounts, is that the news media constantly badger and exploit grieving victims until they are coerced or tricked into participating. Ben Hecht, a famous Chicago journalist, wrote about how he obtained pictures.

> While maturer minds badgered the survivors of the morning's dead for news data, I hovered broodingly outside the ring of interviewers. I learned early not to ask for what I wanted, for such requests only alerted the beleaguered kin, weeping now as much for the scandal coming down on them as for the grief that had wakened them. Instead I scurried through bedrooms, poked noiselessly into closets, trunks and bureau drawers, and, the coveted photograph under my coat, bolted for the street. (Hecht 1954: 123)

Common criticisms of media use of crime victims for news stories include arriving at the crime scene with cameras rolling, camping out on victim's lawns, showing bloody crime scenes and body bags, and interfering with police investigations (Seymour 1986).

When a reporter discovers a newsworthy crime, for most stories crime victims are considered to be secondary, and only certain characteristics will be included in a story. This information is collected from a variety of sources, including the victim, family or friends of the victim, police and other official sources, medical sources, and citizens. The majority of crime stories presented in the media are either tertiary, secondary, or primary. For these stories, if victims decide not to speak to the media, the news media leave them alone, and the information that is included in stories is simply taken from other sources.

Generally, initial contacts with crime victims are made by telephone. If the victim hangs up, the reporter will not bother the victim further because these stories are not important enough. If victims are contacted and are able to provide newsworthy quotes or are willing to go on camera, the news story will be considered more important, and the news organization is more likely to give it news space.

Direct media competition and the need to sell news affect the way reporters react to crime victims when stories are super primary. Reporters not usually inclined to badger the victim are more likely to be pressured by their news organization to do so when a story becomes super primary. A large, diverse range of news organizations is interested in super primary stories, including the local and national press, wire services, tabloids, and free-lancers. Some of these reporters are likely to be extremely intrusive because the stories are of high interest to the audience and every reporter attempts to scoop other reporters. As stated by Wilson (1991: 186): "The television and newspaper media know those cases that have the right earmarks for creating curiosity. Detecting the case when it happens is not the problem: the challenge lies in orchestrating a presentation of the case, with 'exclusive' interviews and story revelations, to outclass the competition. Competition may make the media work harder to be factual and interesting, but it also highlights the priority, especially of television, to entertain."

For most stories, reporters will leave victims alone when they request it. When competition intensifies, some reporters resort to intrusive methods in an attempt to scoop the competition. Other reporters, however, are unwilling to pressure victims—regardless of the importance of the story—and will leave them alone with their grief. For example, the family of Jeffrey Dahmer's first victim was thrown unexpectedly into one of the biggest crime stories since Sam Sheppard was arrested for killing his wife. To the world, Steven Hicks was Jeffrey Dahmer's first victim; to his family, he was their son and a murder victim. The media thought the public wanted to know what Steven Hicks's family felt about the Milwaukee serial murderer. Some news media were relentless. Reporters constantly followed the family, camped out in front of their house for days, and tried to get access through neighbors and friends. Eventually, there were shouting matches between members of the family and reporters because of the media's constant badgering. In contrast, reporters from the Nightly attempted to contact the Hicks family by telephone. When they refused to talk, the station produced stories examining other angles of the case. None of the reporters from the Nightly approached the Hicks family at home because it was the organization's policy to respect the wishes of victims.

The presentation of super primary stories is significant because they can influence public opinions about crime and victims. These sensational cases are not representative of crime, criminal justice, and victimization. They are, however, more likely to leave a lasting impression on consumers because of the space provided to them, because of the importance of the sources cited within them, and because various media (newspaper, television, radio, tabloid, and talk shows) attempt to capitalize on them. Super primary stories become topics of conversation, spilling over into various aspects of our lives.

Certain victims are selected for news presentation because of their ability to entertain and attract consumers. The news media are convinced that crimes against certain victims are more newsworthy and therefore deserving of greater news coverage than others. The news media are able to present only a narrow range of victimization issues because of the need to make news sell. The current presentation neglects the historical and societal contexts from which victimization occurs; moreover, it neglects the underlying sources of victimization. The victims who are prominently presented are the most innocent, usually extreme cases. Defining victimization in this way has limited the ability of professionals in the criminal justice system to respond effectively to the problem. Many of the rights that have been extended to victims have neglected the needs of those who do not fit a particular stereotype. For example, Smith and Freinkel (1988: 172) discussed the way "spouse abuse portrayed battered women as the quintessential victim," precluding those situations in which a woman contributed to the situation or responded by using a similar degree of violence.

Researchers have discussed the fact that one of the primary roles of the news media in society is to balance the need to make a profit against a concern for satisfying social responsibilities in deciding what should be presented to the public (Siebert, Peterson, and Schramm 1956). Currently, profit concerns and entertainment objectives have played increasingly important roles and are the predominate influences on how news organizations interact with source organizations. The impressive ratings achieved by sensational print and electronic media organizations, such as the *National Enquirer* and *Hard Copy,* have forced mainstream media to emulate their entertainment formula for attracting consumers. The bottom line has been pushed to the forefront as the news media have undergone dramatic changes. Some of the new technologies, such as electronic editing and pagination, have made it easier for news organizations to produce their daily product, giving reporters more time to write a story (Willis 1990); newspapers are becoming increasingly available electronically either as videotext (computerized news graphics) or teletext (computerized news text) (see Willis 1990: 161-165); and the cable television industry continues to grow (Kaniss 1991). The public has access to larger amounts of news and more flexibility to individually choose which stories to select, and news organizations can more easily document the types of articles their readers prefer. Will these new technologies change the production of news and ultimately change what is presented to the public? How will they change the formats of news? Will crime news remain as popular? What types of articles will the public select, and how will these choices filter back into the decisions made by the news organizations? These changes in the technologies of news will have to be considered as they become more commonplace in order to determine how media change the news product to continue to capture the largest portion of the market share.

Appendix

A Note on Research Methodology

Past research that has examined crime in the news media has made use of three research methodologies. First, the majority of research has used content analysis. A sample of news items from a particular news medium is selected and content coded for crime, victim, and defendant characteristics (see Graber 1980; Lotz 1991; Mawby and Brown 1984; Sheley and Ashkins 1981). The frequency of each item is then compared with some other construct of reality (such as the Uniform Crime Report) to evaluate the media's depiction of crime. Research using content analysis examines the crimes that are presented to the public. The second methodology is ethnography (see Ericson, Baranek, and Chan 1987, 1989; Fishman 1978; Hall et al. 1978). The research considers news production, observing the organizational processes involved in making news. Selection, production, and editing decisions are scrutinized, providing knowledge on *how* a particular news item gets presented to the public. The third methodology is interviewing. Researchers have interviewed reporters, editors, and management (see Grabosky and Wilson 1989; Kaniss 1991). Studies using interviews examine *why* particular crimes get presented to the public.

Each of these methods has a unique advantage. The present research combines all three—content analysis, ethnography, and interviews—to generate the results, taking advantage of each of their strengths.

Content Analysis

Content analysis of crime news provides data on the crimes presented, as well as what characteristics of victims and defendants and what sources are presented in crime stories. Content data were collected from six print and three electronic media organizations. The media were selected according to city size. In selecting the sample, a list of cities that had at least one newspaper with a circulation of 50,000 or greater was generated.[1] The cities were matched according to population size and number of index offenses for 1990, then stratified into the categories medium, large, and extra-large. Media from two cities in each category were selected in order to represent as many regions of the country and as much variation in crime rate as possible.[2] Content from one newspaper in each of the six cities (two medium, two large, two extra-large) and one television station in three of the cities (one medium, one large, one extra-large) was examined.

Data for the newspaper content analysis were collected from the *Albany Times-Union* (Albany, New York), the *Buffalo News* (Buffalo, New York), the *Cleveland Plain Dealer* (Cleveland, Ohio), the *San Francisco Chronicle* (San Francisco, California), the *Dallas Times Herald* (Dallas, Texas), and the *Detroit News* (Detroit, Michigan). The three sets of papers (Albany-Buffalo, Cleveland-San Francisco, Dallas-Detroit) met the criteria for inclusion in the medium, large, and extra-large categories, respectively. All six are dailies that have morning editions,[3] and half (Albany, Buffalo, Cleveland) stem from single-paper cities.[4]

This analysis provided information about crime and victims in typical crime stories produced by a print news organization. Content was coded from all six newspapers for every fifth day of the first six months of 1990.[5] Thirty-six days of content data were collected per newspaper. In addition, newspaper content from the *Cleveland Plain Dealer* was coded for an additional eighteen days over a three-month period in 1991. This was done for two reasons: It strengthened the reliability of comparisons between the newspaper and television samples because crime stories from the latter were drawn from 1991, and it allowed for a comparison with the results from the 1990 newspaper sample.

Content analysis of late-evening television newscasts complemented the findings from the print analysis, allowing for comparisons across medium.[6] Local evening broadcasts in Albany, Cleveland, and Dallas were coded for seven nights a week over an eight-week time span from May to July 1991. In each city, the most popular station, according to its rating, was selected.[7] Albany and Cleveland broadcasts were thirty minutes in length including commercials; Dallas broadcasts were forty-five minutes. A total of 168 broadcasts were recorded and viewed in their entirety. Crime stories were transcribed and then content coded.

A reliable system of coding classification rules is needed in order to minimize subjective collection of content data (Beardsworth 1980; Holsti 1969; Krippendorff 1980; Weber 1990). A theme analysis of content was therefore completed using a modified version of coding rules from previous research (Graber 1980; Ericson, Baranek, and Chan 1991).[8]

Content was coded from all crime stories reported in a newspaper or an entire broadcast. Defining what constitutes a crime story is difficult—which partly explains why past research has found significant variation in the percentage of stories that concern crime (Cirino 1973; Cohen 1975; Davis 1952; Deutschman 1959; Gans 1979; Jones 1976; Lotz 1991; Meyer 1975; Roshier 1981). This study adopted a fairly broad definition, similar to that used in some past research (e.g., Graber 1980). Stories included were local, national, and international crime stories; stories about specific crime incidents; program stories (e.g., a story on shock incarceration or the efficiency of police sting operations); legislative activities that focused on specific aspects of criminal justice; and statistical reports of crime data. When the stories examined involved a specific crime incident, a clear violation of the law had to be contained in the information provided in order for them to be considered crime stories.

To be included, a newspaper crime story had to be over three column inches in length; a television story needed to be over ten seconds. For three reasons, stories that reported or mentioned crime incidents in a mere three or four sentences were excluded: First, because of the large number of variables collected for each story, excluding these small stories made the number of stories coded and the data set more manageable; second, previous research had employed a similar principle (Graber 1980); and third, these stories were not written as genuine stories and contained very little information. Since crime stories are easily put together, these crimes are fillers chosen for convenience and do not reflect what news reporters and the organization think is important about crime and its victims.

Using these definitional rules, 2,664 crime stories were coded for the content analysis. An additional 375 stories that involved accident, suicide, and auto accident victims were content coded so they could be compared with the media image of crime victims.

This study examined the presentation of crime victims in news stories. All individuals mentioned in a crime story as suffering directly or indirectly as a result of crime were included as victims. Victim data were collected on both primary and secondary victims when they were mentioned. Primary victims are those who suffer directly from a crime; for example, a man who was shot and killed. Secondary victims suffer indirectly from crime; for example, the wife and child of the man who was shot would both be coded as secondary victims if cited in the story.

At times, it was difficult to identify whether an individual noted in a crime story was a victim or a defendant. Sometimes defendants could be considered victims or vice versa. Consider stories involving vigilantes or battered women who murder their abusers. Bernard Goetz was a vigilante who prevented his victimization by shooting at four youths attempting to rob him. He was eventually convicted on a gun charge. The news media presented Goetz as both a victim and a defendant. The key determining factor of who was coded a victim was whether the media portrayed the person as violating the law or as suffering as the result of a crime. In a story about the sentencing of a battered woman who was convicted of killing her husband, for example, the woman's characteristics were coded under defendant.

Ethnography

Ethnographic observation of the crime news-production process was conducted in one newspaper and one television station in a large metropolitan city.[9] Observing across media overcomes the shortcomings of previous research (Ericson, Baranek, and Chan 1987; Garafalo 1981). The ethnographic aspect of this research provides extensive background knowledge about the crime newsmaking process, the relationships within news organizations, and the ways victims and other outsiders are included in crime stories. The ethnographic observations also help to clarify the results produced by content analysis.

The newspaper ethnography took place in summer 1991 at an organization referred to as the *Midwest Tribune*. The *Midwest Tribune* has been reporting news for over 150 years. This newspaper is a large organization with a daily circulation of about 500,000 papers and had recently expanded by building new production facilities, hiring additional staff, and opening suburban news bureaus (*Tribune* Document 1: 1).

Similarly, observations were conducted at a television station in the same city, referred to as the Midwest Nightly. In this city, four broadcast organizations were competing for the nightly television audience. Three of these stations were network affiliated, and one was an independent news station. All four stations were approached in an effort to gain access. The independent station, however, was the only one comfortable with allowing an outsider access to the newsmaking process.

A number of differences between the independent and affiliated stations should be noted. Even though the station observed is among "the top independent news programs in the country" (Arbitron 1991), the observed station had fewer resources available to produce news than did the affiliated stations. This affected the station's ability to "scoop" the other stations and limited its coverage of spot, late-breaking news.

Moreover, this station produced a single one-hour newscast an evening that aired at ten o'clock. The three affiliated stations produced half-hour shows that aired at noon, six o'clock, and eleven o'clock. This gave the independent station the luxury of watching the affiliated news programs and piecing together stories it might have missed.

The most important similarity between the Midwest Nightly and the other affiliated stations was found in the crime news-production processes. Nightly reporters made routine police calls, contacted all relevant sources, and collected sound bites in a similar manner to news production at the affiliated stations. Thus, although there were some differences, I was aware of them and made them a point of inquiry when observing reporters. Most of the reporters at the Nightly had previously worked at some affiliated station and were able to point out how coverage there might differ. Moreover, when interviewing editors and reporters from the affiliated stations—which was the level of access obtained—I asked what they thought some of the differences might be and whether the size of the Nightly affected what news was produced.

Observations occurred across a variety of days, weekends, and hours. The majority of crime stories were produced between eleven a.m. and seven o'clock p.m. at the newspaper, and between three and ten o'clock p.m. at the television station. Most of the observations occurred during these shifts. Some late evenings were spent at the newspaper and early mornings at the television station, however, to see as much of the production process as possible. Approximately 150 hours were spent in each news agency.

Interviews

Forty interviews were conducted to assist with the interpretation of the observational data. Twenty lengthy interviews with crime beat reporters and editors working for the *Midwest Tribune* and the Midwest Nightly accompanied the observational data collected from those organizations. In addition to specific questions about the production process, more structured, open-ended interviews with reporters were conducted for a broader perspective on how each media organization produced stories on crime. Fifteen interviews with reporters and editors from other organizations were also conducted. Some of these were done informally at crime scenes, where several news organizations might gather. This allowed me to gather information from a variety of different-sized organizations and to see how their coverage of crime compared with that observed at the Nightly and the *Tribune*. In addition, I had the opportunity to interview five different sources (both criminal justice and victim) used by the news media in the production of story information. This gave me some preliminary insights into their perspective on what role they play in the production of news.

Notes

1. Determined from a directory of media publications (Koek, K. E., and Winklepack, J. 1990. *Gale Directory of Publications and Broadcast Media*. New York: Gale Research, Inc.).

2. Medium-sized cities are defined as those with between 100,000 and 400,000 inhabitants and between 5,000 and 50,000 index offenses. Large cities have populations of at least 400,000, but no more than 800,000, with the number of index

offenses between 50,000 and 90,000. Extra-large cities have populations between 800,000 and 1,500,000, with the number of index offenses committed between 90,000 and 150,000.

    3. The newspapers in Dallas and Detroit had both morning and afternoon editions. Only the morning editions were coded so they could be directly compared with the newspapers from the other cities.

    4. Technically, none of the cities has a single paper. National press such as the *Wall Street Journal* and *USA Today* compete directly with these papers. In addition, other local newspapers (e.g., suburban weeklies) are also available. This is a study of the presentation of victims in local media. Of the local media considered, Albany, Buffalo, and Cleveland had one newspaper that fit the criteria for inclusion; Dallas, Detroit, and San Francisco had two. The newspaper with the highest daily circulation was selected from each of the cities with two papers.

    5. Every-fifth-day samples were selected based on research that indicates that these samples do not differ significantly from figures for the entire month (Mintz, A. 1949. "The Feasibility of the Use of Samples in Content Analysis." In H. D. Lasswell, N. Leiter, R. Fedner, J. M. Goldsen, A. Gray, J. L. Jones, A. Kaplan, D. Kaplan, A. Mintz, I. De Sola Pool, and S. Yakolsee (eds.), *The Language of Politics: Studies in Quantitative Semantics* (pp. 127-152). New York: George Stewart).

    6. The reason for choosing the eleven o'clock or late-evening news instead of the six o'clock news was that their crime stories were thought to be more representative of those the news organization felt were important for that *entire* day.

    7. The ratings were obtained from the *Television and Cable Factbook*. (Warren Publishing, Inc. 1991. *Television and Cable Factbook*. Washington, D.C.: Warren Publishing, Inc.).

    8. A copy of the codebook is available from the author.

    9. See footnote 2, Appendix.

References

Acker, J. R. 1992. "Social Sciences and the Criminal Law: Victims of Crime—Plight vs. Rights." *Criminal Law Bulletin*, 28(1): 64–77.

Altheide, D. 1984. "TV News and the Social Construction of Justice: Research Issues and Policy." In R. Surette (ed.), *Justice and the Media* (pp. 292–304). Springfield, Ill: Charles C. Thomas.

——— 1976. *Creating Reality: How TV News Distorts Events*. Beverly Hills: Sage.

Altschull, J. H. 1984. *Agents of Power: The Role of the News Media in Human Affairs*. New York: Longman.

American Bar Association. 1988. *Criminal Justice in Crisis*. Washington, D.C.: American Bar Association.

Anderson, J. R., and Woodard, P. L. 1985. "Victim and Witness Assistance: New State Laws and the System's Response." *Judicature*, 68(6): 221–244.

Arbitron Television. 1991. *ADI Book*. Beltsville: Arbitron.

Ash, M. 1972. "On Witnesses: A Radical Critique of Criminal Court Procedures." *Notre Dame Lawyer*, 48: 386.

Bailey, W. C. 1990. "Murder, Capital Punishment, and Television: Execution Publicity and Homicide Rates." *American Sociological Review*, 55: 628–633.

Bailey, W. C., and Peterson, R.D. 1989. "Murder and Capital Punishment: A Monthly Time–Series Analysis of Execution Publicity." *American Sociological Review*, 54: 722–743.

Barak, G. 1994. *Media, Process, and the Social Construction of Crime: Studies in Newsmaking Criminology*. New York: Garland Publishing, Inc.

——— 1988. "Newsmaking Criminology: Reflections on the Media, Intellectuals and Crime." *Justice Quarterly*, 5(4): 565–587.

Bard, M. 1985. "Unblaming the Victim." *Social Policy* (Winter): 43–46.

Bard, M., and Sangrey, D. 1986. *The Crime Victim's Book*. New York: Brunner/Mazel.

Beardsworth, A. 1980. "Analyzing Press Content: Some Technical and Methodological Issues." In Harvey Christian (ed.), *The Sociology of Journalism and the Press* (pp. 371–395). Totowa, N.J.: Rowman and Littlefield.

Belenko, S., Fagan, J., and Chin, K. L. 1991. "Criminal Justice Responses to Crack." *Journal of Research in Crime and Delinquency*, 28(1): 55–74.

Berk, R. A., Brookman, H., and Lesser, S. L. 1977. *A Measure of Justice: An Empirical Study of Changes in the California Penal Code 1955-1971.* New York: Academic Press.

Bittner, J. R.   1989.   *Mass Communication: An Introduction* (5th ed). Englewood Cliffs, NJ: Prentice Hall.

Block, R.   1974.   "Why Notify the Police: The Victim's Decision to Notify the Police of an Assault." *Criminology,* 11: 555–569.

Bureau of Justice Statistics. 1994. *Criminal Victimization in the United States, 1992.* Washington, D.C.: U.S. Department of Justice.

Cannavale, F. J., and Falcon, W. D. 1976. *Witness Cooperation.* Lexington, Mass.: D. C. Heath.

Carrington, F., and Nicholson, G. 1989. "Victims' Rights: An Idea Whose Time Has Come–Five Years Later: The Maturing of an Idea." *Pepperdine Law Review,* 17(1): 1–18.

——— 1984. "The Victims' Movement: An Idea Whose Time Has Come." *Pepperdine Law Review,* 11: 1–13.

Chaffee, S.   1975.   *Political Communication: Enduring Issues for Research.* Newbury Park, Calif.: Sage Publications.

Chibnall, S. 1980. "The Social History of Crime Reporting." In H. Christian (ed.), *The Sociology of Journalism and the Press* (pp. 179–217). Totowa, N.J.: Rowman and Littlefield.

——— 1977. *Law and Order News.* London: Tavistock.

Cirino, R. 1973. "Bias Through Selection and Omission." In Stanley Cohen and Jock Young (eds.), *The Manufacture of News: Deviance, Social Problems and the Mass Media* (pp. 40–62). London: Constable.

Cohen, S. 1975. "A Comparison of Crime Coverage in Detroit and Atlanta Newspapers." *Journalism Quarterly,* 52(4): 726–730.

——— 1972. *Folk Devils and Moral Panics.* London: MacGibbon and Kee.

Cohen, S., and Young, J., eds. 1981. *The Manufacture of News: Deviance, Social Problems and the Mass Media.* London: Constable.

Cole, G.   1992. *The American System of Criminal Justice* (6th ed.).   Pacific Grove, Calif.: Brooks/Cole Publishing Company.

Conklin, J. E. 1975. *The Impact of Crime.* New York: Macmillan Publishing.

Cumberbatch, G., and Beardsworth, A. 1976. "Criminals, Victims, and Mass Communications." In E. C. Viano (ed.), *Victims and Society* (pp. 72–90). Washington, D.C.: Visage Press.

Datatimes. 1992. *Datatimes.* Oklahoma City: Datatimes.

Davis, F. J. 1952. "Crime News in Colorado Newspapers." *American Journal of Sociology,* 57: 325–330.

Deutschmann, P. J. 1959. *News Page Content of Twelve Metropolitan Dailies.* Cincinnati: Scripps–Howard Research.

Dobb, A., and MacDonald, G. 1979. "Television Viewing and Fear of Victimization: Is the Relationship Causal?" *Journal of Personality and Social Psychology,* 37: 170–179.

Einstadter, W. J. 1979. "Crime News in the Old West: Social Control in a Northwestern Town, 1887–1888." *Urban Life,* 8: 317–334.

Elias, R. 1986. *The Politics of Victimization: Victims, Victimology, and Human Rights.* New York: Oxford University Press.

Epstein, B. 1974. *News from Nowhere.* New York: Vintage.

Ericson, R. V. 1991. "Mass Media, Crime, Law and Justice: An Institutional Approach." *British Journal of Criminology,* 31(3): 219–249.

Ericson, R. V., Baranek, P. M., and Chan, J. B. L. 1991. *Representing Order: Crime, Law, and Justice in the News Media.* Toronto: University of Toronto Press.

——— 1989. *Negotiating Control: A Study of News Sources.* Toronto: University of Toronto Press.

——— 1987. *Visualizing Deviance: A Study of News Organization.* Toronto: University of Toronto Press.

Evans, S. S., and Lundman, R. J. 1983. "Newspaper Coverage of Corporate Price-Fixing." *Criminology,* 21(4): 529–541.

Fattah, E. A., and Sacco, V. F. 1989. *Crime and Victimization of the Elderly.* New York: Springer–Verlag.

Fisher, G. 1989. "Mass Media Effects on Sex Role Attitudes of Incarcerated Men." *Sex Roles: A Journal of Research,* 20: 191–203.

Fishman, M. 1980. *Manufacturing the News.* Austin: University of Texas Press.

——— 1978. "Crime Waves as Ideology." *Social Problems,* 25: 531–543.

Forst, B. E., and Hernon, J. C. 1985. "The Criminal Justice Response to Victim Harm." Research in Brief, National Institute of Justice. Washington, D. C.: U.S. Department of Justice.

Forst, M. L., and Blomquist, M. 1991. *Missing Children: Rhetoric and Reality.* New York: Lexington Books.

Friendly, A., and Goldfarb, R.L. 1967. *Crime and Publicity: The Impact of News on the Administration of Justice.* New York: Twentieth Century Fund.

Gans, H. 1979. *Deciding What's News: A Study of CBS Evening News, Newsweek and Time.* New York: Pantheon Books.

Garafalo, J. 1981. "Crime and the Mass Media: A Selective Review of Research." *Journal of Research in Crime and Delinquency,* 18: 319–350.

Garafalo, J., and Laub, J. 1978. "The Fear of Crime: Broadening Our Perspective." *Victimology,* 3: 242–253.

Gibbons, T. 1988. "Victims Again: Survivors Suffer Through Capital Appeals." *American Bar Association Journal* (September), 1: 64–68.

Gitlin, T. 1980. *The Whole World Is Watching: Mass Media in the Making & Unmaking of the New Left.* Los Angeles: University of California Press.

Gittler, J. 1984. "Expanding the Role of the Victim in a Criminal Action: An Overview of Issues and Problems." *Pepperdine Law Review*, 11: 117–182.

Gordon, M., and Heath, L. 1981. "The News Business, Crime and Fear." In D. Lewis (ed.), *Reactions to Crime*. (pp. 227–250). Beverly Hills: Sage Publications.

Gottfredson, G. D. 1989. "The Experiences of Violent and Serious Victimization. In N. A. Weiner and M. E. Wolfgang (eds.), *Pathways to Criminal Violence* (pp. 202–234). Newbury Park, Calif.: Sage Publications.

Gottfredson, M. R. and Gottfredson, D. M. 1988. *Decision Making in Criminal Justice*. Cambridge: Ballinger.

Graber, D. 1980. *Crime News and the Public*. New York: Praeger Publishers.

Grabosky, P., and Wilson, P. 1989. *Journalism and Justice: How Crime Is Reported*. Leichhardt: Pluto Press.

Greenwood, P., and Petersilia, J. 1977. *The Criminal Investigative Process*. Lexington, Mass.: Heath and Company.

Gusfield, J. 1981. *The Culture of Public Problems*. Chicago: University of Chicago Press.

Hagan, J. 1982. "Victims Before the Law: A Study of Victim Involvement in the Criminal Justice Process." *Journal of Criminal Law and Criminology*, 73: 317–330.

Hall, S., Critcher, C., Jefferson, T., Clarke, J., and B. Roberts. 1978. *Policing the Crisis*. London: Macmillan.

Hartley, J. 1982. *Understanding News*. London: Methuen.

Haskins, J. B., and Miller, M. M. 1984. "The Effects of Bad News and Good News on a Newspaper's Image." *Journalism Quarterly*, 61(1): 3–13, 65.

Hawkins, R. O. 1973. "Who Called the Cops? Decisions to Report Criminal Victimization." *Law and Society Review*, 7: 427–444.

Heath, L. 1984. "Impact of Newspaper Crime Reports on Fear of Crime." *Journal of Personality and Social Psychology*, 47 (August): 263–276.

Hecht, B. 1954. *A Child of the Century*. New York: Simon and Schuster.

Hollinger, R., and Lanza–Kaduce, L. 1988. "The Process of Criminalization: The Case of Computer Crime Laws." *Criminology*, 26: 101–126.

Holsti, O. 1969. *Content Analysis for the Social Sciences and Humanities*. Reading, Mass: Addison–Wesley Publishing Company.

Hudson, P. S. 1984. "The Crime Victim and the Criminal Justice System: Time for a Change." *Pepperdine Law Review*, 11: 23–62.

Hulteng, J. L., and Nelson, R. P. 1971. *The Fourth Estate: An Informal Appraisal of the News and Opinion Media*. New York: Harper & Row.

Humphries, D. 1981. "Serious Crime, News Coverage, and Ideology: A Content Analysis of Crime Coverage in a Metropolitan Paper." *Crime and Delinquency*, 27(2): 191–205.

Iyengar, S. 1991. *Is Anyone Responsible? How Television Frames Political Issues*. Chicago: University of Chicago Press.

Jacob, H., and R. L. Lineberry. 1982. *Governmental Responses to Crime: Crime and Governmental Responses in American Cities.* Washington, D.C.: U.S. Department of Justice.

Jamieson, K. H., and Campbell, K. K. 1983. *The Interplay of Influence: Mass Media & Their Publics in News, Advertising, Politics.* Belmont, Calif.: Wadsworth Publishing Company.

Jones, E. T. 1976. "The Press as Metropolitan Monitor." *Public Opinion Quarterly,* 40(2): 239–244.

Kaniss, P. 1991. *Making Local News.* Chicago: University of Chicago Press.

Karmen, A. 1990 [1984]. *Crime Victims: An Introduction to Victimology* (2d ed.). Monterey: Brooks/Cole.

Koek, K. E., and Winklepack, J. 1990. *Gale Directory of Publications and Broadcast Media.* New York: Gale Research, Inc.

Krippendorff, K. 1980. *Content Analysis: An Introduction to Its Methodology.* Beverly Hills: Sage Publications.

Lasswell, H. 1948. "The Structure and Function of Communication in Society." In L. Bryson (ed.), *The Communication of Ideas.* (pp. 243–276). New York: Institute for Religious and Social Studies.

Lee–Sammons, L. 1989. *Television News Reporting of Crime: An Analysis of Three Models of Newsmaking.* Ph.D. Dissertation, Washington State University. Ann Arbor: University Microfilms International.

Levinson, A. 1992. "More States OK Victims' Rights Bills." *Times–Picayune,* 8 November 1992: A8.

Lotz, R. E. 1991. *Crime and the American Press.* New York: Praeger Publishers.

Marsh, H. L. 1991. "A Comparative Analysis of Crime Coverage in Newspapers in the United States and Other Countries from 1960–1989: A Review of the Literature." *Journal of Criminal Justice,* 19: 67–79.

——— 1989. "Newspaper Crime Coverage in the U.S.: 1893–1988." *Criminal Justice Abstracts,* 506–514.

——— 1988. *Crime and the Press: Does Newspaper Crime Coverage Support Myths About Crime and Law Enforcement?* Ph.D. Dissertation, Sam Houston State University. Ann Arbor: University Microfilms International.

Mawby, R. I., and Brown, J. 1984. "Newspaper Images of the Victim: A British Study." *Victimology,* 9(1): 82–94.

McDonald, W. F. 1977. "The Role of the Victim in America." In Randy E. Barnett and John Hagel III (eds.), *Assessing the Criminal: Restitution and the Legal Process* (pp. 295–307). Cambridge: Ballinger Publishing Company.

——— 1976. "Towards a Bicentennial Revolution in Criminal Justice." *American Criminal Law Review,* 13: 649–673.

McGarrell, E. F. 1988. *Juvenile Correctional Reform: Two Decades of Policy and Procedural Change.* Albany: State University of New York Press.

McGarrell, E. F., and Castellano, T. C. 1991. "An Integrative Model of the Criminal Law Formation Process." *Journal of Research in Crime and Delinquency*, 28(2): 174–196.

McGuire, W. 1986. "The Myth of Massive Media Impact: Savagings and Salvagings." In G. Comstock (ed.), *Public Communication and Behavior* (pp. 175–257). New York: Academic Press.

Mendlesohn, B. 1963. "The Origin of the Doctrine of Victimology." In I. Drapkin and E. Viano (eds.), *Victimology* (pp. 3–11). Lexington, Mass.: Lexington Books.

Meyer, J. C. Jr. 1975. "Newspaper Reporting of Crime and Justice: Analysis of an Assumed Difference." *Journalism Quarterly*, 52(4): 731–734.

Mintz, A. 1949. "The Feasibility of the Use of Samples in Content Analysis." In H. D. Lasswell, N. Leiter, R. Fedner, J. M. Goldsen, A. Gray, J. L. Jones, A. Kaplan, D. Kaplan, A. Mintz, I. De Sola Pool, and S. Yakolsee (eds.), *The Language of Politics: Studies in Quantitative Semantics* (pp. 127–152). New York: George Stewart.

Morash, M., and Hale, D. 1987. "Unusual Crime or Crime as Unusual Images of Corruption at the Interstate Commerce Commission." In Timothy S. Bynum (ed.), *Organized Crime in America: Concepts and Controversies* (pp. 129–149). Monsey, N.Y.: Criminal Justice Press.

National Organization for Victim Assistance. 1988. *Victims Rights' and Services: A Legislative Directory 1987.* Washington, D.C.: National Organization for Victim Assistance.

——— 1983. *Campaign for Victim Rights/1983: A Practical Guide.* Washington, D.C.

Newman, G. R. 1990. "Popular Culture and Criminal Justice: A Preliminary Analysis." *Journal of Criminal Justice*, 18: 261–274.

Office for Victims of Crime. 1988. *Report to Congress.* Washington, D.C.: U.S. Department of Justice.

Pasqua, T. M., Buckalew, J. K., Rayfield, R. E., and Tankard, J. W. 1990. *Mass Media in the Information Age.* Englewood Cliffs: Prentice Hall.

Postman, N. 1985. *Amusing Ourselves to Death: Public Discourse in the Age of Show Business.* New York: Viking.

President's Commission on Law Enforcement and Administration of Justice. (1967). *The Challenge of Crime in a Free Society.* Washington, D.C.: U.S. Government Printing Office.

——— 1967. *Task Force Report: Crime and Its Impact.* Washington, D.C.: U.S. Government Printing Office.

Presidents Task Force on Victims of Crime. 1982. *Final Report.* Washington, D.C.: U.S. Government Printing Office.

Pritchard, D. 1986. "Homicide and Bargained Justice: The Agenda–Setting Effect of Crime News on Prosecutors." *Public Opinion Quarterly*, 50: 143–159.

Protess, D., Leff, D., Brooks, S., and Gordon, M. 1985. "Uncovering Rape: The Watchdog Press and the Limits of Agenda Setting." *Public Opinion Quarterly*, 49: 19–37.

Quinney, R. 1970. *The Social Reality of Crime*. Boston: Little Brown.

Reiss, A. 1971. *The Police and the Public*. New Haven: Yale University Press.

Roland, D. L. 1989. "Progress in the Victim Reform Movement: No Longer the 'Forgotten' Victim." *Pepperdine Law Review*, 17(1): 35–58.

Roshier, B. 1981. "The Selection of Crime News by the Press." In Stanley Cohen and Jock Young (eds.), *The Manufacture of News: Social Problems, Deviance and the Mass Media* (pp. 40–51). Beverly Hills: Sage Publications.

Sacco, V. 1982. "The Effects of Mass Media on Perceptions of Crime." *Pacific Sociological Review*, 25: 475–493.

Seymour, A. 1986. "Victim Advocate Suggests Code for Journalists." In T. Thomason and A. Babbili (eds.), *Crime Victims and the News Media* (pp. 31–33). Forth Worth: A National Symposium sponsored by The Texas Christian University Department of Journalism and the Gannett Foundation.

Sheley, J. F., and Ashkins, C. D. 1981. "Crime, Crime News, and Crime Views." *Public Opinion Quarterly*, 45(4): 492–506.

Sherizen, S. 1978. "Social Creation of Crime News: All the News Fitted to Print." In C. Winick (ed.), *Deviance and Mass Media* (pp. 203–224). Beverly Hills: Sage Publications.

Sherman, L. W. 1990. "Police Crackdowns: Initial and Residual Deterrence." In Michael Tonry and Norval Morris (eds.), *Crime and Justice: An Annual Review of Research* (pp. 1–48). Chicago: University of Chicago Press.

Shoemaker, P. J., and Reese, S. D. 1991. *Mediating the Message: Theories of Influences on Mass Media Content*. New York: Longman.

Siebert, F. S., Peterson, T. B., and Schramm, W. 1956. *Four Theories of the Press*. Urbana: University of Illinois Press.

Skogan, W. G., and Maxfield, M. G. 1981. *Coping with Crime: Individual and Neighborhood Reactions*. Beverly Hills: Sage Publications.

Skogan, W. G., Lurigio, A. J., and Davis, R. C. 1990. "Criminal Victimization." In Arthur J. Lurigio, Wesley G. Skogan, and Robert C. Davis (eds.), *Victims of Crime: Problems, Policies and Programs* (pp. 7–22). Newbury Park: Sage Publications.

Smith, D. A. 1986. "The Plea Bargaining Controversy." *Journal of Criminal Law and Criminology*, 77(3): 949–968.

Smith, S. R., and Freinkel, S. 1988. *Adjusting the Balance: Federal Policy and Victim Services*. New York: Greenwood Press.

Sotomayer, E. 1986. "A Victim's Race: Does It Make a Difference?" In T. Thomason and A. Babbili (eds.), *Crime Victims and the News Media* (pp. 11–14). Fort Worth: A National Symposium sponsored by The Texas Christian University Department of Journalism and the Gannett Foundation.

Spelman, W., and Brown, D. K. 1981. *Calling the Police: Citizen Reporting of Serious Crime.* Washington, D.C.: Police Executive Research Forum.

Stack, S. 1987. "Publicized Executions and Homicide, 1950–1980." *American Sociological Review,* 52: 532–540.

Stanley, H. W., and Niemi, G. G. 1988. *Vital Statistics on American Politics.* Washington, D.C.: Congressional Quarterly.

Stark, J. H., and Goldstein, H. W. 1985. *The Rights of Crime Victims.* New York: Bantam Books.

Surette, R. 1992. *Media, Crime, and Criminal Justice: Images and Realities.* Pacific Grove, California: Brooks/Cole Publishing Company.

——— 1989. "Media Trials." *Journal of Criminal Justice,* 17: 293–308.

Taylor, S. E., Wood, J. V., and Lichtman, R. R. 1983. "It Could Be Worse: Selective Evaluation as a Response to Victimization." *Journal of Social Issues,* 39: 19–40.

Tuchman, G. 1978. *Making News: A Study in the Construction of Reality.* New York: The Free Press.

——— 1973. "Making News by Doing Work: Routinizing the Unexpected." *American Journal of Sociology,* 79(1): 110–131.

Tunstall, J. 1971. *Journalists at Work.* London: Constable.

Viano, E. 1987. "Victim's Rights and the Constitution: Reflections on a Bicentennial." *Crime and Delinquency,* 33: 438–451.

Von Hentig, H. 1948. *The Criminal and His Victim.* New Haven: Yale University Press.

Voumvakis, S., and Ericson, R. 1984. *News Accounts of Attacks on Women: A Comparison of Three Toronto Newspapers.* Toronto: Centre of Criminology, University of Toronto.

Walker, S. 1989. *Sense and Nonsense about Crime: A Policy Guide* (2d ed.). Pacific Grove, Calif.: Brooks/Cole Publishing Company.

Warren Publishing Inc. 1991. *Television and Cable Factbook.* Washington, D.C.: Warren Publishing Inc.

Weaver, D., Drew, D., and Wilhoit, G. C. 1986. "U.S. Television, Radio and Daily Newspaper Journalists." *Journalism Quarterly,* 63: 683–692.

Weber, R. P. 1990. *Basic Content Analysis.* Newbury Park: Sage Publications.

Wickersham Commission Reports. 1931. *Report on Police.* Washington, D.C.: U.S. Government Printing Office. Report no. 14.

Willis, W. J. 1990. *Journalism: State of the Art.* New York: Praeger Publishers.

Wilson, J. Q., and Herrnstein, R. J. 1985. *Crime and Human Nature.* New York: Touchstone Books.

Wilson, J. V., and Fuqua, P. Q. 1975. *The Police and the Media.* Boston: Little Brown.

Wilson, W. 1991. *Good Murders and Bad Murders: A Consumer's Guide in the Age of Information.* New York: University Press of America.

Windhauser, J. W., Seiter, J., and Winfree, L. T. 1990. "Crime News in the Louisiana Press, 1980 vs. 1985." *Journalism Quarterly,* 67: 72–78.

Wolf, R., Thomason, T., and LaRocque, P. 1991. "The Right to Know vs. the Right of Privacy: Newspaper Identification of Crime Victims." *Journalism Quarterly,* 67: 503–507.

Wolfgang, M. 1958. *Patterns of Criminal Homicide.* Philadelphia: University of Pennsylvania Press.

Young, M.A. 1989. "Emerging Issues in Victim Assistance." *Pepperdine Law Review,* 17(1): 129–143.

Ziegenhagen, E. A. 1977. *Victims, Crime, and Social Control.* New York: Praeger Publishers.

About the Book and Author

The portrayal of crime victims in the news media has played a significant role in stimulating political and public concern regarding their treatment in the criminal justice system over the past three decades. Using content analysis of nearly 3,000 crime stories and in-depth ethnographies conducted at a midwestern city daily newspaper and an urban television station, Steven M. Chermak examines the presentation of crime victims in newspaper and television media, providing insights into the images generated about crime and its victims. Exploring how victims are presented in the media and how the media exploit certain characteristics and reactions to sell news, Chermak discusses the implications of presenting victims this way and considers how this practice may alter public knowledge of crime.

Steven M. Chermak is assistant professor in the Department of Criminal Justice at Indiana University–Bloomington.

Index

Advertising, 22–23, 138, 153
Age
    and crime newsworthiness, 63, 67, 79–
        82, 86, 129, 169, 175
    of defendants, 60(table), 77(table), 79,
        80, 82, 127(table), 158(table)
    of victims, 59, 60(table), 62, 65(table),
        126, 127(table), 155(table), 162–163,
        166, 174
Albany, 135(table)
    crime news in, 134, 136(table),
        137(table), 138–139, 140(table),
        141(table), 142–143, 152–153
    sources in, 145(table), 147(table),
        148(table), 149(table)
Albany Times-Union, 138
AP. *See* Associated Press
Ashkins, C. D., 24, 110, 119
Associated Press (AP), 14
Audience, 23–24, 28, 32, 111, 165

Barak, Gregg, 177
Baranek, P. M., 19, 30, 95, 119–120, 122
Barry, Marion, 38, 56, 130
Beardsworth, A., 5
Blomquist, M., 4
Boesky, Ivan, 47, 57, 121
Brooks, S., 5
Brown, J., 80
Buffalo, 135(table)
    crime news in, 136(table), 137(table),
        139, 140(table), 141(table), 142–143,
        152–153
    sources in, 145(table), 147(table),
        148(table), 149(table)

Cable News Network (CNN), 18, 45

Celebrities, 47
Chan, J.B.L., 19, 30, 95, 119–120, 122
Chicago Tribune, 24
Child abuse, 81, 170
Children, as victims, 8, 10, 51(table),
        54(table), 59, 86–87, 120, 178. *See
        also* Age
Citizens Against Crime, 18
City size, 186(n2)
    and crime index, 135(table), 186(n2)
    and crime news, 139, 141(table), 142–
        144, 150–153, 160–161(table), 162–
        166
    and defendant image, 151–153, 157–
        159(table), 164, 166
    and sources, 146, 147(table), 148(table),
        149(table), 150, 166
    and victim image, 151–153, 154–
        156(table), 162–164, 166, 175
Cleveland, 135(table)
    crime news in, 134, 136(table),
        137(table), 138–139, 140(table),
        141(table)
    sources in, 145(table), 147(table),
        148(table), 149(table)
CNN. *See* Cable News Network
Cohen, S., 133
Comprehensive Crime Control Act, 7
Content analysis, 2–3, 13–14, 21, 183
    methodology of, 83(nn 8, 9), 166(n2),
        183–185, 187(nn 4, 5, 6)
Courts, 33, 37, 45
    and media format, 123, 124(table), 125
    in news, 21, 22(table), 111–112, 116–
        117
    and reporters, 16–17, 19, 21, 25–27,
        86–87, 116–117

as source, 29(table), 85, 89(table), 90,
    92(table), 95, 98, 147(table),
    148(table), 149(table), 171
  See also Criminal justice system
Crime index, 135(table), 186(n2)
Crime news, 1–6, 11–13, 21–24
  and city size, 139, 141(table), 142–144,
    150–153, 160–161(table), 162–166
  crime impact in, 70, 71–72(table), 73,
    153, 160–161(table), 164–165, 170
  crime information in, 122–123,
    124(table), 125–126, 169
  and crime rate, 133–134, 142–144
  crime types in, 47(table), 50(table), 51–
    52(table), 53, 54(table), 55–57,
    140(table)
  crime waves in, 4, 12(n3)
  limitations of, 151, 170–172, 176–177
  local, 138–139, 142, 144, 146, 154–
    161(tables), 162, 165–166, 175
  marketing of, 23–24, 28, 32, 111, 171–
    172
  and media format. *See* Media format
  prevalence of, 43, 47, 48(table),
    49(table), 134, 136(table), 137–139
  production of. *See* News production
  study of, 1–5, 183
  societal role of, 167–168, 176–177
  sources for. *See* Sources
  status checks in, 44–45
  story levels in, 32–33, 34–35(table), 36–
    41, 53, 64–66(table), 68–69, 71–
    72(table), 76–78(table), 79–80
  story selection in, 18–19, 22, 24–25,
    31–32, 40–41, 49. *See also*
    Newsworthiness
Crime rate, 6, 133–134, 142–144, 151, 175
Crimes, 11–13
  bias-related, 8, 52(table), 53, 54(table)
  categories of, 49, 50(table), 53
  domestic, 52(table), 53
  impact of, 70, 71–72(table), 73, 130,
    131(table), 153, 160–161(table), 164–
    165, 170
  newsworthiness of, 24, 27–28, 32, 44–
    46, 53, 54(table), 55–57, 168
  property, 24, 67, 73

  sources for, 89(table), 90, 94–95, 122–
    123, 124(table), 125–126, 146,
    147(table), 150, 169
  against special groups, 118(table), 119–
    120, 125–126, 132, 140(table)
  victimless, 51(table), 53, 54(table), 57,
    118(table), 140(table)
  violent, 119, 133, 142, 172
  white-collar. *See* White-collar crimes
  See also individual crimes
Criminal justice system, 24, 29, 30(table),
    36–37, 153
  crimes against, 51(table), 53, 54(table),
    118(table), 121, 140(table), 164
  and media format, 116–117, 123, 125
  media relations with, 4, 9, 20–21,
    22(table), 168–169, 176–178
  as source, 19–21, 34–35(table), 41(n3),
    97–98, 132, 170–171, 174–177
  victims in, 5–9, 67, 85, 169
  See also Courts; Police
Cumberbatch, G., 4

Dahmer, Jeffrey, 39–41, 44–46, 75, 105,
    179
Dallas, 135(table), 152–153, 175
  crime news in, 134, 136(table),
    137(table), 138–139, 140(table),
    141(table), 142–143
  sources in, 145(table), 147(table),
    148(table), 149(table)
Defendants
  characteristics of, 58–59, 60–61(table),
    75, 76–78(table), 79–82, 126, 127–
    128(table), 130, 157–159(table)
  information sources for, 89(table), 90–
    91, 94–95, 122, 124(table), 126, 146,
    149(table), 150
  and media format, 122, 124(table), 126,
    127–128(table), 129–130
  naming of, 153, 157(table), 162
  newsworthiness of, 25, 58, 59, 74, 79,
    82, 151–153, 164
  as source, 89(table), 90, 92(table),
    124(table), 147(table), 148(table),
    149(table)

victim relationship to, 80–81, 93, 128(table), 155(table)
Detroit, 135(table)
  crime news in, 136(table), 137(table), 139, 140(table), 141(table), 143, 152–153, 175
  sources in, 145(table), 147(table), 148(table), 149(table)
Detroit News, 134, 137
Domestic violence, 8, 170
Drew, D., 25
Drugs, 51(table), 53, 54(table), 56–57

Editors, 31, 40
Elderly, 8, 63, 67, 81, 82, 86
Ericson, R. V., 19, 30, 95, 119–120, 122
Ethnography, 2–3, 183, 185–186
Evans, S. S., 57

Families, 89–90, 93–96, 125, 149–150, 166, 170, 172
Fishman, M., 4
Forst, M. L., 4
Freinkel, S., 180

Gender
  of defendants, 59, 60(table), 75, 76(table), 127(table), 157(table)
  of victims, 59, 60(table), 64(table), 127(table), 130, 154(table), 162, 166, 169
Genovese, Kitty, 9
Goetz, Bernard, 10, 185
Good Murders and Bad Murders (Wilson), 55
Gordon, M., 5
Graber, D., 3, 24, 56, 57, 133
Grabosky, P., 10

Hard Copy, 180
Harding, Tonya, 47
Hecht, Ben, 178
Herman, Pee Wee, 47
Hicks, Steven, 179
Homicide. *See* Murder

Hospitals, 90–91, 92(table), 93, 126, 147(table), 148(table), 149(table), 150–151
Houston Chronicle, 134
Hulteng, J. L., 168
Huntsville Item, 134

Ideology, 176–177
Interviews, 96, 100–103, 106, 183, 186

Jackson, Michael, 47
Jacob, H., 4

King, Rodney, 39, 130, 172

Leff, D., 5
Lineberry, R. L., 4
Lotz, R. E., 166(n1)
Lundman, R. J., 57

MADD. *See* Mothers Against Drunk Driving
Marital status, 58–59, 60–61(table), 62, 65(table), 78(table)
Marketing, 111, 171–172
Marsh, H. L., 133, 134
Mawby, R. I., 80
Maxfield, M. G., 133, 139
Media, 3–5, 12, 22–23, 167–169, 176–179
  competition between, 23, 104–105
  crime coverage by. *See* Crime news
  format of. *See* Media format
  marketing by, 165, 171–172, 180
  news production in. *See* News production
  as source, 14, 15(table), 144, 145(table), 175
  source use by, 88, 89(table), 94–95, 168, 170–172. *See also* Sources
  technology in, 180–181
Media format, 109–113, 121, 132
  and crime coverage, 113, 114(table), 115–117, 118(table), 119–122, 125–126, 130, 131(table), 132
  and defendants, 122, 124(table), 126, 127–128(table), 129–130

and source use, 111, 116–117, 121–123,
124(table), 125–126, 132, 132(n3),
173–175
and story types, 11, 139, 143, 173
and victims, 122, 124(table), 125–126,
127–128(table), 129–130, 131(table)
See also Newspapers; Television
Men, 162. *See also* Gender
Midwest Nightly, 2, 75, 87, 168, 179, 185–
186
news production at, 17–18, 37, 39–40,
44–47, 69–70, 111–113, 116–117
sources used by, 20, 28–29, 96, 100,
121, 123
Midwest Tribune, 2, 68, 73, 75, 79, 168–
169, 177
news production at, 19–20, 36–38, 40,
41(n3), 55–56, 112–113, 120, 142
readership of, 23, 185
reporters for, 14–17, 22–23, 25, 116–
117, 146, 172
sources used by, 28–29, 95–96, 98–99,
101–102, 107, 121, 123, 175
Milkin, Michael, 47, 57, 121
Mothers Against Drunk Driving (MADD),
7, 18
Murder, 93, 135(table), 151–152
coverage of, 51(table), 121, 133, 139,
140(table), 141–144, 150–153, 165–
166
and media format, 110, 117, 118(table),
119
newsworthiness of, 24, 53, 54(table),
55, 80, 82, 168, 173, 175

National Advisory Commission on
Criminal Justice Standards and Goals,
8
National Crime Victims' Week, 7
National Enquirer, 180
National Organization for Victim
Assistance, 7
Nelson, R. P., 168
Nesler, Ellie, 10
New York Times, 14, 18

News, 48(table), 49(table), 83(nn 2, 3),
136(table), 138–139. *See also* Crime
news; News production
Newspapers, 3, 11, 12(n1), 22–23, 111
crime impact in, 130, 131(table)
crime prevalence in, 113, 114(table),
115–117, 132, 134, 136(table), 137–
138, 173
crime types in, 118(table), 119–121,
140(table)
defendants in, 76–78(table), 124(table),
126, 127–128(table), 130
news-item sources in, 144, 145(table)
news production by, 14–17, 110, 112–
113
sources in, 13, 91, 92(table), 112, 122–
123, 124(table), 125–126, 132(n3),
173, 175
victims in, 64–66(table), 71–72(table),
126, 127–128(table), 129–130,
131(table)
white collar crimes in, 118(table), 120–
121, 130, 173
News production, 10–11, 13–14, 18–26,
28, 31–32, 40, 153
and media format, 109–113, 121
by newspapers, 14–17, 110, 112–113
story levels in, 32–33, 34–35(table), 36–
41, 174
story types in, 47(table), 51–52(table),
53, 54(table), 55–57
by television, 18, 44–46, 111–113, 116,
186
victim influence on, 1, 11, 27, 85–86,
178
Newsworthiness, 1, 24–28, 88, 91, 168,
176
and city size, 151–152
and crime impact, 70, 71–72(table), 73,
87, 165, 170, 174
of crime types, 24, 27–28, 32, 44–46,
53, 54(table), 55–57, 168
of defendants, 25, 58–59, 74, 79, 82,
151–153, 164
and media format, 109–110, 113, 132
of murder, 24, 53, 55, 80, 82, 168, 173,
175

of occupations, 67, 87, 129, 152, 163–164, 169–170, 175
and victim age, 63, 67, 79–82, 86, 129, 169, 175
and victim behavior, 93–100, 103–104, 107, 151–152, 162–163
of victims, 58–59, 60–61(table), 85–87, 169–170, 174–175, 180
Noriega, Manual, 56

Occupations
of defendants, 58–59, 60–61(table), 75, 77(table), 79, 81–82, 128(table), 129, 158–159(table), 164
newsworthy, 67, 87, 129, 152, 163–164, 169–170, 175
of victims, 58–59, 60–61(table), 62, 66(table), 128(table), 129, 156(table), 162–164, 166, 174–175

Photographs, 104, 152
Police, 9, 55–56, 168
media evaluation of, 21, 22(table)
and media format, 123, 124(table)
reporter use of, 14–16, 19–22, 25–27, 30–31, 69–70, 85–88
as source, 29(table), 33, 89(table), 91, 92(table), 95, 147(table), 148(table), 149(table), 166, 177
See also Criminal justice system
President's Commission on Law Enforcement and Administration of Justice, 8
Primary stories, 137(table), 153
characteristics of, 34–35(table), 36–38, 53, 168
defendants in, 76–78(table), 79–80
sources for, 91, 92(table), 93
victims in, 63, 64–66(table), 68, 71–72(table), 99–100, 102–104
Protess, D., 5

Race
of defendants, 58, 59, 60(table), 76(table), 79, 127(table), 130, 157(table)

of victims, 58, 60(table), 62, 65(table), 79, 127(table), 130, 154(table)
Radio, 3
Rape, 9, 53, 24, 110
victims of, 7, 63, 87, 120, 170, 178
See also Sexual assault
Ratings, 23
Reagan, Ronald, 7
Reporters, 17, 25–26, 28, 31, 40
court, 16–17, 19, 21, 25, 27, 86–87, 116–117
interview techniques of, 100–103, 106
police, 14–16, 19–22, 25–27, 30–31, 69–70, 86–87
Rose, Pete, 47

San Francisco, 135(table)
crime news in, 136(table), 137(table), 139, 140(table), 141(table)
sources in, 145(table), 147(table), 148(table), 149(table)
San Franciso Chronicle, 138–139, 144
Secondary stories, 137(table), 153
characteristics of, 33, 34–35(table), 36, 41, 53, 91, 92(table), 174
defendants in, 76–78(table)
victims in, 64–66(table), 69, 71–72(table), 97–99, 102
Seiter, J., 166(n1)
Sexual assault, 8, 9, 51(table), 54(table). *See also* Rape
Sheley, J. F., 24, 110, 119
Skogan, W. G., 133, 139
Smith, S. R., 180
Smith, William Kennedy, 63, 172
Sources, 13–21, 26, 28, 29(table), 170–172
citizens as, 123, 124(table), 168
and city size, 146, 147(table), 148(table), 149(table), 150, 166
courts as, 85, 89(table), 90, 92(table), 95, 98, 123, 124(table), 125, 147(table), 148(table), 149(table), 171
for crime information, 89(table), 90, 94–95, 122–123, 124(table), 125–126, 146, 147(table), 150, 169

criminal justice, 19–21, 34–35(table),
    41(n3), 97–98, 132, 170–171, 174–
    177
  for defendant information, 89(table),
    90–91, 94–95, 122, 124(table), 126,
    146, 149(table), 150
  defendants as, 89(table), 90, 92(table),
    124(table), 147(table), 148(table),
    149(table)
  families as, 89–90, 93–96, 125, 149–
    150, 166, 170, 172
  hospitals as, 90–91, 92(table), 93, 126,
    147(table), 148(table), 149(table),
    150–151, 171
  and media format, 111–112, 121–123,
    124(table), 125–126, 132, 132(n3),
    173–175
  news-item, 14, 15(table), 144,
    145(table), 175
  and newsworthiness, 88, 91
  police as, 29(table), 33, 89(table), 91,
    92(table), 95, 123, 124(table),
    147(table), 148(table), 149(table),
    166, 171
  and story level, 91, 92(table), 93, 96–97
  for victim information, 89(table), 90–
    91, 92(table), 93–95, 122, 124(table),
    125–126, 146, 148(table), 150, 171–
    172, 178
  victims as, 89(table), 90–91, 92(table),
    93–96, 98, 124(table), 126, 150, 172–
    173, 178–179
Stalkings, 9
Super primary stories, 34–35(table), 38–
    41, 83(n6), 104–107, 174, 179–180
Surette, R., 5

Television, 3–4, 11, 12(n1), 23, 111, 185–
    186
  crime impact in, 130, 131(table)
  crime prevalence in, 13, 114(table),
    115–117, 134, 136(table), 137–139,
    173
  crime types in, 18, 118(table), 119–121,
    125–126, 132, 140(table), 143
  defendants in, 124(table), 126, 127–
    128(table), 130

  local news in, 144, 146
  news production in, 17–18, 44–46, 110–
    113, 116, 186
  sources in, 111–112, 122–123,
    124(table), 125–126, 144, 173, 175
  story levels in, 137(table), 174
  victims in, 124(table), 126, 127–
    128(table), 129–130, 131(table)
  white-collar crimes in, 118(table), 120–
    121, 132(n2)
Tertiary stories, 137(table), 153
  characteristics of, 32–33, 34–35(table),
    41, 53, 174
  defendants in, 75, 76–78(table), 79
  sources for, 91, 92(table), 93, 96–97
  victims in, 63, 64–66(table), 67–68, 71–
    72(table), 96–97
Tyson, Mike, 38, 47, 63, 172

United Press International (UPI), 14
UPI. *See* United Press International

Viano, E., 171
Victim and Witness Protection Act, 7
Victim information
  and media format, 122, 124(table), 125–
    126
  sources for, 89(table), 90–91, 92(table),
    93–95, 122, 124(table), 125–126, 146,
    148(table), 150, 171–172, 178
Victims, 1–3, 5–6, 8–10, 80, 175, 180
  age of, 59, 60(table), 62, 65(table), 126,
    127(table), 155(table), 162–163, 166,
    174
  behavior of, 85, 93–100, 102–104, 106–
    107, 151–156, 162–164
  children as, 8, 10, 59, 86–87, 120, 178
  and crime rate, 133, 151
  in criminal justice system, 5–9, 55–56,
    85, 169
  defendant relationship to, 80–81, 93,
    128(table), 155(table)
  characteristics of, 58–59, 60–61(table),
    62–63, 64–66(table), 93, 126, 127–
    128(table), 169
  and city size, 153, 154–156(table), 162–
    164, 166, 175

elderly as, 8, 63, 67, 81, 82, 86
families of. *See* Families
gender of, 8, 59, 60(table), 64(table),
   127(table), 130, 154(table), 162, 166,
   169
naming of, 63, 73, 126, 127(table), 153,
   154(table), 162, 178
in newspapers, 64–66(table), 71–
   72(table), 126, 127–128(table), 129–
   130, 131(table)
in news production, 1, 11, 27, 85–86,
   178
newsworthiness of, 25, 58–59, 60–
   61(table), 67–70, 73–74, 85–87, 169–
   171, 174–175, 180
occupations of, 58–59, 60–61(table), 62,
   66(table), 67, 87, 128(table), 129,
   156(table), 162–164, 166, 169, 174–
   175
organizations for, 6–7, 9, 170
policies concerning, 168–169, 178–179
race of, 58, 60(table), 62, 65(table), 79,
   127(table), 130, 154(table)
of rape, 7, 63, 87, 120, 170, 178
as source, 89(table), 90–91, 92(table),
   93–100, 124(table), 147(table),
   148(table), 149(table), 150, 172–173,
   178–179
and story level, 63, 64–66(table), 67–69,
   71–72(table), 80
suburban, 68–70
in television, 111, 126, 127–128(table),
   129–130, 131(table), 132
Victims of Crime Act, 7
Vigilantes, 9, 10
Violence, 8, 24, 53, 133, 142, 170, 172
Vox pop, 85

Walsh, Adam, 9–10
Weaver, D., 25
White-collar crimes, 24, 47, 53, 54(table),
   57, 67, 164
and media format, 118(table), 120–121,
   130, 132, 132(n2), 140(table), 173
Wilhoit, G. C., 25
Wilson, P., 10
Wilson, W., 55, 179
Windhauser, J. W., 166(n1)
Winfree, L. T., 166(n1)
Women, 8, 57, 126, 162. *See also* Gender